School of American Research
Advanced Seminar Series

DOUGLAS W. SCHWARTZ, GENERAL EDITOR

SCHOOL OF AMERICAN RESEARCH BOOKS

The Pottery of Santo Domingo Pueblo
KENNETH CHAPMAN

The Pottery of San Ildefonso Pueblo
KENNETH CHAPMAN

Reconstructing Prehistoric Pueblo Societies
EDITED BY WILLIAM A. LONGACRE

New Perspectives on the Pueblos
EDITED BY ALFONSO ORTIZ

Structure and Process
in Latin America

STRUCTURE
AND PROCESS
IN LATIN AMERICA
Patronage, Clientage and Power Systems

EDITED BY
ARNOLD STRICKON
AND
SIDNEY M. GREENFIELD

A SCHOOL OF AMERICAN RESEARCH BOOK

UNIVERSITY OF NEW MEXICO PRESS · Albuquerque

Preface

This book is the product of a seminar sponsored by the School of American Research and a symposium held at the 71st annual meetings of the American Anthropological Association, on the subject "Patronage, Clientage, and Power Structures in Latin America." Although both sessions took place in 1969, the idea of bringing together a group of empirically oriented anthropologists, each of whom had given individual thought to the role of patronage and clientage in the social structures of the region, to share their thinking goes back several years before that. As I recall, the idea originally was suggested by Anthony Lauria in the course of a discussion at the 1966 meetings of the association in Pittsburgh.

That year I had presented a paper (see Greenfield 1966) in which I tried to combine some of the then-current thinking on patron-client relations with developments in network theory in an effort to summarize the results of a field project I had just completed in Brazil. Lauria, at the time, was working on a proposal on the subject of patronage that he had hoped to develop into a doctoral dissertation. After he read my paper we began what was to be the first of a series of lengthy discussions on the subject. After several hours on the second day, he noted that the ideal way for us to proceed would be to organize a conference to which would be invited several of the people who were working on the subject, because we all would gain from sharing our experience and data. The problem was to find a source of funds for the venture.

The following year Tony and I met again at the meetings of the as-

198311

sociation, discussed our respective progress, and went over some papers we had exchanged during the year. At the time Tony was living in Puerto Rico and I in Milwaukee. The annual meetings were our only opportunity to discuss our mutual interest.

The idea of the conference sounded even more attractive when we raised it in 1967. Neither of us had any ideas as to possible funding, but we did begin to discuss the format and participants.

At the association meetings in Seattle in 1968 we were joined in our planning by Nancie Gonzalez. Nancie had been conducting fieldwork in the Dominican Republic the year before and Tony had spent some time with her there.

When Nancie returned to Albuquerque, where she was teaching at the University of New Mexico, she telephoned Douglas Schwartz, who recently had assumed the post of director of the School of American Research in Santa Fe. He responded with enthusiasm, and Nancie drafted a proposal, which was approved by the board of the school.

In Seattle, and in our later correspondence, we had raised the possibility of inviting both European and Latin American scholars to participate. We also raised the possibility of not restricting our examination of patronage and clientage to Latin America. However, given the experimental nature of the venture and the limited budget with which we were working, we decided to keep the group of participants small and to focus our attention on Latin America. We did, however, insist on inviting at least one Latin American scholar to participate.

Although the airline fare from Buenos Aires to Santa Fe was more than we could manage, we all agreed that we wanted M. Esther Hermitte to participate. Fortunately, the Instituto Torcuato Di Tella was able to assist with transportation. We are grateful both to Esther and to the *Instituto* for their contribution.

Several scholars who would have added substantially to the final product were unable to join us. Field projects, writing commitments for unrelated materials, university obligations, and personal commitments kept some of our colleagues from participating.

Our budget enabled us to invite nine participants. We hoped to obtain overall coverage of Latin America—geographically, and in terms of levels in the complex, hierarchically ordered, national sociocultural systems of the region. We sought participants who had first-hand experience and knowledge both of Portuguese and Spanish America. Also, we wanted scholars able to draw upon experience in the highlands of western South America, the interior of the continent both north and south, the east coast, and the islands of the Caribbean. Everything considered, we feel that we were fortunate is getting the range of geographical and sociocultural diversity we did in such a small group.

We tried to get other kinds of diversity in our small group. Two of our nine participants were women. Two others had not yet received their Ph.D's. We ranged in age from the late twenties to the early fifties. We combined senior scholars with up to a quarter of a century of professional experience with others who had only completed their first field project. We covered the range from instructor to full professor; and to our great pleasure the group functioned with complete unity and without pressure or deference. From the outset we were a group of scholars, each with his own point of view, but each willing to listen to the others and to respect them for what they had to say.

The task of sending off the formal invitations and charging the participants with their responsibilities fell to me. Previously we had decided that each participant would be requested to prepare a working paper, to be circulated in advance of the conference, that would be a point of departure for our discussions. I am grateful to Arnold Strickon, and to a previous conference we both attended, for a suggestion that I believe to have been critical.

It has become conventional practice to ask conference participants to prepare working papers to be submitted and circulated in advance of the meeting. Then most of the interaction of the group during the collaborative sessions becomes centered on the individual presentations. In far too many cases, however, conference participants organize their working papers around the presentation of tentative conclusions, providing only the data and analysis needed to reach the conclusions. In a post-mortem following another conference, Strickon had pointed out that working papers generally suffer from the fact that they depart from what most anthropologists would agree to be the greatest strength of our discipline. They are primarily theoretical and analytic, often containing only a minimum of descriptive data.

We decided to instruct our participants to prepare working papers that emphasized situational and behavioral data. The invitation letter requested participants to select from their field notes materials describing and illustrating patronage and clientage.

The working papers provided the group with a body of diverse materials to which we were able to turn each time new theoretical and methodological questions arose. As a result, we were able to reach theoretical, conceptual, and methodological conclusions based upon the cooperative examination of the same data.

In planning the conference we had decided that the session in Santa Fe would best be followed by a symposium some six weeks later at the annual meetings of the American Anthropological Association in New Orleans. Our thinking was that in the interim each participant would be able to at least outline a revision of his working paper that would incorporate the criticisms, suggestions, and theoretical and conceptual conclusions reached at the conference. The expectation then was that the final version of the papers would be written after the conference, with the authors having benefited from exposure to the dynamics of both the conference and the symposium. In addition, the symposium would give us the oportunity to present our conclusions, in a tentative form, and have them discussed and criticized by colleagues working in the same area who could not be invited to the conference. In this way we had hoped to add the wisdom of their thinking and experience to this publication.

The conference in Santa Fe accomplished more than Lauria and I ever imagined it might. Not only did the data presented, and included in the pages of this book, make what we believe to be a valuable substantive contribution to our knowledge of Latin America, but the theoretical and methodological discussions they generated resulted in what we also believe to be significant contributions to theory and method both in anthropology and in Latin American studies.

Unfortunately, Lauria, for personal reasons, was unable to complete the revision of his working paper. Strickon and I have tried, however, to include the essentials of his contribution in the introduction, citing him where appropriate. We acknowledge his contribution, and although he is not one of the authors of a chapter, we all consider him as a collaborator and associate in this collective venture.

The same may be said for William Mangin who, also for personal reasons, was unable to complete his manuscript in time for publication.

Sidney M. Greenfield

Contents

Figures

Tables

The Analysis of Patron-Client
Relationships: An Introduction

ARNOLD STRICKON
Department of Anthropology
The University of Wisconsin, Madison

SIDNEY M. GREENFIELD
Department of Sociology
The University of Wisconsin, Milwaukee

The chapters in this volume grew out of an advanced seminar held in Santa Fe, New Mexico, October 1–4, 1969, sponsored by the School of American Research and entitled "Patronage, Clientage, and Power Structures in Latin America." The organizers and participants had intended to use the same title for this book. However, in the period following the conference and the symposium on the same subject held at the annual meetings of the American Anthropological Association in New Orleans November 22–24, 1969, the two of us who had assumed the editorial responsibility for transforming the papers and other materials presented and discussed into a book discovered that we had moved considerably beyond the examination of patronage and clientage as these concepts had been developed in the literature of social anthropology and allied disciplines (see, for example, Boissevain 1965, 1966; Campbell 1964; Foster 1961, 1963; Galjart 1964, 1967; Hutchinson 1966; Kenny 1960; Lande 1964; Paine 1969, 1971; Pitt-Rivers 1961; Powell 1970; Schneider,

J. 1969; Schneider, P. 1969; Scott 1970; Weingrod 1968; Wolfe 1966a). While preparing this introduction, which was intended to summarize the papers and discussions at both sessions and to relate our contributions to anthropological theory, we came to realize that we had moved beyond the narrow area of patronage and clientage as defined in the literature, into much more fundamental matters with more far-reaching implications both for the discipline of anthropology and for Latin American studies.

For the reader to understand this and thereby grasp what we believe to be the major theoretical, methodological, and substantive contributions of this collective endeavor, it is necessary for us to go back and reconstruct the intellectual currents and developments upon which we have built.

The point of departure for most contemporary work on patron-client relationships by anthropologists and political scientists is the seminal paper on *compadrazgo* by Sidney Mintz and Eric Wolf (1950). In that paper Mintz and Wolf pointed out that although the "co-godparent-hood" relationship operated within the broad framework of the formal structure of the Catholic church and its requirement that each initiate have a sponsor who stands in the relationship of godparent, the more significant social relationship throughout most of Latin America was that between the parents of the initiate and the godparent, not that between godparent and child. This relationship of compadrazgo, or ritual co-parenthood, although derived from the formal tradition of the church, was not a part of it. The *compadre* relationship existed, therefore, to use an analogy suggested later by Wolf (1966a) in another, though related, context: in the interstices of the formal institutional structure. It was not a part of the formal institutional system, but was both derived from and dependent upon it.

In conventional terms the positions of both godparent and compadre may be thought of as being achieved. After all, parents did select those persons they wished to sponsor their children. Although those asked could refuse, there were no limits on the number of initiates any active member of the church could sponsor. Also, there were no limits on the number of compadres any individual could have.

In practice, the selection of godparents, and hence compadres, appeared to correlate positively with social status. That is, those asked to be godparent—and compadre—more often than not were of a higher social status than the child to be initiated or his or her parents.

The relationship between godparent and godchild, according to the formal requirements of the church, may be thought of as an exchange. In return for sponsorship, which gives the initiate access to the sacraments, the godparent is given obedience and deference. Informally, material exchanges (for example, presents) also may be added to the godparent-godchild relationship.

The relationship between compadres also takes the form of an exchange, but one that in practice is most often of material goods and services, although deference and support, as we shall see, also are relevant elements. These exchanges, though derived from the formal situation of initiation into the church, are independent of the relationship between godparent and godchild.

Because parents select the sponsors of their children, they also choose their own compadres. And because the exchanges of the compadre relationship often are of considerable material importance, especially to people who for the most part are poor and underprivileged, care is given to the selection of godparents and hence compadres. Because a request for sponsorship can be turned down, negotiations invariably precede selection. Consequently, the effective role of compadre might be described as one negotiated within the framework of the needs, available resources, and goals of the parties involved, and not as one achieved or ascribed.

The preceding analysis, although derived from Mintz and Wolf (1950), is not to be found there. Their presentation, like most of the anthropology of the period and much of the later literature on patron-client relations, focused on structural arrangements within society and on transformational and evolutionary trends. The primary interests of anthropological theory at the time were structural-functional, with society seen as being composed of groups and institutions (in contrast to the culture traits and complexes by which it was described in a previous period). Research and analysis, especially in complex cultures, for the most part tended to concentrate either on the contribution a group or institution made to the maintenance of the societal whole, or on it as an example of an interest group in conflict with and competing with other groups in the dynamic that became manifest in social change and cultural evolution. Individual negotiations within a given cultural framework were bypassed by the mainstream of the discipline, and culturally specific, actor-oriented analysis—in the tactical rather than the psychological sense—was not to be expected of the time.

Consistent with the structural emphasis, Mintz and Wolf focused their analysis of compadrazgo on the social positions of the actors involved in the relationship—social position relative to the society viewed as a totality—rather than on their specific actions and behaviors. This in turn led them to think in terms of categories and social types. Consequently, compadre relationships could be viewed according to whether the participants were status equals—that is, members of the same social class—or members of different classes in positions of subordination and superordination.

Exchanges of goods and services then could be viewed as either between equals (for example, when a woman took care of the home and children of an ill compadre in anticipation of reciprocity should she herself become ill) or between unequals (as when a wealthy compadre provided his poor co-parent with money, credit, or access to and influence with government in return for labor, votes, or business). In neither case were the exchanges to be viewed as market transactions in which payment balanced the accounts of the participants; the general reciprocity of transactions between compadres produced constant imbalances that resulted in continuing relationships and exchanges.

Consistent with the structural-functional perspective, compadrazgo also was analyzed in terms of its "function" for the society. Vertical relationships (for example, those between members of different social classes) were viewed as a means of linking social strata whose disparate interests otherwise might drive them apart. This, in turn, was related to neoevolutionary theory by arguing that compadrazgo operated in specific "types" or "stages" of society, particularly agrarian, preindustrial stages of an assumed developmental continuum.

Outside forces then were hypothesized to introduce changes that would result in the replacement of compadrazgo by other social arrangements resulting from the changing relationships between the various social classes. This hypothesis was illustrated by Mintz and Wolf (1950: 351–52) with examples drawn from pre-Reformation England, where the importance of the institution declined as the society began to modernize.

The significance of the example was that the decline in importance of godparenthood and ritual co-parenthood could be related to changes in

4

technology and economic arrangements rather than to specific developments in a single cultural tradition or to contacts between peoples or groups. Mintz and Wolf then hypothesized a decline in compadre relationships in Latin America as industrialization and modernization would carry the region to the next evolutionary stage.

Students who went into the field in the years following the Mintz and Wolf analysis of compadrazgo returned to report other relationships paralleling those between compadres, especially in Latin America and Mediterranean Europe. However, for the most part these relationships lacked even the indirect institutional support and religious sanctions of compadrazgo proper.

It was the isolation of these relationships along with their similarities to compadrazgo as analyzed by Mintz and Wolf that resulted in the isolation and recognition of patronage and clientage, and the patron-client relationship, as legitimate interests of anthropology and later political science not only in Latin America and Mediterranean Europe but around the world (see Scott 1970; Powell 1970; Paine 1971).

In a series of articles based upon his research in Tzintzuntzan, Mexico, George Foster (1961, 1963, 1965) took the next step in the analysis begun by Mintz and Wolf. In the first paper on the "dyadic contract," Foster (1961) addressed himself to social relations between pairs. Contrasting his data collected in the Mexican village with the models of society produced by British structural-functionalists working primarily in Africa, he emphasized that instead of corporate groups, interlocking to form a coherent whole that ordered social life, the dominant feature of social organization in Tzintzuntzan seemed to be a series of dyadic relationships,[1] each negotiated by the participating pair, with each party ready to abandon the relationship should it prove disadvantageous to him or should he be presented with a better opportunity. These "dyadic contracts," however, lacked even the secondary religious support of compadrazgo and seemed to be based more on random interaction and the recognition of self-interest and potential benefit by the actors than on any formal principle. In contrast to the highly structured crystal latticework of African societies, at least as they were presented by classical British social anthropology, a better analogy for Tzintzuntzan, and perhaps other "peasant" villages of Latin America, seemed to be that of a jar of gases in which the constituent molecules bounced around lacking a coherent structure to regularly and predictably link atom to atom and

5

molecule and molecule. Instead, they transacted individually to form paired relationships, which, although of short duration and constantly changing, did give a degree of order to the whole. Only the family, or nuclear household, appeared to Foster to be a stable and continuing group in Tzintzuntzan.

Many students of anthropology and related disciplines working in Latin America, including the present authors, while recognizing the value of Foster's presentation, felt somewhat dissatisfied with the degree of randomness implicit in it. After all, things did get done predictably and with regularity even though there appeared to be no formal rules for the organization of activities. Fields were planted, markets were held, and officials were elected and installed in office. In addition, formal national institutions did exist and function within most villages—a fact with which Foster never really dealt—but their relationship to local life was not to be understood in terms of dyadic contracts or the activities of nuclear families.

As had been the case with Minz and Wolf before him, Foster was unable to find in the anthropological theory of the period a framework that could help him in addressing this order of problem. In the tradition of his predecessors the best he could do was to establish a typology of relationships that used as criteria not the characteristics of the relationships themselves, but rather the social class positions of the participants.

Two types of dyadic relationships were delineated, paralleling in their relevant criteria those made in the analysis of compadrazgo. *Colleague contracts* were those between status equals (Mintz and Wolf's horizontal compadrazgo); *patron-client contracts* were those between parties of unequal status (Mintz and Wolf's vertical compadrazgo).

With respect to patronage and clientage, the consequence of both the Mintz and Wolf and the Foster analysis was that the concepts, and the social relationship they attempted to isolate and examine, came to be severely restricted by a definition that placed primary emphasis on the different social status or class position of the participants and paid only peripheral, secondary attention to the details of the negotiations, reciprocities, and exchanges that brought them into being and maintained them.

In Foster's analysis the processes involved in negotiating a colleague contract were taken to be largely the same as those involved in a patron-client agreement. Each participant was assumed to be seeking his own goals and exchanging his own resources for those of another in an effort to achieve his objective. To accomplish this he sought the partner who most likely would enable him to do this. The primary difference in the two types of contract was not in the process of their formation and dyadic exchange, but instead in the kinds of resources each partner commanded, which was based on his social position in the society.

Thus far Foster's analysis and the ordering of the descriptions upon which it is based did not stray far from that of Mintz and Wolf; he, like them, had generated a structural typology. From this point on, however, he moved in a very different direction. While Mintz and Wolf had focused on social structure—and the role of compadrazgo in the class system of the larger society—and the possible implications of evolutionary change, Foster turned his attention to an examination of religion, symbolism, and ritual. Consequently, whereas Mintz and Wolf directed the investigation of compadrazgo and related relationships in the direction of cross-cultural comparison (structurally and evolutionarily), Foster came to look more closely at the features of the particular culture within which the dyadic relationships were imbedded.

In the behavior of the believer, and in his interaction with the church, the saints, and ultimately with God, Foster found what he took to be a symbolic representation of the relationship between men in Tzintzuntzan. The predominant form these representative magico-religious relationships were to take were what he had referred to as the patron-client contract.

The church, with its formalized system for the distribution of powers and desiderata, constituted the formal institutional framework within which the interactions of individuals and their social relationships then were to be examined. Within the church was an established, formalized, and ritually elaborated set of means, with appropriate acts and powers to work through, in order to obtain the benefits available: assistance in this world, personal peace and satisfaction, and ultimate blessing and eternal salvation.

According to the beliefs of the people of Tzintzuntzan, all ultimate power and authority are vested in God. He is the source of all benefits. However, they also believed that a personal relationship could be established between a congregant and a saint, who represented another level of supernatural that did not have direct control over resources but who

7

was assumed to stand in a position that gave him direct access to the source of all value. Through this personal relationship with the saint the congregant believed that he could gain indirect access to God, the source of all value and benefit.

There were, however, a large number of saints, each of whom was believed to have different access to God and the ability to obtain different benefits for a worshiper. The congregants, in their individual efforts to approach the Almighty to obtain the benefits he controlled, established relationships with saints who they hoped would be able to serve successfully as intermediaries. Sociologically, these relationships could be either ascribed or achieved, but in both cases detailed analysis revealed that they were negotiated. For example, the saint on whose day one was born, the patron saint of the town or community in which one lived, the patron saint of the occupation one followed, and so on, might each be thought of as a saint with whom one stood in a relationship of ascription. However, the worshiper was not bound to these saints, nor was he required to interact with them; he could turn if he chose to any other supernatural with whom he could establish some basis for expecting assistance. The basis for all relationships with supernaturals in the final analysis was negotiated. The congregant could turn to any one with a request; in return he would have to offer to perform some act or do something for the saint.

The essence of any such relationship, from the perspective of the worshiper, was its utility in obtaining the valued resources from the Almighty. If the saint could deliver, so to speak, which implied that he was close to God, the congregant would reciprocate by performing his part of the bargain. The reciprocity then would validate their relationship, which could be appealed to repeatedly by the worshiper in the future. Should the saint be unable to deliver, however, there would be no reciprocity by the congregant and the relationship would end. In the event of failure, which was always a possibility, the worshiper then could appeal to other saints in a succession that hopefully would lead him to the "right" one, with whom he would establish a more permanent relationship of reciprocity that would bring rewards and benefits to both parties.

What Foster had been examining and analyzing, of course, was not a mere dyadic relationship between a saint and a petitioner. Although he appears at the time not to have appreciated all the implications, the interaction between the two was dependent upon and influenced by the interactions of others. While Foster could focus on the relationship between worshiper and saint, it was obvious from his analysis that the negotiations between the two were conditional with respect to yet another dyadic exchange: that between the saint and God.

The congregant, according to the assumptions prevalent in Tzintzuntzan, did not have direct access to the source of benefits. It was assumed that the saint did. The appeal and negotiations that might result in reciprocity and a relationship between man and saint, then, were predicated on the fact that the supernatural could serve, as the result of another set of transactions, as the intermediary to God and the benefits he controlled. There were at least two linked, interdependent dyadic relationships to be considered, both dependent upon negotiations. However, the details of the negotiations and the reciprocities of each, and the ensuing relationships between the parties, depended upon the outcome of the other.

The church then provided the formal institutional framework within which the prototype of negotiated, transactional behavior called patron-client relationships took place. Its formal rules and structure set the constraints and limitations for individually negotiated relationships that were believed to bring to men the benefits and values they desired. However, the negotiations and exchanges were not a part of the formal church structure. Instead they were supplementary to it, but dependent on it and its rules and functions. The informal system of exchanges that resulted in the ideal type for the social relations and social structure of the society therefore was to be understood only insofar as it was imbedded within the matrix of the formal institution.

The secular social parallels to the relationships of patronage and clientage between man and saint within the religious sector, as Foster saw it, were those between persons of different status and social class who had access to different kinds of resources and power.

The assumption was that the sources of desiderata were located outside the arena in which ego was operating and that he could obtain them only through the intermediacy of someone at a social level higher than his who had access to them. From the perspective of the Tzintzuntzeños, on whom Foster focused the analysis, the system of social stratification and its implicit social classes provided the analog with the supernatural world. The resources in question differed, but there were striking parallels in the way in which individuals went about obtaining them. And the model of patron-client exchange was applicable to both.

As in the supernatural relationships, individuals appealed to superiors with access to resources they themselves did not have. They negotiated exchanges that, if successful, resulted in continuing relationships. If the reciprocities were not forthcoming, the parties moved on to try again with other partners.

Although Foster emphasized the dyadic relationships and the exchanges between Tzintzuntzeños, who were at the terminal levels of the national stratification system and who had minimum resources, and the immediate superior, or patron, with whom they exchanged, it was obvious that, as had been the case with the saints, the superiors were at best intermediaries; themselves lacking control over the resources in question, they could yet provide access to those resources.

Questionable in many ways, Foster's analysis of patron-client relationships opened up new and fruitful avenues for research and analysis. Instead of more typologies of different kinds of dyadic links, he began to ask about, and open the door to questions about, the basis of the links, the larger systems of relationships to which they articulated, and their relationship to formal institutions. These questions and the framework in which Foster placed them made it possible, among other things, to relate the analysis of dyadic exchanges of patronage, clientage, and compadrazgo to conceptual, methodological, and later theoretical advances being made by some British social anthropologists (see Barnes 1954; Bott 1957; Epstein 1961; Mayer 1966; Mitchell 1966). Working in societies without corporate groupings, these students of social networks began to raise questions about the articulation of individuals to the larger social arena and the formal institutions of society. In so doing, they shifted the emphasis of their analysis from the traditional preoccupation with the functions of patterned behavior for the society to an examination of the goals and motivations of the actors who formed the networks that articulated and made operational the formal institutional system. This shift in the level of analysis made it possible to see individuals establishing the networks in the process of obtaining the means for the attainment of their individual goals.

The examination of network behavior, analogous to some of the earlier descriptions of compadrazgo, colleague, and patron-client relationships, made it clear that the networks were based upon negotiations

Introduction

that related the actors to the resources of a variety of different formal structures. And while the processes of linkage—the negotiated exchanges —appeared to differ in detail according to whether the transactions were between equals or unequals, fundamentally they were the same. The differences stemmed from the structural position of the actors and the differing resources to which they had access. Consequently, their specific goals and strategies and tactics for attainment differed, but not the processes of negotiating relationships and exchanges that were the means. If viewed processually, therefore, colleague and patron-client transactions were similar; if viewed structurally, that is, from the social class or status position of the actors and the functioning of the total society, they differed markedly. Yet both analyses were based upon the same behavioral events; the difference was analytic and conceptual. At the time, however, there still was little in anthropological theory to facilitate a shift from the structural level of analysis to that of the actor and the process of interaction by means of which relationships were established and activities organized. Most writers continued to speak about patronage and clientage and vertical compadrazgo from a structural perspective.

Foster's third article (1965), also based primarily on his work in Tzintzuntzan, broke yet more new ground and paved the way for relating the subject matter to other theoretical and conceptual developments.

In contrast with the tradition of social anthropology, in which order is seen as the coherent relationship among institutions, Foster, in an effort to provide order to and account for the disparate behavior he described earlier in his analysis of the dyadic contract, turned to the world view of the actors, and specifically to what he termed their "image of the limited good."

The image of the limited good, he maintained, represents a basic assumption regarding the nature of the universe made by the Tzintzunzeños.[2] In practice it means that the members of the community act as if they believe that the valuables, resources, and general desiderata of the universe are in short and finite supply. Therefore, any additional resources of valuables obtained by one person must be at the expense of someone else. Man's wants are infinite, the resources to satisfy them finite and limited; therefore, the more any one person has, the less is available for each of the others.

Given this assumption, it follows that, among other things, as each man seeks his own ends, he protects what he has from others who may want it because if they should take it from him his only recourse will be to try to take it back from someone else. It follows also that a man should not try to obtain too much of anything, lest he attract the attention of others who will believe that he has taken that which is theirs and will attempt to take it from him.

The assumption of the limited good leads to the conclusion that men will behave so as to maintain and protect what they have, but not to obtain much more than their fellows.

The reaction to Foster's proposal of the image of the limited good in the professional journals was largely negative (see, for example, Kaplan and Saler, 1966). Although admitting that peasants were generally conservative, which was consistent with the model, critics also noted that at times they were innovative, progressive, and even radical—behavior inconsistent with that to be expected from the model. Also, it was noted, many peasants regularly left their native villages for the cities, where their behavior changed so that they appeared no longer to be bound by the image of the limited good. Finally, it was added, the image and the behavior it ordered were not exclusive to peasants—a point noted by Foster himself in a footnote (Foster 1965:311). If this were so, however, the image of the limited good as the world view held by peasants could not account for the differences between peasants and nonpeasants. Furthermore, it was argued, Foster's analysis was reductionist in that it sought to explain social and cultural phenomena in terms of the psychology of the actors.

The most serious weakness of Foster's position, more significant in our judgment than those touched on by others, lay not in the argument itself, but in the implicit assumption that the image was somehow a reality, a psychologically true statement about the mental states and processes of the actors.[3] Instead, consistent with the logic of scientific explanation, it should have been presented as an analytic assumption posited by the investigator-analyst, the value of which depended upon its ability to order the data, and for models derived from it to generate hypotheses and to predict behavior. Even here, however, as presented by Foster the assumption of the limited good was a single determinant. If it were psychologically true, it followed that people would behave in a specific way. Instead, we would say that the assumption might better have been proposed as one of a series of variables that would produce different outcomes, depending upon the specific weight of each of the variables in the situation under consideration.

When the image of the limited good is recast from something taken to be real in the minds of the actors to an analytic premise posited by the researcher, however, it translates into a model of a zero-sum game, with the peasants of Tzintzuntzan applying a variety of minimax strategies in the playing of the game. Thus the peasant who migrates and he who stays, the traditionalist (conservative) and the radical, all may be seen as following different strategies within the same game. Their varying strategies or courses of action depend upon such factors as their individual circumstances, individual estimations of probable outcomes, access to information and resources, and so on.

Applying the image of the limited good in this way, however, requires a theoretical foundation that was not available in anthropological theory at the time Foster, Mintz and Wolf, and most others to study patron-client behavior did their work. Recent contributions building on the lead taken by students of social networks, specifically by Frederik Barth (1966, 1967a, 1967b) elaborating on the earlier suggestive work of Raymond Firth (1951) and F. G. Bailey (1969), have provided the theoretical foundations for the approach and the type of analysis presented in this volume.

Unlike either structural-functionalism or conflict approaches, which have predominated in the study of complex cultures to this point, the new analytic stance enables us to concentrate on and examine the decisions and behaviors of social actors, rather than the outcomes of their actions alone, that is, the institutionalized patterns, social groups, and consequent structure and functioning of the society. The actors from this perspective, may be viewed as game players seeking personal goals within analyzable social, cultural, and situational fields.

Within this framework one can examine the processes by means of which negotiated relationships are established, and the variety of strategies employed, along with the factors relevant to their formation. As a result, one can now do sociological analysis at what might be considered a lower level than previously.

This actor-oriented level of analysis rests on the assumption that individuals operating in social situations seek to maximize their chances of achieving some set of specific goals. Several points should be made about the assumption. First, it is precisely what we have said it is: an assumption. It is not intended and in no way should be construed as an epistemologically true statement. Its value rests solely on its utility in enabling us to order and predict the behavior of individuals in social situations.

Second, with respect to the goals of the actors, no a priori conclusions are to be made about their content. We must be careful not to impute goals in specific situations (financial, political, religious, and so on). Instead, along with the strategies selected to attain them, goals must be ascertained by investigation.

Finally, the assumption underscores the *actor* orientation of the level and type of analysis. It forces us to focus on the social participant, not on what the observer infers or concludes about him. His definition of the situation is what counts, not that of the observer or any third party. The actor's goals and strategies and tactics for attaining them, inappropriate though they may be when judged with respect to conditions as determined by an "objective" third party (whatever that may mean), are what we want. Since it is the behavior of the participant, and not the observer, that we wish to understand, we need his view of the world. The "loser" in the game, he who does not obtain the goals, is therefore as important as the "winner," since the behavior of both is to be understood in terms of the same set of variables.

At this level of analysis we are interested primarily in the question "Why does Juan Fulano behave the way he does?"—not "Why is Juan's society or culture the way it is?"

Within this framework we can examine the processes through which negotiated relationships are established and the variety of strategies employed by actors in attaining ends, along with the factors relevant to their formation. This level of analysis, of course, is not an alternative to structural studies; it is complementary, and most constructively viewed as a preliminary to structural analysis, to be combined with it in the expansion of our analytic tool kit.[4]

If patron-client relations—and all negotiated relationships—are to be viewed within the framework of the gaming analogy, the strategies and tactics employed by the various actors have to be viewed as the outcome of the interplay of a number of variables rather than as the result of simple structural demands or psychological states. The variables isolated in the chapters that follow, which were examined in detail by the participants at both the conference and the symposium (see Greenfield

14

1969; Strickon 1969) are: (1) the Ibero-American cultural tradition—which in Anthony Lauria's terms constitutes the idiom in which the negotiations and transactions are conducted; (2) the system of formal positions within the institutional system of the nationally organized, complex cultures of Latin America; and (3) the resources available to the specific actors that may be employed by them in the transactional process.

In most of the papers, and in most discussions of Latin America, the idiom is treated as a constant. However, in specific cases (for example, Nancie Gonzalez's discussion of transactions between elites in the Dominican Republic and USAID personnel and Dwight Heath's examination of the Aymara articulation with national Bolivian culture) where there are cultural differences, the idiom may be seen as a variable to be used in a sense as a resource by the parties negotiating.

Perhaps the most important variable in our analyses of situations that resulted in the patterned behavior that has come to be called patron-client (and colleague) relationships was the resources available to specific actors seeking to enter into transactions as a means of attaining goals. Resources, as viewed here, could be material (land, money, minerals, precious stones and metals, livestock, control over fighting men, and so on) or nonmaterial (specialized skills and expertise, the ability to manipulate symbols, access to or control over supernaturals and so on).[5]

The system of formal positions, which in addition to prestige and status in Latin America also may be seen as a source from which incumbents gain access to resources that effect their ability to negotiate, constitutes another significant variable. The positions vary in terms of quality and quantity of resources that each controls, as does the distribution of positions within the population. The specific location of an actor in the formal positions of the institutional system of the society has a significant effect on his behavior, and in the understanding of his goals and strategies and tactics for attaining them.

Cultural idiom, formal institutional positions, and access to and control over resources, then, are used in the following studies as variables in analyzing situations in which actors seeking goals employ divergent strategies and tactics to negotiate exchanges. The exchanges establish relationships referred to in other places in the literature of anthropology (and allied disciplines) as ties of patronage and clientage. It will be obvious to the reader that, although all of the authors share a concern with this type of situational analysis, they are by no means in agreement about which level—the situational, the structural, or the evolutionary—they wish to focus upon in their own work. In fact, the problem focus of the individual chapters varies according to which level of analysis the author considers most important.

Strickon and Greenfield concentrate primarily on the decisions of individuals—in Strickon's case those of a rancher and in Greenfield's those of the actors involved in the cases of the charwoman, the cesspool, and the road—taking the changing institutional frameworks first of Argentine and then of Brazilian society as constituting the parameters for the analysis. Heath, Hermitte, and Shirley give relatively greater emphasis to the structural features that constitute the parameters—Heath to changes brought about by the Bolivian revolution of 1952, Hermitte to changes and developments of markets for ponchos, and Shirley to changes in the political structure of Brazil as they related to the establishment of cooperatives—that in turn affect the scope within which individual strategies may be developed and choices made. Gonzalez and Stuart place primary emphasis on the cross-cultural and evolutionary implications of their analyses, which use structural factors—in Gonzalez's case, the national systems of two societies (the Dominican Republic and the United States), and in Stuart's case, which may be considered a negative one used to test the variables, the almost zero input into the local community that precluded the development of the negotiations and exchanges associated with patronage and clientage—as parameters for the choices and decisions of the actors being discussed.

Differences among the studies, it appears to us, derive not from differences in the value attributed to situational analysis or its versatility but rather to differences in what the individual authors take to be the most important questions to be addressed. This is nothing new to anthropologists. In the broadest sense, the differences that emerge from the papers —and these differences were discussed at length during the conference and the symposium—parallel the old distinction within anthropology between cultural relativists and evolutionists. At the risk of oversimplifying and hence offending, we can say that the former seek greater in-depth understanding of particular cultures. Hence traditional structural-functionalism and situational analysis tend to be compatible as research orientations to those who lean in this direction. Cultural evolution, in contrast (again at the risk of oversimplifying), seeks cross-cultural parallels and directional trends. This, of course, requires another orientation with which both situational analysis and structural-functionalism are not necessarily, but in fact may be, compatible. The first position may be said to seek more accurate predictions in particular situations and therefore requires that as much detail as possible be controlled about a particular culture at a particular time (see, for example, Geertz 1965). The other, in contrast, may be said to seek prediction in broader, cross-cultural terms. Therefore, it requires less detail about specific cultures and greater uniformity in the ordering of data.

Each position is based on differing interests and objectives, and hence asks different questions that are to be answered with different conceptual abstractions taken from the same body of observed events.

Anthropologists, as we have indicated, have long disagreed on the relative priority to be given each position. Our intent here is not to argue for or against either orientation. We feel that both are valid, and that the choice—and therefore the appropriate questions to be asked and hence emphasized in presentation—is to be made by the individual scholar. We believe that situational analysis as presented in the case studies in this volume adds a dimension that strengthens both positions and advances the understanding of the phenomena of patronage and clientage and of the cultures and civilizations of Latin America.

NOTES

1. The choice of the term *contract*, which normally implies the existence of some third party able to force compliance if the terms are not met, to describe the relationship was unfortunate. As Foster readily admits, no third party can force the parties to a "dyadic contract" to live up to their obligations. A term like *dyadic alliance* probably would have been more appropriate to describe the relationship and emphasize that fulfillment of the obligations in the relationship is ultimately dependent upon the self-interest of the parties involved.

2. In the article he extrapolated from Tzintzuntzan to claim that the image characterizes all "peasants" (Foster 1965).

3. A position Foster continued to hold through 1971, judging by a paper he presented, and the discussion following it, at the annual meetings of the American Anthropological Association in New York in November of that year (Foster 1971).

4. The relationship between the two levels of analysis, the situational and the more abstract structural, and the way of moving from one to the other to deal more adequately with questions of social and cultural change and persistence, also were grounded in the new approach (see Barth 1967b).

5. Political scientist Charles Anderson (1964) provides an interesting analysis of the relationships among political symbols and rhetoric, street demonstrations, and political careers in Latin America to demonstrate this point.

2

The Explanation of Patron-Client Systems: Some Structural and Ecological Perspectives

WILLIAM T. STUART

Department of Anthropology
Lawrence University

INTRODUCTION

For some time, social scientists, historians, and others have agreed that some salient structure and functional analogies may exist between such matters as "hacienda" systems and "feudal" societies and between these and "patron-client" blocs, "frontier" societies, and Melanesian "big man" systems. Certain scholars have noted also the similarity of "entrepreneurs" to the leaders characteristic of at least some of the structures just mentioned.

If we are to sort out the structural identities from the disanalogies in the above considerations we must proceed deliberately; initially by proposing an analytical approach equal to the task. Such a stance for the analysis of anthropological data will be one that allows us to comprehend sociocultural phenomena, customs, and institutions as the results of the interplay between particular human populations and the selective environmental pressures they face. In our discipline this approach has commonly been called "cultural ecology." What is important here is that the stance of cultural ecology is informed by a systematics usually termed "general systems theory" (GST).

Accordingly, in the tentative formulations that follow, I shall (1) supply what I feel is a useful theoretical basis for the ecological analysis of patron-client systems—some of the necessary programmatics for using general systems theory in analyzing sociocultural phenomena; (2) generalizing somewhat, discuss patron-client phenomena as characteristic of a peculiar structural type that arises only under certain conditions— phenomena associated with a particular form of state integration, which I shall for convenience describe as weakly centralized; I shall then compare the causes and systematics of patronage phenomena with other kinds of loosely structured social forms.

CULTURAL ECOLOGY AND GENERAL SYSTEMS THEORY

Systematics and Systems

General systems theory [1] is not a single set of reduction rules of a single well-worked-out axiomatic theory to explain all concrete systems. Rather, it represents some standards for a systematics that can guide natural scientists in exploring order and behavior in the world around them.

A review of the literature on general systems theory suggests that progress in the field has often been delayed by confusion between the related concepts of systems and systematics. Thus, I repeat, GST represents a kind of *systematics*, rather than a kind of *system* per se: an inventory of theoretical concepts, assumptions, and so forth, which inform and constrain identification, description, and explanation of operating physical systems.

Peter Caws has made a distinction similar to the one I am emphasizing here. He speaks of "theoretical systems" on the one hand and "physical systems" on the other—my "systematics" and "systems." As Caws sees it, general systems theory involves an initial ontological assumption that there are indeed some physical, natural systems out there somewhere, susceptible to identification, description, and explanation. These physical systems are existentially prior to the theoretical system (or systematics) in terms of which the former are to be explained. According to Caws, any theoretical system thus "confronts the physical system of which it is the theory and this confrontation is not a bad image of the human activity we call science" (1968:3).

The failure of many social scientists to make explicit this dichotomy has led, I believe, to a great deal of confusion. For instance, Peter Winch (1958) appears to have confused a kind of system (for example, a society) with the systematics involved in the explanation of it (that is, social science).

Despite the fact that *systematics*, as I employ the term here, may represent a broader usage than that implied in *theoretical system* as Caws construes the term, I think we could both agree that as a particular theoretical science (or its systematics) develops, it should become increasingly the case that "the two systems (theoretical and physical) have the same form," that is, that they are isomorphic. Caws continues with a point that is worth reiterating many times over, especially because it is too often forgotten on the part of mentalistic social scientists. In what I feel is one of the most concise expressions of the essential empirical quality of natural science, he argues:

> Now, isomorphism [between "theoretical" and "physical" systems] is not something that belongs to the theoretical system and the physical system separately; it appears only when they are taken together, and this has to be done from a vantage point outside them both. It is not the function of a theory to reflect on its adequacy to the world; its function is to *be* adequate to the world. Questions about the adequacy of scientific theories, like questions about their logical structure, their origins, their usefulness, etc., are *metascientific* questions (1968:3).

General systems theory is, in part, then, a body of conceptual, interpretative, and explanatory principles that will ideally allow us to recognize, explain, and in some cases anticipate the existence and distribution of nomic analogies between particular physical systems. In this fashion, the physical systems themselves ultimately act as the empirical test against which the general (but always conjectural) explanations must prove themselves. I hope to be able to demonstrate in this chapter that an approach to natural science informed by general systems theory represents a non-dogmatic basis for scientific inference that cautions against an a priori acceptance of what ought to remain problematic, namely, the character of the structure and causality associated with any particular system under examination. Our concepts must be flexible enough both to enable us to recognize diverse organizational features of systems as we find them and to facilitate their explanation.

Basic Assumptions of General Systems Theory

Some of the more important assumptions underlying a general systems systematics include: (1) that the external world is knowable in natural terms; (2) that the kind of philosophy of science appropriate to the general systems theory is that of natural science (cf. Hempel 1965, Nagel 1961) rather than a distinct "cultural" science for the comprehension of emergent sociocultural phenomena; (3) that natural systems can best be comprehended from a materialist position wherein it is maintained that all systems exist in a matter/energy universe ultimately subject to the laws (or principles) of thermodynamics; the ecologist must, at least by implication, adopt a materialist stance; (4) that since systems of various sorts exist and indeed often interact, a posture of methodological collectivism is called for—that is, as sets of structured constraints, systems (for example sociocultural ones) may be said to "exist" in more than a metaphorical sense as simply the summation of individual actions.[2]

Kinds of System

There are two general kinds of system: the "closed" and the "open." In the strict sense, there is only one closed system, the universe. All other natural systems are open in the sense that there is some actual or potential flow of matter or energy across the system boundaries. Open systems may be further divided into "nonliving" and "living." The principles of chemical reactions and laws of physics are usually meant to describe the former. The steady states characteristic of nonliving systems are essentially of the "equilibrium" sort, in that they are not maintained through any internal direction of matter or energy flows across their boundaries. Such an internal source of direction (often described as "quasi-teleology") is typical of all living systems—be they organisms or populations. This should not be taken to mean that living systems violate the laws of thermodynamics; rather, they can counteract the course of entropy only insofar as run-down parts and processes are revitalized by the input of new matter or energy from sources outside the system.

Structural and Ecological Perspectives

When we mention the steady states of living systems, the attributes that set them off from nonliving systems are homeostatic. The structures of those systems that are so regulated are explicable in terms of environmental parameters. Finally, it should be emphasized that not all the variables of a given *substantive* system need be in a formal sense part of it (I shall return shortly to the distinction between "formal" and "substantive" systems).

There are many kinds of living systems. In sociocultural systems our concern is with populational rather than with individual systems. The latter are neither few in number nor altogether unimportant, but an individual natural system (such as as organism) does not, in fact, evolve (in the sense of having the capacity to change its own structure); rather it adjusts or acclimates in terms of the range of the variables characterizing it. Populational systems do possess just such a quality of evolution—morphogenesis—wherein by generating new variety and having it "subjected" to environmental selective pressures a system may become altered in terms of new arrangements of variables. A new system emerges!

This matter of how human sociocultural systems evolve new homeostatic mechanisms (often described prosaically in terms of "institutions") or lose them, or in other fashion qualitatively alter them, ought to be a paramount interest for anthropologists. I shall be arguing, for instance, that the "institution" of patronage-clientage characterizes only certain systemic arrangements that exist in peculiar environments.

Multi-individual (populational) systems, be they "breeding isolates" in biology or "cultures" in anthropology, may be seen to evolve—that is, to change structurally or systemically primarily as a result of the selective pressures of environment on system-produced variety.[3] I belabor this point a bit because I sense that much of the discussion of social structures in anthropology (especially that of social anthropology) has too often been phrased in terms of an *organismic* (single individual) analogy. The shortcomings of such an analogy are now well documented and universally recognized. We need not, however, retreat from a science of sociocultural change in a determinant sense simply because this one analogy has proven deficient. I hope to demonstrate here that a *populational* systems referent can explain sociocultural phenomena.

Following Hall and Fagan (1968:87) I suggest we use the term *adaptation* to characterize "the ability [of living systems] to react to their environments in a way that is favorable, in some sense, to the continued operation of the system." Excusing for a moment the assumption implicit in Hall and Fagan's statement as to the inevitability of success in such adaptation, it seems useful to distinguish between subcategories of adaptation: "adjustment" or acclimatization (for individual systems) and "evolution" (for populational systems), in accord, I believe, with contemporary biological usage.

Perhaps it is appropriate now to elaborate the distinction between "formal" and "substantive" systems, a clarification that I hope will obviate disputes that often intrude at this juncture. It is possible to be very much confused by the trees of ethnographic data and as a result to miss the structure of the forest altogether. I propose that when we speak of a given concrete instance as "a people" or "a society" or "a culture" we are making reference to a *substantive* sociocultural system or configuration. By such holism we are forced to confuse the unregulated variety with the regulated variables. We may be, in addition, including under a single rubric concern with certain variables only some of which are "integrated" (or organized) in one manner and at one locus and concern with others integrated differently and elsewhere. The concept of "formal system" is intended to help us out here. In the sense in which I employ it, *formal system* refers only to those variables that are in systemic, causal relationship. We are concerned specifically with describing the appropriate value ranges of those variables and the process relationship statements that obtain between the variables. This will allow us to keep distinct the variety from the formal structure of the substantive cases. Thus we may say, in the formal sense, that the sociocultural system has changed or "evolved" only when we are able to specify either (1) new variables becoming, or ceasing to be, systemically regulated at a particular locus, or (2) alterations in the appropriate value ranges for such variables and, concomitantly, changes in the relationship statements obtaining between variables.[4]

Now in all but trivial cases, a given substantive system ("people," "society," or "culture") will, when systematically analyzed, be seen to consist of a number of formally distinct systems in terms of which individual members are constrained to act. Some of these may be hierarchically integrated as subsystems of a single analytically superordinate system; others may not be. We must realize that all substantive sociocultural systems are formally *multidimensional*. For instance, to use one common scheme, many of the same individuals in a given society will be involved (as statuses and roles) at one time in several formal systems, such as "village," "tribe," and "chiefdom." [5] Certainly much of what we have come to call "levels" of sociocultural integration is an attempt to make distinctions such as I am discussing. It is worth emphasizing, too, that formal systems are constraint systems on the action of lower level substantive entities. Such is the internal material linkage between formal and substantive.

To continue, we must recognize that the formal systems are *multistate* systems; especially this seems to be the case with populational systems. I do not mean simply the number of formally distinguishable systems that control substantive inferior entities within higher level substantive systems. I mean a superordinate system may, and often does, regulate subsystems the states of which may not at all times be substantively present. Examples include "developmental cycles" of domestic groupings (which involve temporal, though still system-regulated, process-directed change) or seasonally large-scale groupings as evidenced by Plains Indian groups that would degenerate into smaller scale substantive entities and action at other times. Such alterations between states do not imply structural systemic change except in their origin or in their termination. Substantive elements may be, and commonly are, regulated by and make up multistate systems.

The distinction between "individual" and "populational" systems is not, strictly speaking, a formal distinction. It is not necessarily the case that individual systems cannot change their own structures (evolve). Commonly, of course, they cannot. With particular reference to human beings, individuals may be seen to be capable of some degree of evolution (as evidenced in ideological restructuring by the human mind). However, from the perspective of sociocultural systems, the variety thrown up by such "thinking machines" is relatively unimportant unless and until it is either selected for or systemically "dampened" by the sociocultural system as it responds to external parameters.[6]

Before moving on to other matters I should like to emphasize one very important implication of the preceding arguments: that change in the formal system may be seen always to be *external* (or exogenous) in origin to that system. This seems to me to be the case for at least two reasons: (1) analytically, the variety that is the raw material of change is not "of" the system formally, but only "in" it in a substantive sense; (2) more significantly, it is only in terms of environmental (external) parameters that we are able to explain how and what substantive variety will be systemically restructured and/or is likely to be selected for.

Let me recapitulate. I have argued that there are certain assumptions for the systems stance I adopt here. I believe this structural approach can facilitate the explanation of cultural change and the evolution of sociocultural systems. Specifically, we need some paradigm for the materialist analysis of such systems. The one I have in mind is cultural ecology; it is firmly grounded in a general systems framework and I turn to it now.

CULTURAL ECOLOGY

Cultural ecology is the unfortunately now faddish term used to describe one kind of approach to the nomic explanation of cultural diversity and similarity. As a matter of fact, cultural ecology relies heavily on the paradigm worked out by biologists over the last several decades. Despite such a legacy I insist that this in no way implies that cultural ecologists are reducing our analysis to biology. Rather, the formal, systems framework that underlies each cultural and organic ecology is equally appropriate to both in the sense that general systems represents the source of "nomic analogies" for both these disciplinary endeavors. Nonetheless, the fact remains that, for a number of reasons I need not go into here, biological ecologists were the first to work systematically from this perspective now held common to both our pursuits.

Minimally then, ecology [7] is the study of the determinant relations that obtain between the numbers, distribution, and organization of living systems, especially those of the populational sort, and their effective environments. As I view the matter, it is the task of the cultural ecologist to isolate those environmental factors that, as parameters, put a strain on the organizational properties and complexities of particular sociocultural systems and that may be seen to select for some alternate structurings of constraints. Ideally, if we can go beyond the particular instances and specify the general or nomic character of selection for particular social structures we shall be well on our way to more than simply vague, impressionistic, or metaphorical uses of terms like "ecology" and "evolution" in anthropology. There is no need to adopt wholesale the particular concepts worked out by biologists for the analysis of their peculiar data—rather, the use of such concepts should depend upon their utility not only in the problem of classifying cultural data but in the framing and testing of specific hypotheses.[8]

Enough, then, of the formal promise of cultural ecology, and on to the programmatics! Specifically, I think we need to be able to specify the location of the system's "action" and then proceed to describe and measure it. And finally we shall wish to *explain* its occurrence. In the sense intended here any adequate explanation of structure ought simultaneously to be an explanation of change—accordingly we are able to sidestep another of the cans of worms that have distracted too many anthropologists even in the recent past.

I have found it useful to think of sociocultural systems in terms of one or more of three dimensions. Notice that I do not use the words *component* or *subsystem* as is common in entertaining these topics. The three dimensions of sociocultural systems are the "organizational," the "control," and the "energetic." [9] These dimensions are just that: they represent in no way distinct systems. Rather they represent different formal perspectives from which to appreciate the structure and behavior of any single substantive living system. In a complete or holistic sense, every living system can be said to "have," that is, to be analyzable in terms of at least these three dimensions. In addition, each of these dimensions refers to matters commonly dealt with by at least some social scientists; finally, the variables structured along these dimensions are fairly easy to operationalize in anthropological research and analysis. In this chapter I shall emphasize the organizational dimension for reasons that should become obvious.

It is the competence of the variables described as the *control* dimension to express the capacity of a sociocultural system to generate variety (in terms of symbols or ideas). More importantly it is with reference to this dimension that we are able to discuss culture as "the dead hand of tradition." Often incorrectly termed "information" in the systems literature, the control dimension is a description of the structuring of the system's "people-processing." [10] It will be possible and fruitful to discuss this dimension as the culture's ability to provide, through socialization and enculturation, both in terms of instrumental and affect manipulation, the constraints necessary to ensure behavior consonant with the organizational structures selected for; that is, *continuity* of structure. It is of no small moment that in substantive systems such systemically unregulated symbolic variety described along this dimension may be critical as we examine its manipulation by such social types we call "patrons." For our purposes here, it is structured ideology, on the one hand, and minority or alternative symbol arrangements, on the other, that represent most saliently the controlled structure and the uncontrolled variety, respectively, of a given substantive sociocultural system.[11]

Living systems can be seen also as representing kinds of energy capture and energy processing and storage "machines." Thus it is necessary for us to allow a place in our analyses of sociocultural systems for a consideration of this ultimately most critical, if not most interesting, dimension of living systems. Accordingly I have isolated the *energetic* dimension in terms of which we are able to appreciate just such matters as the extractive and energy storage capacity of a given system, whereby it is able to buffer out changes in external environmental parameters so as to maintain, say, the organizational steady state required of or selected for in the system itself. Indeed, for many problems, there is reason to assign causal, or at least critical enabling, priority to the energetic capacity of a system. Especially this is so if we wish to comprehend the why and the how of the operation and change of structured variables along the other two dimensions, the control and the organizational. Once more, at any one time it is possible to isolate the energetic salience of systemically regulated variables as well as to note (for instance, Boserup 1965) the energetically measured variety "in" but not yet "of" the system.

When we turn to the *organizational* dimension we are on somewhat more familiar ground anthropologically. For it is here that we have reference to the systems of variables that seem to be at the very interface with the environment. Albeit any given living sociocultural system must in a formal sense "people process" and energetically enable, very often we can shorten our systems modeling by playing the "as if" game—by assuming or holding constant matters of control and energetics—and feasibly proceed to the consideration of the varying selective strains that environments place on diverse formal structurings of statuses and roles, power and reciprocity. So we are dealing with system structures that may sometimes comprise a multitude of statuses that articulate large numbers of people; at other times we may be concerned with role systems for small numbers. Often we may be dealing with corporate integration and group or quasi-group structuring; or, again, we may be faced with network and noncorporate structuring. The point to be emphasized, however, remains that it is the formal character of the organizational structures of sociocultural systems as such, and not simply otherwise reducible collections of individuals, that are often selected for or against, in the course of sociocultural evolution. As Catton (1966:81) puts it so well: "In both the organic world and the social world . . . it is less a question of individuals of varying degrees of fitness, struggling against each other for survival, than a question of survival of the best adapted structures."

As I suggested before, the formal structuring of sociocultural systems does not vary randomly. Rather, particular organizational structures may be seen to be instrumentally best suited (or at least minimally suited) to certain environments and, given that minimal enabling matter energy capture or storage and redistribution structuring prevail, are selected for.

We might now turn profitably to some other aspects of the nature of structuring itself. I have in mind two things; first, the matter of structural tightness or looseness (often called "integration"), and second, that of hierarchy. Especially when we wish to consider such phenomena as those that are the subject of this book, we shall find when talking of integration that it is necessary to distinguish between the two things. By *structural tightness or integration* I mean not only the numbers of variables that are systematically regulated at a particular locus as opposed to those variables not so regulated.[12] Equally important is the range of alternative values a given variable may assume before it "activates" substantive elements. For instance, as we examine patronage phenomena we will note that they typically occur where there is considerable unregulated or loosely integrated variety along the organizational dimension of the system. It is precisely here that there is room for the wheeling and dealing associated with the establishment of patronage "bridging transactions." In this sense I think that we can extend Barth's comment (1967a: 171) beyond the solely economic aspects of entrepreneurial activity he described in the following terms: ". . . entrepreneurs will direct their activity preeminently towards those points in an economic system where the discrepancies of evaluation are greatest, and will attempt to construct bridging transactions which can exploit these discrepancies."

Hierarchy in systems structuring is an issue of particular significance when we attempt to explain patronage. I refer here to the utility of the notion of formal "levels" of substantive sociocultural system. On the

29

one hand it is of course possible that many of the lower level systems (formally speaking) of a given substantive society or culture will be directly regulated "from above," as it were, and thus be formally regulated subsystems of the larger formal identity. To the degree that this is the case and such superordinate control is pervasive and "rationalized" we would expect, I suggest, little room for the effective operation of patronage. On the other hand, we would expect rather greater prospects for the presence of patrons [13] in those circumstances where either the superordinate (hierarchical) regulation is restricted, that is, where it formally concerns *few* activities of the subsystems, or where it is loose, that is, where there is wide latitude in the values of those variables that obtain between suprasystem and subsystem. All this is by way of background for remarking that much of the activity we commonly associate with patronage is systematically (structurally and hierarchically) interstitial in nature. I shall return to a more detailed consideration of some of these issues in the concluding section of the chapter. For now, and in anticipation of some other points to be raised shortly, it is necessary to note that such hierarchical integration or regulation is clearly and determinantly associated with the relative as well as absolute form of energetics structuring characteristic of the systems and subsystems respectively.

At this point I should like to introduce the question of how the cultural ecologist might systematically go about explaining how it is that in some environmental circumstances some individuals are able to exercise effective power over the actions of others. In essential agreement with some of my colleagues, I suggest that we need to isolate and ideally to measure the various kinds of resources that individuals or groups are able to manipulate in given systems contexts. In anticipation of the concluding section of this paper I might note that patrons, and indeed clients also, are likely to have peculiar limitations and accesses to empirically relevant resources. Strickon has proposed that, at least with respect to patronage, we can usefully distinguish between three sorts of resource variables: the "idiom," the "positions," and the "material resources." Now not surprisingly these three fit in rather well with the three systems dimensions I noted earlier. In order both to avoid misconstruing Strickon's meaning as well as to suggest a more general utility to the distinctions raised I propose the terms: "symbolic," "social," and "energetics" power resources. By analyzing the relative and absolute concentrations of each of these in the hands of particular persons or groups in the sociocultural system, it ought to be possible to understand just how particular "adaptation gambits" come to be generated by particular sociocultural systems. I use the term "gambit" to emphasize the fact that not all systems responses to environment will necessarily be successful. To explain the success of any given adaptation gambit we need to analyze the degree to which it effectively copes with the (exogenous) environmental parameters.

THE NOTION OF PATRONAGE: COMPARATIVE PERSPECTIVES

Arnold Strickon concluded in an earlier session of our original symposium held at Santa Fe that many of the papers members of the group had presented were actor oriented, and not society or culture oriented. He suggested that in these papers the authors were not addressing themselves to the questions, "Why is sociocultural system X the way it is?" In some way then this chapter represents a different analytic emphasis: an "ecological" (and structural) one rather than a "situational" one. Specifically I feel that, given my negative instance of patronage in San Miguel (chapter 9), some account of patronage that is adequate in the larger (explanatory) and not only the situational (descriptive) sense would be useful.

Indeed, the question that seems to me to be of particular importance is precisely that relating to the special environmental circumstances under which we should expect to find such political irresolution and structural looseness as that which is customarily expressed as patronage systemics. I maintain that our answer will be, at least, twofold. *First,* in the broad sense of environment, we may expect that the flexibility and short structural duration that characterize the patronage adaptation gambit will coincide with those cases where environmental parameters vary sufficiently and erratically so as to render any concrete centralized regime ineffective over long periods of time. *Second,* in the narrower system-specific sense, we should expect patronage systems to arise in those circumstances where power of the larger system is diffuse, at least interstitially, so as to present zones of unregulated substantive variety that would provide the basis for a tentative, uncertain development and relative instability of social differentiation and accordingly be associated

31

with weakly rationalized intersystem regulation—namely patron-client systemics.

I am using the terms *patronage* and *patron-client relationships* in a more restricted manner than do some of the other contributors to this volume. In this section I hope to isolate and account for some of the critical structural features of this peculiar institution. Patronage, it should be obvious, is not universally pervasive as an organizing principle —even in Latin America. My demur is not simply a definitional one, though it is of course at least that. Rather, and more to the point, I wish to suggest that most societies or cultures have been and are able to work out more concrete, substantive, and permanent adaptations to environmental challenges than the short-term and precarious resolutions we are calling "patronage."

In this concluding section then I shall discuss several problems related to the character and occurrence of patron-client systems: (1) the features of individual flexibility and loosely regulated macro-sociocultural structures; (2) the entrepreneurial and brokerage aspects of patron-style social action; (3) the structural similarities and differences among the big-man, the chief, and the patron; (4) the importance of "state" integration and the significance of derived power in patron-client systems; (5) the differences between sociocultural structurings such as feudal societies and manorial systems and rationalized state bureaucracies on the one hand and patron-client orderings on the other; (6) some of the characteristics of resource manipulation peculiar to entrepreneurs as the paradigm for patronage systems.

PATRONAGE AND LOOSELY STRUCTURED SOCIOCULTURAL SYSTEMS

One of the more obvious facts about patron-client systems is that they occur in circumstances that may be described minimally as loosely structured or integrated. It is, of course, the presence of unregulated flexibility among variety in the substantive populational system that makes it possible for certain individuals or subgroups to creatively exploit them to their own advantage. This is accomplished, as I remarked before, through some person's or some group's being able to manipulate a particular set of resource variety in order to set up a transaction of Barth's "bridging" sort. Now, obviously, in all societies or substantive socio-cultural systems there is some degree of flexibility even for that variety which is regulated as variables; there also is a pool of variety unregulated at higher systems levels. However, in most cases it seems that either the payoffs are insufficient in scale to underwrite widespread patron manipulation, or in the event or anticipation of significant success experienced by a particular manipulator, his comrades "realize" that his advantage is at their expense; accordingly, countering negative feedback mechanisms are either developed or, once more, activated. I am suggesting, then, that probably in most cases in history (that is, most of the time), the "adaptation gambits" characteristic of sociocultural systems were set up precisely as structured constraints on individual action in environmentally conditioned "zero-sum games." It is precisely such circumstances that inhibit the wheeling and dealing of patrons. More broadly, we can see that it is only in those cases where either sociocultural and environmental circumstances allow the occupation of a new or changing range of operation (i.e. new adaptive niches) or where a runaway positive feedback on the part of the system itself keeps the environment changing, that the sociocultural system is unable to maintain any consistent concrete organization as its permanent adaptation gambit. The result, given certain other features, may be the phenomenon of patronage.

PATRONS, ENTREPRENEURS, AND BROKERS

I suggest that it is the entrepreneur who best represents the prototype for agents of sociocultural adjustment and change, including the patron as he attempts to set up his bloc. The patron is, in other words, a special kind of entrepreneur. He shares with others in this class the fact of operating for maximal parochial advantage in the formally relatively unregulated sectors and interstices of the larger substantive populational system.

This brings us to the fact that a patron is a broker as well as an entrepreneur. Barnes (1969:73), for instance, distinguishes between patron-client relationships, on the one hand, and broker-client relationships, on the other. I do not wish to split definitional hairs at this juncture. However, I also suggest that the two, the "patron" and the "broker," may be seen as more than only slightly different representations of the same phenomenon. For when the patron operates to set up any kind of bridging transaction he is doing so at the interstices of formally regulated systems. By the term *brokerage* we emphasize the instrumental significance of exchange in the patron-client relationship, while by the term *patronage* we stress the associated status asymmetry that results from or is a part of the very same relationship. Now I do not maintain that all entrepreneurial brokerage involves patron-client asymmetry; nor do I hold that all brokerage is entrepreneurial in character. Respecting the first of these matters, I do suggest, however, that all patronage necessarily involves some form of brokerage functioning, competences, instrumentalities, and payoffs. For it is precisely the presence of the local-level sorts of brokerage, as found in San Miguel though restricted even there, that initially suggests the possible presence of patronage systems. In San Miguel, however, such brokerage is almost invariably accomplished through the traditional generalized reciprocities of kinship and related mechanisms. Thus, while neither brokerage nor entrepreneurship represents sufficient definitions of patronage, they are both essential parts of an adequate definition.

I have distinguished between brokers and patrons. It is worth some effort to make clear that I do not intend to identify all entrepreneurs with patrons. I maintain that an entrepreneur is the general model for any number of resource manipulators, including patrons. Furthermore, I argue that the strategies of patrons are appropriate only in certain game situations. I suggest that the frequency and significance of entrepreneurs in any society is not a function of any McClelland-like motivational makeup, nor even a result of a Hagen-like educational profile peculiar to them. Rather, their presence and frequency are to be adequately explained only in terms of the presence of structural looseness of the sociocultural system and the potential payoff of the entrepreneurship endeavor, as both of these may be seen to be conditioned by particular sets of environmental parameters—those conducive to hierarchical structural looseness as well as to flexibility of actor (client or patron) alliance.

KINSHIP, SOCIAL HIERARCHY, AND PATRON-CLIENT SYSTEMS

Turning to the matter of the importance of status asymmetry as a *sine qua non* of patronage systems, I have taken pains to emphasize this aspect partly since it seems to be one of the best distinguishing markers between the hierarchical character of many peasant groups in Latin America, on the one hand, and the relatively flat social differentiation typical, for instance, of San Miguel, on the other. What is especially important in the San Miguel case is the dominant limiting effects of generalized exchange reciprocities which, operating primarily through the kinship idiom, act to dampen out status distinctions. I suggest that this is just what one may expect of what Fortes (1970) calls a "kinship polity" rather than an otherwise centralized polity.

However, it is not entirely appropriate to argue that all sociocultural systems that emphasize kinship idioms as the substantive means whereby their formal systems are realized are therefore nonhierarchic in character. Nor is it useful to hold that wherever we have hierarchic social orderings of status, we therefore have patronage. Specifically I propose we now consider such types of social persons as "chief," "big man," and "lineage head," in order to place in relief the differences among them.

The "big man," so typical of Melanesia, is often cited not only as a kind of "primitive capitalist," which he is not, but also as a kind of "primitive patron," which I similarly hold he is not. To be sure, the big man shares some features in common with both. Like the patron, he is continually forced to recruit, mobilize, and maintain a following through his ability to manipulate resources of various kinds, often those of a symbolic character. Such personal qualities as possessed by the big man imply a kind of "personalismo," in some ways not strikingly different from that of the patron. In both instances too they at least commence their machinations often aided by little ascribed status of ascendancy. Indeed, because they are so intricately embedded as *part of* the very social person of patron or big man, such qualities may give us as well some understanding as to the limitations on the duration of the power blocs they build. That is, seldom if ever can the power and influence of such social types as these be simply transferred or inherited from one person to another. Indeed, the second in command often is just the sort of person, by virtue of the very traits that make him an excellent lieutenant, who is least capable of maintaining the mantle of power received from a deceased or abdicated leader of either sort. This suggests, it seems to me, another similarity between the big man and patron; namely, that symbolic resources, rather than clear-cut and permanent access to either ascribed power over social persons or energetics monopoly, represent some critical dimensions of both types.[14] It is precisely because they must continually rely upon symbols as their basic resources that they remain big man and patron instead of transforming, for instance, into chief and feudal or manorial lord.[15]

Still, I think there are salient differences between the patron and the big man. I believe that the relative unimportance, for the big man, of deriving additional power resources from domains superordinate to and outside of his own relatively restricted sources is in great contrast to the patron. The latter is able, after his own successful competition for leadership, to tap into important derived (state) power. By contrast the big man is extremely limited in the arena of his social activity and is confined to his own localized resources or those of his immediate faction (cf. Sahlins 1968:86–90), and to his own skill to manipulate them. The patron may, on the other hand, through resources not inherently or locally his own, attain such derived clout and at least momentarily be transformed into an office occupier on the local level.[16] Thus he may cease to be subject, temporarily or for the rest of his life, to the indeterminancy of constant patron-izing. Finally, while the salience of big man ranking is intrasystemic in focus, that of the patron is hierarchically intersystemic.

Within tribal circumstances big men contrast to at least two other social types commonly discussed in the literature. These are the "lineage headman" and the "chief." (The latter is characteristically the highest, or at least an important, kind of influential person in many of the same circumstances of *rank society* described so clearly by Fried [1967:109–84].) Following Meggitt (1965) I suggest that at least one environmentally significant difference between the circumstances that give rise to the big man and those that produce the lineage head is the presence of a set of environmental constraints that define a zero-sum game [17] for the sociocultural system under examination. Under such conditions it seems plausible to expect that increasingly severe constraints may be placed by the corporate core-group (whatever it is) on the independent and thus selfish operations of a would-be big man. Although my case of San Miguel is obviously not a Melanesian tribe, we find at least a structural isomorphism between the constraints on lineage headmen in Melanesian sociocultural systems and those that obtain in the "limited good" corporate philosophy of the campesinos of San Miguel.

The chief in tribal society offers still another contrast with the patron, although once again some similarities as well. The chief and his several subchiefs are entangled in an arrangement involving several sorts of status distinctions. In chiefly societies, the kind of clientage that exists between so-called noble and commoner implies a set of traditional hierarchical constraints much more predictable and durable than any we have evidenced in patron-client systems. I do not mean that in the latter case the immediate effect of status differential may not, in fact, be more exploitative than that associated with chiefdoms. In fact it often is. Rather, I maintain that the single thing that sets the chief off from the patron is the former's traditionally based (internally oriented) power, which suggests that the whole chiefly system with its paramountcies and emphasis on ascribed statuses not only can make unnecessary the wheeling and dealing (except at the system's boundaries) but also can maintain a severalty of homeostatic mechanisms to frustrate just such runaway individual efforts as those of patron.

PATRON-CLIENT SYSTEMS AND THE STATE

I now turn to another very important feature that sets off patron systems from *all* the tribal instances I have discussed in the preceding. In some particulars I have indeed already anticipated the argument I make here. This is that patron-client systemics are a phenomenon characteristic only of state-organized societies. I wish to emphasize this factor, since it seems to me to be the case that state societies alone are able to possess and distribute to lower echelons any large amount of power not already specifically conditioned and constrained by the universe described by the subordinate units themselves. For instance, by contrast with the chiefly instances, states (and the derived power typical of patrons) are characterized by a significant degree of "unaccountability" to lower levels. Again, borrowing from Bailey (1965:13), this may be described in terms of an "elite" sort of status reference group behavior and constraints. That is, I maintain that there is one thing, especially, about the critical environmental parameters of individual actors who operate in sociocultural systems characterized by pervasive patron-client relations that distinguishes them from nonstate forms of entrepreneurship and wheeling and dealing. This is the presence of derived state power, a resource that patrons, as a structural type, are able to exploit.

37

Importantly, the brokerage function most typical of a patron is that in which he is able to exploit the favor and the other resources of the superordinate state in a fashion impossible for many others in the larger sociocultural system. It is such derived power that allows the patron to leapfrog the constraints of lower echelon resources, and at least temporarily to aspire to, and in some instances to realize, a social status radically different from any possible at the more local levels alone.

Following Adams (1966:3–21) I think it is possible to evaluate the power of integration of state societies in terms of their ability to exercise power over subordinate units: "Two kinds of power sources can be distinguished. . . . If the superior has the control in his own hands and does not need to turn to another party for aid, then he holds *independent power* and exercises an *independent* domain. If the superior depends upon another party, however, he is exercising *derivative power*; he stands, in short, within the domain of the third party upon whom he depends for power" (Adams 1967:40).

The patron is just one such manipulator of derived power. And, of course, not all beneficiaries of derivative power are patrons. At least two other sorts of social statuses are possible, depending on the nature and scale of the superordinate state power exercised by each. These are the "feudal lord" and the "bureaucratic official."

It is in weak state systems that we expect to find patron-client systems both pervasive and continual. However, quite clearly we should not expect all weakly centralized states to evidence, in the long run at least, patronage systems. In certain cases we will discover that, after some brief period of flexibility and structural looseness typified by patronage maneuvering, things become increasingly firmed up and traditionalized. One of the common outcomes of such a transformation is some sort of "feudal" arrangement.

Boissevian (1966), among many others, has seen a kind of identity between certain feudal circumstances (for instance cases of East African feudalisms) and patron-client relationships. It is easy to see however, even as Boissevain does, that all such cases and those of Medieval European feudalism are at the opposite end of the continuum from the cases most of us deal with in this volume as being typically patron-client in character. With the latter we have been concerned with less formalized kinds of brokerage, where "the exact nature of the rights and obligations are not clearly defined culturally" (Boissevain 1966:18); in other words, where the very structuring itself is almost continually being re-negotiated. The distinction I am making between the patron per se and the feudal lord (and, indeed, the "hacendado" as a kind of manorial lord) relates to the fact that the latter possesses some clear-cut continuity of derived or monopoly power over social persons, whereas the patron, although also characterized by brokerage functioning, needs to demonstrate repeatedly the mutual advantages of the arrangements to those both above and below him in order to maintain such power. What Adams (1966:3–21) calls "unitary" as opposed to "multiple" power domains parallels the kind of distinction I am making between feudal lord and patron. That is, it is useful, I think, to raise the question, with respect to a relatively powerful broker, of whether his clients have any option in changing their allegiance. Thus, as Wolf (1966a:16–18) notes, the patron-client relationship holds out the promise of mutual support. From the perspective of the client, the motivations initiating such a relationship might well include such matters as an attempt to level inequalities, by getting a piece of the scarce pie or simply defense or security. But as we have seen, under conditions of "retreatest" corporate society, we would not expect patron-client relationships. For in the jargon of "systems" analysis, the homeostatic leveling mechanisms in this case are sufficient to frustrate these special patron-client ties. But where such mechanisms are finally broken down, for whatever reasons, one may expect that relations of the patron-client sort will appear and will be maintained so long as the whole system is not brought under the pervasive direction of a powerful and "rational" state apparatus. And until such occurs, the client may be forced to seek access to economic goods and services, to protection and buffering of state institutions, by setting up personal ties with a patron.[18]

It is my point here that patronage-clientage systems are structurally transitional forms; transitional, that is, between "earlier" and lower level corporate local systems and a "later" strongly rationalized and higher level state apparatus. Nonetheless the fact remains that in a temporal sense patronage systems (though not specific patron blocs) may prevail for considerable periods of time. There is no conflict here; as I argued earlier, so long as weak state structure prevails the "rational" bureaucratization of the structure cannot proceed far enough to liquidate the patronage systems. Indeed even in highly rationalized and high-energy state systems such as our own some spheres of activity remain decentralized; the result is often patron-like "ward healer" and ghetto boss relationships.

CONCLUSION

I have tried to weave together several of my thoughts on matters ecological, economic, and political. I hope to have been successful in arguing that all these issues make sense when considered from an ecological stance informed by general systems theoretics.

Thus, the cultural institution of patronage-clientage is sensible partly and immediately in terms of political facts on the ground. These, in turn, are often inextricably based in economic affairs—at least in the broad sense of the relative distribution of, and access to, scarce resources. Further, any adequate account of the significance and continuity of access to such resources necessitates an informed ecological discussion.

Finally I hope it is obvious now that in the explanation of patron-client systems, reference to only similarities of the elements or traits in and of substantive systems is insufficient; recognizing and describing the formal regulation of such variety as variables is critical.

NOTES

1. The literature on systems theory is even now rather large. In my statement I shall deal with my own version of the important matters. Those interested in other views, sometimes similar and often not, might refer to Buckley (1968) and Bertalanffy (1968) for general introductions. A. Strickon quite correctly remarked in our earlier discussions that what I argue for is hardly yet to be dignified as a bona fide "theory" of general systems. Rather, I should propose, the general systems approach is, in effect, a form of elliptical explanatory phrasing which, in addition, directs, constrains, and informs this and similar sociocultural analyses—that is, it underpins our "explanation sketches" (cf. Hemple 1965).

2. It seems to me likely that of the assumptions mentioned, the first two would stimulate little debate. More discussion, however, is probably appropriate regarding the latter two assumptions. *Materialism* as a philosophical position is usually opposed to what is often called Mentalism. As a result there exist a number of misconceptions about the salient differences between the two. First of all, the difference is not that only the followers of the latter position entertain the concept of ideas. Rather, the issue concerns the relative importance and priority of ideas in the changing of systems. Specifically, the materialist would allow for the existence of ideas in some systems (e.g., human living systems) but argue that it is not ideas themselves that compete but rather the individuals or populations possessing them. Even more important, perhaps, is the argument that the ultimate decision as to the merit of a particular ideological structuring in a sociocultural

system lies in the effectiveness of such informational directives in mobilizing human beings to cope in a matter energy universe. In essence, I suppose, the best justification I know of for materialism is that it is broader and more ambitious in explanation—that is, it ties together more of the universe in a single explanatory framework.

As to the matter of *methodological collectivism*, the intended opposition is to that of methodological individualism. As I argue it, one has demonstrated the existence of a system if he is able to isolate the determinant relations that obtain between the variables held to constitute the system itself, and if, further, he is able to effectively operationalize this formal model. The system, as we shall see, is analyzable in terms of both the number and constraints on the values of its variables.

3. For the moment it is not of importance whether this variety in the system is in fact developed internally or diffused into the substantive system.

4. Although I am not prepared to demonstrate it here, I suggest that ideally we should be able to describe a particular system in terms of some mathematical formulae (such as some differential equations). Certainly, however, our discursive attempts at systems description ought at least to entertain the possibility and desirability of such a mathematical "functional" statement.

5. The only full-length ethnography undertaken in the vein I am discussing now is *Moala* by Marshall Sahlins. Undoubtedly others exist and have escaped my notice, thus far.

6. Something of the sort of argument I am now making appears to be implied in Boserup's book, *The Conditions of Agricultural Growth*, wherein she argues that unregulated variety was inconsequential until the altered environmental circumstances selected for a new system incorporating the variety.

7. For those who care to pursue the matter of ecology I suggest Odum, *Fundamentals of Ecology*, and Andrewartha, *Study of Animal Populations*. Especially useful in light of my present analysis are the papers by Odum, "The Evolution of Ecosystems" and Simon, "The Architecture of Complexity." The paper "Ecology: Cultural and Non-Cultural" by Vayda and Rappaport is also a useful survey.

8. This is not the place for a detailed discussion of the role of classification and typology in anthropology. Suffice it to say that I have more ambition for the "ecological" approach than that it simply supply just one more "cognitive grid" for plugging our data into.

9. Although there is a general similarity between my "three dimensions" and White's "layer cake model," we differ somewhat in both theoretical and analytical perspectives (White 1949:55 ff.).

10. I owe this term to L. R. Binford. If I were to acknowledge all my debts to him, even those that pertain only to this paper, it would be much longer.

11. It seems that what I am calling the "control" dimension is the primary concern for members of the Chicago "Cultural Systems" school. Nonetheless, I feel that Nadel's concluding chapter in *Nupe Religion* contains the best explanation of "competences" as I use them here.

12. When I say that some variables are not regulated at a particular level or by a particular formal system, this should not be taken to mean either that the

variables are not determined or caused in some fashion or that they are not systematically regulated by another formal system.

13. I am aware of Lauria's distinction between "patron" and "padrino" and there is the possible confusion between the two in my present usage. Nonetheless, for sake of simplicity and in light of received usage I shall stick with "patron."

14. I am arguing, as also have many of the others represented in this volume, that the consideration of "idiom" in Strickon's terms is critical for an adequate understanding of patrons and patronage. Initially it might seem that this emphasis on symbol manipulation is exaggerated. However, its importance lies in the fact that if and when a given patron-type entrepreneur can come to rely directly on material resources or be assured of ascribed or deprived power over social persons, that individual is no longer a patron at all but rather some other social type such as feudal lord or hacendado.

15. Nancie Gonzalez (chapter 8) suggests the provocative idea that as a general rule patronage systems, such as those characteristic of the Dominican Republic, evidence a definite "limitation of evolutionary potential." In a similar vein I would be prepared to maintain that where the next lower decomposable unit (Simon 1965) of a given social structure, say a patron-client bloc, is that of the individual himself possessed only of his symbolic manipulatory powers, we can expect to find a precarious system severely limited in its evolutionary potential.

16. Such, indeed, is exactly what occurs in many cases of modern-day democratic politics where, after a patron-like pursuit of votes, the winner is assigned to an office replete with derived power and often access to resources for the payoff.

17. For Meggitt's analysis, the critical substantive parameter was that of population pressure on scarce land resources; his instrument of measure was thus population density.

18. As Wolf (1966a) notes, although the exchanges flowing toward the patron may not be as immediately tangible as those in the direction of the client, they are by no means inconsequential. The patron receives, in addition to esteem, critical information about the functioning of local activities under the aegis of his derived power as well as about the state of his rival's power bloc. Finally, he may recruit additional personnel to swell the ranks of his own bloc; this increase acting as a clear sign of his right to the mantle of "patron." In other words, it may be worth it to the patron, in order to guarantee his continued success, to maintain and increase ramifying relationships with underlings.

3

Carlos Felipe:
Kinsman, Patron, and Friend

ARNOLD STRICKON

Department of Anthropology
University of Wisconsin, Madison

INTRODUCTION

In the past decade or so, increasing attention by anthropologists has centered on noninstitutionalized (or at least nonformalized) groups in attempts to analyze the ways in which these groups mediate between individuals and institutions. It seems to be a hallmark of such groups that they exist, as Wolf (1966a) points out, in the interstices within and between the formal institutions of the societies in which they occur. These informal groups have been examined from varying points of view and classified under a number of different structural "types," from the dyads of the compadrazgo to wide-ranging interpersonal networks. There seems to be a growing consensus, however, that these various phenomena, as well as relationships of kinship and friendship (Wolf 1966a; Paine 1969), are all somehow, at least for certain purposes, related.

The manner in which informal action groups relate to each other, and their significance for anthropological theory and concepts, raises questions about the character of sociocultural systems, cultural evolution, and even the relationship between psychology and anthropology. Most of these questions are too broad to be considered here, although a few are discussed in this book's introduction.

In this paper I focus on a single individual, Carlos Felipe,[1] as a participant in different action groups: as a member of his family, as the manager of one of his family's business operations (and, in that context, as an employer dealing with his employees), and as a friend among friends in the rural neighborhood where he manages a cattle ranch for his family.

The three action groups to which Carlos Felipe belongs would be described, structurally, in different terms: "family," "patron-client sets," and "peer group." The question I wish to raise is whether these structural "types" are distinct structural entities or whether their distinct structural characteristics are, rather, epiphenomena resulting from attempts to raise, organize, and allocate resources (human, material, and moral) for a variety of goals, in different situations with different systems of reinforcement and constraint.

The following case material illustrates some of the variables that influenced specific decisions (or classes of decision) in Carlos Felipe's action groups; appropriate goals for specific types of action group (or, alternatively, the kind of goal that generates one as opposed to another kind of group); and the strategies used to obtain the ends desired. The spotlight is on the actor, Carlos Felipe, and his kinsmen, employees, and friends, rather than on the action groups as structural entities.

FELIPE HERMANOS, S.A.: THE CHANGING ORIENTATION OF A FAMILY FIRM

The firm now known as Felipe Hermanos, S.A., was founded in Buenos Aires about the time of World War I by an Italian immigrant and his wife. Felipe, who had been a skilled cabinetmaker in Italy, found in Argentina a booming economy and a rapidly growing upper and upper middle class attuned to the furniture-making traditions that he knew.

Three Felipe sons, of whom Carlos was the youngest, and one daughter were born in Argentina. The sons attended school through the secondary level, and the two elder entered the family business. The firm prospered during the depression of the 1920s and 1930s and into the early 1940s. It received awards at public exhibitions for its products, and this reinforced its standing with its wealthy clientele.

The firm's workers were not unionized, and good personal relationships existed between the workers, who were also mostly Italian immigrants, and the Felipes. The Felipes say that they helped workers' children through school, paid ill employees for months, and hired the grown sons of their workers if they too wanted to be furniture makers. Even today, most of the dozen or so Felipe Hermanos factory employees are older men who have been with the firm for many years. (The owners complain, however, that the sons of the workers no longer come into the firm, and that the young men whom the Felipes are now forced to hire impersonally are undependable.)

During the twenties and thirties the business expanded into real estate in Buenos Aires; during the forties it expanded into cattle ranching. In the nineteen thirties the firm and family bought a half-block lot in Buenos Aires and transformed it into a headquarters. On about two-thirds of the lot they erected a two-story building with a factory, showroom, and office at ground level and a massive apartment for the parents and unmarried children above. Connected to the factory and parental residence was a four-story apartment house for the married sons (and later some of their children) and a few senior factory workers.

During World War II the firm (by this time under the management of the elder brothers) reached its peak in furniture manufacturing. From the start of the Perón administration in 1946 its furniture-making activity began to decline in importance, and with it the importance of the two elder brothers. The decline, according to the Felipes, was brought about by the economic, labor, and social policies of the Perón regime, the economic difficulties of the post-Perón period, and, not unimportant, changing tastes in furniture in the postwar period and the refusal of the Felipe management to adapt to them.

The decline in the urban fortunes of Felipe Hermanos, S.A., was balanced by a rise in their rural business. Paralleling this rise was an increase in the personal and family influence of the youngest brother, Carlos Felipe.

From the late twenties to the early forties Carlos Felipe had played grasshopper to the elder brothers' role as ants. He had come to maturity in the parental household as the economic fortunes of the family were rising to a peak. Few demands were made on him to participate in the family business. He used the money available to him to play a classic Argentine role, that of the *niño bien,* described (at a considerably higher economic level) by Vicente Blasco Ibáñez in *The Four Horsemen of the Apocalypse.* Carlos raced horses and cars (he won a Grand Prix), and generally lived "the good life." He played no significant role in the family business.

Carlos claims that it was he who, shortly after the start of World War II, persuaded his father and brothers to buy a small estancia (cattle ranch) in central Buenos Aires province as a place to spend weekends and vacations and to entertain friends. It served the status functions often ascribed to land ownership in Latin America, and also served the quasi-status, quasi-economic purpose of raising thoroughbred race horses. The management of this minor end of the Felipe business was delegated to Carlos. "To keep me out of trouble," he adds wryly.

As the war progressed, however, and the prices paid for beef and grains began a long, steep rise, Carlos was increasingly attracted to the more mundane aspects of estancia management. New to the business, he sought more expert advice than did other owners and managers in his zone. He introduced a number of production and breeding practices on his ranch that were new to the area. The innovations paid off handsomely both economically and in terms of his status among his local peers.

At this time Carlos met and married a schoolteacher, the daughter of one of the leading middle class business families in the county seat (*cabeza del partido*), which was the administrative and market center for the area in which the Felipe ranch was located. Through his brother-in-law, Carlos Felipe became a partner in a hotel and bar in the county seat. The place was an estancieros' hangout and provided a local home away from the ranch for Felipe and other ranchers and large farmers of the area.

In the late nineteen forties, during Perón's administration, the Felipes decided to expand their ranching operations. The family provided the capital to purchase an additional 3,000 acres. Then shortly before Perón was overthrown they acquired another 2,000 acres. The manner in which this land was obtained is worth considering in terms of the sociopolitical constraints on the market.

The 2,000 acres for sale were—legally—the personal property of a member of the Gómez family, a pseudonym for a wealthy, politically and economically powerful, traditional elite landowning family. The land was managed as part of the 90,000-acre Gómez estancia in the *partido*. This estancia, in turn, was managed as part of the Gómez holdings all over Argentina. The Gómez family, like the Felipes, is also a legal corporation (Strickon 1962).

The individual owner of the 2,000 acres was a young man deeply involved in the anti-Perón movement. He had been arrested for his activities but somehow had escaped and left Argentina. He placed the 2,000 acres on the market to raise money. His best offer came from a high official in the Perón administration, but before the sale closed the Gómez family stepped in and prevented it. Whether they did this for political, economic, or personal reasons is not clear. The word went out that the land was for sale again—to someone who could be "trusted." At this stage, Felipe entered the picture. His reputation was good. He could be trusted, and he had, as we shall see, significant personal connections with people who could intercede for him with the Gómez group. The land went to the Felipes and brought their holdings up to the present 10,000 acres, a medium-size ranch by central Buenos Aires province standards.

Of course, the Felipes did have to buy the land with hard cash. The fact that they were men of honor simply gave them entrée into the Gómez marketplace. The purchase represented a significant proportion of the firm's resources in available capital and credit. The decision by the firm to purchase the land, and the livestock and equipment to stock it, meant a shifting of emphasis in terms of not only the business itself but also its leadership. Carlos Felipe, once the family lightweight, was to be in charge of the major family economic undertaking and *de facto* head of the family. His new status was symbolized by the fact that upon the death of the parents it was Carlos Felipe and his family who took up their urban residence in the apartment over the factory, while the elder brothers, still managing the furniture factory and other urban interests, remained in their smaller quarters in the adjacent apartment house.

Why was the decision made to develop the firm's rural interests, and what were the alternatives to this decision?

According to Carlos Felipe, the money spent for land, livestock, and

47

equipment could have been used to expand and modernize the factory or to develop further the family's real estate interests (particularly apartment houses) in Buenos Aires. In either case, according to Carlos, they could have expected a return on their investment larger than the 4 percent that he said they were earning in 1959 on the land. However, expansion of the factory would have meant expansion of the labor force far beyond the core of "family retainers" then employed. Although the workers were legally unionized during the Perón administration, relations within the factory continued to be handled on a personal basis. The risks of getting involved with the Peronist unions was perceived by the Felipes as too risky. The factory also was losing its market, as tastes in furniture changed.[2]

Similar problems existed for them in expanding their interests in apartment housing in Buenos Aires; they felt that Peronist regulations had put them, as landlords, in a weak and uncertain position vis-à-vis tenants.

They were further dissuaded from investing capital in the city by the economic and political uncertainties of the early fifties, as the years of the Perón government drew to a close.

The risks and difficulties inherent in expanding their rural interests were the smallest of all. They believed that the value of the land itself would increase faster than would inflation. The return on agricultural products was good, and given the economic history of Argentina as of 1954, there was little reason to doubt that the importance of cattle and grains would increase no matter what the political future held. Although ranch workers were officially unionized, relations on the cattle ranches were still largely personal. No strikes had occurred among the cowhands and agricultural workers in the vicinity of the Felipe ranch during the Perón regime.

The reasons that the Felipes give for deciding to stress rural over urban interests seem clear, phrased as they are in terms of undeniable economic and political considerations. But additional thought reveals that there had to be other variables, of which the Felipes were at least tacitly aware, in their analysis of their situation. If the decision to stress ranching was simply the result of the reasons they stated, for example, then all similar businesses operating at that time in Argentina should also have changed their emphasis. Obviously, they did not. Some were able to cope successfully with the problems that the Felipes chose to avoid. The factors that the Felipes offer as their reasons for expanding into ranching might perhaps better be viewed as changes in the parameters of the business, compared to what those parameters were in the great days of the furniture factory. Our problem then is to seek the resources, constraints, and opportunities provided by these changed parameters and contrast them with those provided by ranching.

Changes in the Character of the Furniture Market

The Perón years, in fact, provided opportunities for such firms as Felipe Hermanos. People were streaming into Buenos Aires from the outlying provinces and the standard of living in the city was indubitably increasing. In order to tap this new market, however, it would have been necessary for Felipe Hermanos to produce cheaper furniture, changing production methods and design. Similar steps were called for even if quality were to remain high but styles were to shift away from the firm's heavy Victorian and baroque specialties. A decision to shift the market orientation of the furniture business would have represented a major management action, which they chose not to take. I cannot be certain why they did not, but I suggest two hypotheses; the first relates to the characters of the managers, the two elder brothers, the second to the family's access to certain financial and political resources.

The Characters of the Managers

The two elder brothers became active in the family business as soon as they left school. Through the years in which their father managed the concern, they worked chiefly as his assistants, with little voice in setting company policy. The father's policies were successful, and the changing parameters of the world in which the business operated were still not fully appreciated by him when he died. In the years following his death the two brothers faced a rapidly changing business, social, and political climate. They had no experience in independent decisionmaking but were still in the shadow of an extremely successful father, whose example of business acumen they had no basis for changing. Well into the fifties, their mother continued to represent the father's business policies.

The Financial-Political Variable

Even if the elder Felipe brothers had opted to try to exploit the growing market opportunities in their industry, they would have faced a number of serious constraints. If they had decided to change the quality or design of their product, they would have found it necessary not only to finance the changes, which they could have done without difficulty, but also to gain access to foreign exchange and permits for the importation of new machinery. Under the Perón government, neither of these would have been simple for the Felipes.

Today the Felipes take great pride in their anti-Peronism and their refusal to "knuckle under" to the Peronists. They delight in recounting how they never "contributed" to Eva Perón's charitable causes or distributed Peronist literature to their workers. They look with disdain upon those they knew who were against Perón but who "cooperated" with him in order to guarantee their own security and the success of their businesses. As far as I know, the Felipes were not on good terms with Peronist officials or sympathizers. Given this, I doubt that, had they attempted to obtain the requisite foreign currency and import licenses, they would have had the slightest chance of receiving them.

The Decision to Emphasize Ranching

What decided Felipe Hermanos to emphasize their rural over their urban interests, to stake practically everything on a major shift in emphasis?

I believe that the critical resource in this decision was Carlos Felipe himself, and the career trajectory he had followed up to this critical point in the family fortunes. Unlike his brothers, Carlos had not become his father's assistant. Drawing on the fortunes of the family, he had gone his own way—that of a *niño bien*, a playboy, a racer of automobiles and horses. By both North American and Argentine middle and lower class standards, this is a wastrel's role, an unproductive way of life. Yet it proved to be the entrée to people and resources that were decisive in the Felipe family's shift to ranching.

When the Felipes were permitted to purchase an estancia from one of the old elite families, it was Carlos's reputation and contacts that allowed them to enter the marketplace. His brothers did not have friends who moved in the circle of the Jockey Club and the Sociedad Rural, but it was through his involvement with such people that Carlos built his reputation. Where but in the paddocks of the thoroughbred racing tracks or the pits of the Grand Prix circuit, and the social world that revolved around them, could Carlos Felipe have made such friends?

Carlos, then, brought the Felipe family contacts with persons who had access to valuable resources in the ranching world, contacts that offset the family's lack of influence in Peronist circles. In effect, the family's decision to shift to ranching followed the development of influence in circles that offset their growing isolation in Buenos Aires. (It is interesting to note that a number of internationally famous Argentine athletes have invested in ranches following, or even during, their active careers. I would argue that this is due to more than the high prestige according to ranching; that, rather, the prestige accorded to this occupation is a kind of social shorthand recognition of the material, social, economic, and political resources needed to operate a big ranch. Ranching also continues to be the one area where the power associated with landholding, traditional elite groups still holds sway. And the one area where a person of relatively humble background can establish the contacts necessary to operate in such a situation is the *dolce vita* world of athletics and entertainment, of the *niño bien*, where Carlos Felipe "wasted" his younger years.)

The Felipe family followed its contacts into ranching, but the decision to follow this route was nonetheless costly to some members of the family. Influence within the family shifted away from the elder brothers to Carlos. The change, however, required family agreement, since the resources that had to be redirected into the ranch belonged to the family corporation. By agreeing to the shift in emphasis, the elder brothers decreased business risks at the cost of reduced personal prestige and power within the family and, presumably, outside it as well. Their willingness to go along with this change makes sense only if we assume that their interests in personal wealth, power, and prestige were secondary to their interests in the security of the family as a whole. The actions of Carlos and his brothers are comprehensible only if we look at the Felipe family not only as a corporation in the legal sense, which it is, but also, more important, as a corporate group in the anthropological sense.

The corporate character of the family and its effect upon the actions of Carlos Felipe stand out even more clearly when we examine the other action groups (patron-client dyads and networks and peer groups) in which Carlos Felipe participates.

CARLOS FELIPE: THE ADVANTAGES OF BEING A PATRON

One of the explicit variables in the Felipe Hermanos decision to expand their rural interests was the relative simplicity of dealing with ranch hands compared to effectively organized urban workers. To admit this is not to say that there are no difficulties in dealing with the former as well, though the problems are different.

Cattle ranching is a labor extensive operation, as is the highly mechanized form of agriculture carried out on the ranches. In the Felipes' part of Buenos Aires province it takes two men to put 2,500 acres, and its capacity of 1,000 cattle, to effective use. The low labor demand in reference to acreage and livestock capacity is one of the outstanding benefits of ranching as a business (Strickon 1965). This benefit is linked to a technology and body of techniques concerned with handling large numbers of livestock from horseback. This body of techniques, in turn, is linked to a social and cultural status associated with a particularly intense form of the European male way of life and values—that of the cowboy, gaucho, charro, vaquero.

The job, physically dangerous, is perceived by its practitioners and others to require a great deal of courage. Associated with the value of physical courage are the values of personal independence, competitiveness, egalitarianism (of a personal sort, and perhaps stressing etiquette more than substance), personal honor; in a word, *machismo*.

Both worker and employer believe that the culturally valued personal characteristics are linked with professional competence. The belief creates problems for both, for the very characteristics that make a good cowboy make a fractious and undependable employee. The conflict between professional competence and manageability of the work force results in what might be considered a perceived, as opposed to a *de facto*, labor shortage. This, of course, is not meant to imply that the numbers of men available to fill the jobs available do not affect the character of the market. Rather, the *de facto* labor potential is mediated by and through the perceptions of those in the market as either buyers or sellers of gaucho labor.

Part of the solution to the problem of dealing with a labor force that is presumed to be intractable in direct proportion to its competence is for the person who deals with the workers to himself operate, at least partially, according to their norms. If he does this, he is not requiring them to be subservient to a lesser being than the workers perceive themselves to be. If the owner cannot assume this role, then the manager must; if the manager cannot, then his assistant must; and so on, down the line, so that the man in the most immediate and continuous contact with the workers, the capataz or foreman, is always a man up from the ranks of the gauchos themselves. At any given supervisory level, if the man holding the position is unable or unwilling to operate in terms of gaucho norms, he has, in effect, relinquished control and general influence over his workers to whomever lower down the supervisory structure will fulfill the mounted workers' expectations of proper behavior.

A good many owners and managers do play, or attempt to play, the gaucho role. This role is of considerable symbolic and romantic importance in Argentina, as it is in the United States, and being able to play it does not detract from but rather adds to a man's prestige, in and out of ranching. This role does not always add to the influence, outside of the specific work context, of the owner or manager; some are just playacting; others are not interested in using it outside of work; still others, in spite of gaucho abilities, are despised on personal grounds by their employees and others in the area. In other words, the ability to play the gaucho is required in order to control the work force; it can be a resource harnessed for other ends as well, but is not always.

Carlos Felipe does indeed play the gaucho. He is no master horseman, but he has attempted to master the horseman's skills, and to some degree has been successful. He will defer to his workers over technical problems of horsemanship and herding. He has agreed to play by their rules and recognize their standards within those special contexts where they feel that they are more expert than he. They lose nothing by accepting his direction, since he sometimes accepts theirs. Carlos Felipe has a secure and reasonably disciplined mounted work force.

The ability to operate within gaucho values and standards, then, is part of the answer in dealing with a work force whose recalcitrance is in direct proportion to its competence. This pattern of control is further reinforced by a network of patron-client relations that not only tie owner or manager (both, in Carlos's case) to employee but ramify beyond the boundaries of the ranch into the rural neighborhood and village.

The goals of employer and employee, patron and client, are complementary. Out of a "labor pool" larger than the ranches in the area can possibly use, the owner-manager must select competent, stable employees. An employee must bring himself to the attention of the owner-manager in order to obtain a desired position. There are, however, constraints upon the labor market. Government and union regulations set minimum limits on incomes and fringe benefits, and members of the labor pool have alternatives they can turn to, so that they place considerable emphasis on the income and benefits of the jobs. They will not make personal sacrifices in order to be ranch employees. Many withdraw from the cowboy market, usually by migrating to the cities.

A number of occupational and status categories are relevant to the analysis of patron-client relations on cattle ranches. The first are those of day workers and seasonal workers, significant categories chiefly because they permit the worker to demonstrate his competence and personal characteristics. Such demonstrations are one way to enter the complex of personal relationships and networks that lead to desirable full-time ranch positions. The full-time positions are those of mounted worker and the senior foreman (capataz), section chief (puestero), horse trainer (domador), and a few others. Most men, in fact, never get beyond the day and seasonal worker category, and ultimately migrate to the cities.

One rule governs the owners' search for regular hands: "Never ask another rancher to recommend one of his own people." Since competent, stable workers are perceived as a scarce resource, it is assumed that an owner will never recommend one of his own good people, but, because of the constraints imposed by the government and unions on firing workers, only those he wants to get rid of. An approach to another owner, therefore, is made only when an owner or manager is new to an area, and then only to ask the first owner to find a recruiter.

The effective recruiter is an established senior employee, usually a foreman or section chief, not necessarily in the employ of the owner doing the recruiting. Owners and managers in a zone try to get to know the senior workers on the ranches around them with just such future recruiting in mind.

Carlos Felipe: Kinsman, Patron, and Friend

The foreman, once he has been notified of the opening, has four sources to draw on: his kindred; his fellow senior employees on surrounding ranches (who are almost always his friends and often his kinsmen as well); other employees on the ranch where he works; and daily or seasonal workers in the locality—in that order of desirability.

The senior employee is strongly motivated to bring his employers a good stable worker. The foreman's standing with his employer and the advantages to be gained from it largely depend upon the degree to which he can run an efficient operation. An incompetent, a perennial drunk, a fighter, or a troublemaker in the ranks reflects discredit on the competence of the foreman or section chief as a leader of men—an aspect of both the *macho* complex and managerial abilities. Thus the foreman will go for a man he thinks he can control, and the multiplex relations within the kindred of a zone make such control somewhat easier to achieve with consanguineals and affines than with strangers. But kinship connections are not the only, or even the major, criterion. I know of at least one case where a man would not recommend his own father for a job, in spite of their having a good relationship. The son felt, accurately, I think, that the father, a heavy drinker, would be undependable in that job and might endanger the son's future relations with his patron (who happened to be Carlos Felipe).

The other foremen and section chiefs to whom the primary recruiter passes word of the job opening go through much the same process. At times it takes a turn that results in a short-term loss for an owner or manager, as when a foreman of one ranch receives word that another ranch is looking for a man to fill a good opening, and recommends one of his own subordinates. His own employer loses a good hand, and the owner will grumble and complain a bit, but will do nothing. The ability of one's senior employees to attract good workers is related to the belief of the junior employees that the seniors will help them improve their positions. The foreman and section chiefs are, themselves, patrons to the junior workers, the resource that they command being job referrals. This resource is also a factor in the ability of a foreman to control his subordinates, reinforces the masculine image of the senior, and rebounds to the obvious economic and administrative self-interest of the owner. The senior employee also benefits because his juniors will help him in some of his personal economic or social activities.

In addition to the direct negative effects of interfering with the patronage activities of a senior employee, any attempt by an owner to interfere with the hiring away of one of his hands could produce problems with other owners. The employer losing the good worker in this situation, of course, has a neither legal nor moral basis for interfering. The only step he could take would be to appeal to the hiring owner not to take the man, as an act of friendship. It should be obvious that this would place the new employer in a difficult situation indeed. By acceding to the request he would endanger his own position in the complex social networks that structure the cowboy labor market of the zone. Normally, tempting an employer to interfere with the hiring away of one of his people is prevented by simply not telling him about it until it is a *fait accompli;* or the employee concerned may approach the present employer to see if he will better the offer.[3]

As a man rises along the mounted worker's career trajectory his resources increase, as does his direct dependence on the owner or manager. The section chief usually is alloted a hectare of land for his own purposes, but whether or not he can raise his own sheep or cattle or produce commercial crops on it depends upon the owner's feelings. Generally, the more important a man is to his owner-manager, the greater the number of privileges he can claim. At the top of the ladder is the foreman, the capataz, and here both the dependence upon and the benefits derived from the owner are overwhelming.

By the time a senior hand becomes a capataz, he is looking for his own place. He is a rare and valuable economic, administrative, and social resource for his employer. If the capataz is good, and there are very few poor ones, it becomes critical for the owner to hold on to him permanently. The desire of the capataz for a small ranch or farm of his own is the key to ensuring this.

Land, of course, is expensive, and credit, even through government banks, is almost impossible to obtain for a person from the economic class that produces most capataces. The owner, through his own circle of contacts, can intervene in his foreman's application for credit. Only by such intervention will the foreman be able to get a loan at all. Some owners will even arrange for land to be sold to their foremen, or sell some of their own land. Once the foreman has his own ranch,[4] the owner of the estancia will lend him equipment, let him use ranch personnel when he needs additional hands, help him arrange for the buying of breeding stock and the sale of his animals, and so on. At this point, of course, the capataz is tied to the owner far more closely than is any other employee, but the nature of these ties provides him with the resources that are the basis for his own role of patron to his subordinates.

The advantages of such arrangements for the ranch owner are clear: effective informal controls over a labor force whose stated values are against formal on-the-job discipline; access to a large and known (indirectly) labor force; involvement in a widespread, multiplex network that effectively organizes the labor market of the zone.

The foremen, too, derive obvious advantages from the arrangement, as do the younger men who are following traditional career patterns. For those not plugged into the network either as workers or as owners, the only solution is to get out. The system as it exists today operates to fill the employment needs of an industry that cannot possibly use all the people who are born in, or move into, the zone.

The complex steplike patron-client relations that tie owner-manager to foreman and section chief, and these in turn to men lower on the ladder, at one time served also to organize the political activities of the cowboy. As late as the 1930s the votes of the local lower class flowed back up this network to be used by the ranch owners and managers and their associates, a political flow that paralleled the flow of the region's economic product.

In the years since Perón, however, the political patron-client relationship between *estanciero* and ranch hand has lost its significance; political powers and alignments have changed. The political and administrative favors of patron for client, owner for capataz, capataz for lower employee, continue. They are, however, no longer paid off with a vote.

CARLOS FELIPE: THE ADVANTAGES OF HAVING FRIENDS

For Carlos Felipe, "friends" are peers. He may like and respect his foremen and hands, and they him (though the more usual feeling between them is cool, detached respect), but they would never describe their relationship as friendship. Similarly, consanguineal kin are *parientes*, who may or may not be liked and respected. Friends are nonkin peers, or are so perceived, although their wealth and other resources may, in fact, vary greatly. Affinal kin are discussed and evaluated in the same terms as friends, rather than in those applied to kinsmen. (This differs from the practice of the traditional lower class and, very likely, from that of the old elite landowning families.) The relationship with friends is seen as being based upon the personal characteristics of a man. The friend must be, of course, *simpático*, that wonderful word that defies any simple translation into English. A social subordinate, however (for example, a ranch hand or foreman), may be simpatico but not a friend.

Carlos Felipe's friends are in the *cabeza del partido* of the country. His circle of friends includes his brother-in-law, with whom Felipe is a business partner, a number of professionals, businessmen, and government and civil servants, and, of course, the ranchers and large farmers of the zone.

A second, somewhat overlapping group of friends is located primarily in Buenos Aires, where Felipe maintains a second home. The Buenos Aires group has a common interest in *gauchismo*, and its members collect nineteenth-century gaucho lore, literature, and artifacts. Most of them are also ranchers whose holdings are distant from the Felipe ranch. Almost all of them are actively involved in the Sociedad Rural. Some, including Felipe, have been on various committees of the society at the national level and some, again including Felipe, have held national-level offices in the society. Some of Felipe's Buenos Aires friends can trace connections to major, traditional elite landholding families. These families often have profound influence at the higher levels of the Sociedad Rural, which, in turn, has a profound influence on national agricultural policy and therefore on national policy on a great many other matters. The minister of agriculture of Argentina is usually himself a member of the Sociedad Rural or, at very least, has received their imprimatur.

My chief interest at the moment are Felipe's friends in the *cabeza del partido* and the way in which they organize and allocate different resources to desired ends.

Obtaining Capital

Among the most important of the group of friends are the livestock and grain buyers, who represent the chief market for the area's product and control a major source of credit for landowners and operators in the area. Through them the zone's products move to the national and international markets. The buyers' control over capital in the form of cash or credit is crucial to the economic flexibility of the landowners. New de-- velopments in breeds and techniques, the purchase of additional land, and other needs often are funded by livestock or grain marketing concerns rather than by banks. The buyer's advantage in such an arrangement is that the terms of the loan call not only for payment of interest but also for the buyer to have first option (if not a monopoly) on the purchase of the producer's output. From the borrower's point of view the arrangement is advantageous because of the speed and flexibility of response compared to that of a bank or other more usual credit source.

The buyers offer capital only to landowners with substantial holdings (or smaller ones who have the support of larger ones), and only to those with whom they have standing relations. No buyer, of course, has un-limited resources, and they rarely attempt to expand the market for credit services. When a buyer helps to capitalize a small farm or ranch it is usually as a favor to one of his larger producers and as a means of reinforcing their relationship, not as an undertaking for the sake of economics.

Growing Crops

Closely connected to the operations of grain and cattle dealers are the agricultural (as opposed to livestock) operations. Agricultural production in this zone is largely of wheat, maize, and sunflowers, destined for national and international markets, and a variety of forage crops for consumption by local livestock. Agricultural production within the zone is profitable in its own right and also is an important conservation measure, as particular fields cycle between crops and pasture.

At the present time [5] argicultural activities are organized and financed by contractors, although these may include ranchers who serve as con-tractors for their own holdings. The labor is provided by a variable combination of local day and seasonal workers, local machine operators, and itinerant teams of agricultural machine operators who come from far outside the zone and leave after the harvest is in.

The primary resource that the ranch owners or managers can offer the agricultural producer is, of course, large stretches of land that the rancher wants either to cycle out of pasture for a time or to raise crops on because of a differential between grain and livestock prices.

There are also constraints upon the rancher in agricultural activities.

Financing agricultural operations is quite different from financing live-stock; the latter generally requires long-term, the former short-term fi-nancing. The work cycle, personal characteristics, and relationships of agricultural workers and likestock workers are quite different. Invest-ment in agricultural machinery is heavy. In brief, if the rancher were to finance, organize, and manage the agricultural operations on his own ranch, it would amount to running two independent operations on the same place at the same time.

The solution is the use of agricultural contractors who arrange financ-ing, provide machinery and labor, manage and oversee the operation, arrange for marketing the product, pay the rancher in cash or by share for the use of the land, and, finally, once the field is withdrawn from agricultural use, plant it to grass or other forage crops so it will be ready to return to pasturage for the ranch's livestock. The rancher's responsi-bilities are to see to it that the ranch's livestock operations do not inter-fere with the agricultural activities, to decide which pastures are to be put under the plow, and, most important from our present viewpoint, to select the contractor or contractors who will use the ranch's lands.

The contractors are all men who by national standards would be con-sidered middle to lower upper class, but they all fill significant control-ling positions within the community and are the local upper class. The contractors include a few larger resident owners, of whom Carlos Felipe is the most important, the professional managers of a few still larger elite-owned ranches, owners of the largest stores in town (two of whom are also grain dealers, and one of whom is also the local representative of a provincial bank), the two town physicians, and the local represen-tative of an important national livestock auction concern whose contract-ing activities are independent of the concern for which he works.

Carlos Felipe contracts his own ranch. He has invested in some of the required machinery but still depends on itinerant work groups for har-vesting. He also does agricultural contracting for others. He is the only man I know of in his zone who tries to combine the two activities on his own land. The other contracting arrangements can be described in terms of structural "types" based upon the status of the contracting parties.

Horizontal contracts. These are essentially contracting relations be-tween peers, such as occur when Carlos Felipe contracts with another owner in his area or with the owner of a large local *chacra de ganado*, or when one of the town businessmen contracts with one of the larger resident landowners. The general influence of the contracting parties is about the same and the resources that each control are complementary. Each could, in theory, make a contracting arrangement wherever he wished. Therefore, the tie that holds the two together tends to be "friendship"; in fact, a "multiplex relationship" with social, perhaps kinship, and noncontracting economic links between the parties. Thus Carlos Felipe, who usually contracts his own lands, will occasionally permit a town businessman who is one of his chief suppliers to contract one of his pastures.

Descending contracts. These are contracts where the social and economic position of the landowner is inferior to that of the contractor. Here the subordinate party is not really free to seek other contractors for a more profitable arrangement. Carlos Felipe contracts the land of his foreman and a number of smaller farmers who arrange some of their town purchases through him. By refusing the contract, of course, these smaller landowners would endanger, in fact destroy, their access to the scarce and important resources that Felipe offers them.

Ascending contracts. The ascending contract is one in which the contractor is the social or economic subordinate and has fewer resources and less social "clout" than the party supplying the land. Ascending contracts are, universally, those made with the managers (not the owners or central administration) of a few massive elite-owned cattle ranches. Here it is the manager, rather than the contractor, who can arrange the most beneficial terms. The key man in such an arrangement is the large ranch manager who has the authority to select contractors. In spite of the disadvantage of their position, some contractors are very eager to enter into the arrangement. This is true of the storeowners, the grain dealers, and the cattle dealer. The elite ranch manager has more land to dispose of than any single owner in the zone; the ranch is the biggest source of livestock and grains for the market, and the largest single customer for the wares sold in the town's shops.

The advantages seem all to be with the elite ranch manager. He uses them to forge agreements with the contractor-storekeepers for his personal benefit, such as the granting of discounts for his private purchases. Other factors, however, give the contractor-shopkeepers a hold on the manager. This often occurs when, for example, false billing is arranged so that the stated prices charged to the ranch are higher than the real prices. The difference between what the ranch pays and the real cost is split among the shopkeeper, the manager, and ranch office personnel (such as the bookkeeper) directly involved in the graft. As a result, the managers are bound by the contractors' silence to guarantee the contractors access to the elite ranch's pastures.

Arrangements such as these are, of course, illegal, but they very rarely come to court. In cases I know of where ranch managers were fired by their employers, such stealing was not the reason for the termination of employment. There is almost always a good deal of friction between elite owners and their paid managers, and suspicion of such activities is one element in this friction. On the other hand, the government-controlled salaries for ranch managers are so low as to be ludicrous for the manager of a large cattle ranch, and the ranch owners recognized this. One of the benefits of a managerial position is the right to allocate agricultural contracts on the ranch, including the right of the manager to allocate them to himself and his immediate assistants. I find it difficult to believe that owners and "city management" are completely ignorant of the arrangements that result and the costs to the ranch. It is the price they pay for competent field management.

An elite ranch manager and local businessmen do not enter into the full complex of such contracting agreements lightly or with carelessly chosen partners. The ties between the parties are too critical and dangerous to be entrusted to anyone except an *hombre de confianza* in the literal sense.

The difference between what I have called an ascending contract and a descending contract concerns more than the structural positions of the contracting parties. The ascending contract turns into a peer relationship, as the reciprocal rights, obligations, and duties of the contracting parties cancel out the initially overwhelming advantage of the large ranch manager. The resources of each are different but, ultimately, complementary. In a descending contract the advantages of the contractor are never offset by the reciprocity of the small farmer or *chacarero de ganado*.

A man like Carlos Felipe rarely becomes involved in an ascending contract. His ranch is relatively small and he can handle his own contracting arrangements. As a contractor he has little to offer the large ranch managers; the resources he controls, unlike those of the shopkeeper, are much the same as those the manager controls, though on a smaller scale. His contracts, therefore, are horizontal or descending. Such contracts do not provide the lavish under-the-counter profits that the ascending contract does, but they pay off well for Felipe in areas other than the strictly economic.

As a man operating with peers and social subordinates, as a man who not only owns but manages a significant economic unit in the area, Carlos Felipe is a man of some importance. As a man not tied to the large ranches and their managers, he is considered to be his own man and an independent. Furthermore, his relations with the town businessmen lack many of the tensions that characterize their relations with the large estate managers. Felipe is a man of honor and confidence, in local eyes, and much more likely to speak for local interests and concerns than someone with interests in the large elite-owned ranches. What Carlos Felipe loses in the profits of ascending contracts he gains in personal stature and prestige in his own and surrounding *partidos*.

Gaining Access to Public Resources

The resources of government—national, provincial, and even international—that flow down a variety of institutional pipelines to the *partido* are of various kinds. I consider examples of two resources: (1) people and the positions they hold, and (2) public services and the equipment necessary to provide those services.

The lowest level of government in Buenos Aires province is that of the *partido*. The government and administrative arm of the *partido* is the *municipalidad*. For electoral purposes, the *cabeza del partido* is inseparable from the *partido* as a whole. All citizens of the *partido* vote for the intendente and other officials. Government representatives in the rural areas, *delegados*, are appointed by the party winning the election at the *partido* level. Prior to the Perón regime the electoral victors were always a party locally controlled by one or another clique, including local businessmen, large farmers, and ranchers or their managers. The local representatives of the winning party would "recommend" one of their number to the victorious intendente as the local *delegado*. The *delegado* was traditionally the owner of a large farm or small ranch. A resident owner-manager of a large estancia, or the manager of an elite estancia, would never deign to hold such a position.

This traditional arrangement changed with the start of the Perón regime in 1946. Perón, of course, rejected the traditional patterns of political control, as did his local representatives. Interestingly enough, however, the first *delegado* to be selected by the *partido's* new Peronist administration was a bar owner in a rural village who, in the 1930s, had been a rural policeman and the local strong arm for the conservative party. In addition to his duties as *delegado*, this man organized the workers into a local of the national Peronist stevedores' union and turned it into a rather effective hiring hall for nonlivestock workers. When he gave up the position of *delegado* in the Peronist administration in the early fifties he owned a large bar, a general store, land, and several cars that served the rural localities as taxis. During his regime the union had never struck.

The second, and last, Peronist *delegado* was recommended to the intendente by a group of local ranchers and farmers, Felipe among them. This man did so well that after the removal of Perón in 1955 the local powers recommended to the intendente, who at this time was a military appointee, that he ignore the policy of the military junta and keep the Peronist as *delegado*. The man remained in office until the elections of 1958, when there was a return to the pre-Perón method of *delegado* appointment.

The Peronist intendente was known as a fire-breather, much given to flights of rhetoric directed against the "oligarchy" in general and the ranch owners of the area in particular. The ranchers and their business associates did not care for this, but "arrangements were made." The intendente was an auto mechanic and during his tenure obtained the contract to maintain and service the vehicles of the large Gómez ranch. By the time he was removed from office in 1955 he owned the largest garage in the county seat.

But factors other than immediate personal gain were also involved in the cooperation between the local elite and the Peronist leader. The *municipalidad* operated within an inadequate budget. At the same time, of course, the intendente had to get certain services performed. I will look at just one of these, road maintenance.

The *municipalidad* is responsible for road maintenance within the *partido*. This is acomplished, through the proper bureaucracy, by two different procedures: a pool of equipment and labor stationed at the cabeza and dispatched where and when needed, and the assignment of resident road service workers (*camineros*) and their equipment to places scattered throughout the rural areas. Under neither arrangement are there sufficient funds to meet all the legitimate demands on the service. Connections with the *municipalidad*, therefore, are activated to see to it that these services are provided when needed.

The government pays the *camineros'* wages. A group of local ranchers, however, may get together and donate a plot of land, some livestock, or horses to provision and house the *caminero* in the countryside. They also dip into their own recruiting pools and networks for people to hold these jobs. The men recommended are tied to the locality by their involvement with the cowboy networks and by their dependence on the landowners and managers for important resources. The fact that Carlos Felipe and his friends recommend a man for a *caminero's* job is far more important than whether or not a man meets the formal government-defined criteria and passes the written test for the job. One *caminero* I know is illiterate; nevertheless, he "passed" the written examination and was appointed to the position. It is assumed that a man such as this will do his work well and diligently, whereas one who is not tied by the kin, friendship, and patronage relations that are normally activated to obtain this kind of position [6] is assumed to be less diligent and serious about his work. It is also assumed that the latter will not be in the assignment for very long.

Somewhat different procedures are used to gain access to the equipment pool that the *partido* maintains at a central location for road maintenance and repair work. The intendente or his appropriate subordinate must make a direct decision to assign the equipment to a particular location at a particular time. The Sociedad Rural acts as a go-between, "offering" to provide workers and fuel to the *municipalidad*. The intendente can state that a group of public-spirited, selfless citizens have offered their own time and resources in order to carry out the services that the *partido* requires but that are so difficult to do given the financial restrictions within which the *partido* must operate. The public-spirited citizens, of course, see to it that the feeder roads to the railroad and the main highways in their particular zone are kept open during critical periods in the livestock and agricultural cycles.

I need hardly add that the *partido's* Sociedad Rural is, effectively, Carlos Felipe and his friends, in their formal positions as the board of directors of the local chapter of the society.

CARLOS FELIPE: EPILOGUE

In the spring of 1966 a military *golpe de estado* removed the elected government of Arturo Illia from power. In his place a military governing junta was established in Buenos Aires and military officers, or their civilian allies, "intervened" the provincial governments. It was patently impossible, however, to appoint military interventors to each locality. The junta therefore decided that local officials would be appointed by the provincial interventors and the governing junta from among "the people" of the locality. The requirements set for the new local level officials reflected the junta's public position that the military had had to act because of the inefficiency, mismanagement, selfishness, and general lack of concern with the "real" national interest of all the established political parties.

There were two criteria for a local official under the new junta: (1) the man was to be recommended by his "neighbors," and (2) the man was to have no past history of involvement in politics.

In the summer of 1966 Carlos Felipe was appointed intendente of his *partido*. He had, after all, never signed his name to the rolls of any political party.

CONCLUSION

Although Carlos Felipe had never joined a political party, had never been active in organized politics, had never held any formal political position, it is clear that he managed (quite unintentionally, I am convinced) to gather the various reins of local power into his hands. He did this completely informally, with the exception of his formal positions in the Sociedad Rural, operating only in the context of noninstitutionalized action groups consisting variously of kinsmen, clients, patrons, and friends. For Carlos the formal institutions of his world—governmental, economic, and social—presented resources and opportunities that could be used to further the ends of himself and his family. He was geared not to changing society but to utilizing it for ends that he sees as personally rewarding and also, not insignificantly, as socially valuable as well.

Of the three action groups that have been described here in which

Carlos Felipe is involved, the family stands forth as markedly different from the patron-client networks and the peer groups.

The Felipe family operated as a corporate group and, in fact, had a legal corporate identity. Whether the kin ties reinforced the legal corporate ties or vice versa is moot. What is important is that the decisions and actions of the Felipes as individuals and as participants in a corporation seem to me comprehensible only insofar as they were operating within a framework of familial values and goals (Benedict 1968).

While the Felipe family controls common property and therefore as individuals have common interests at least in managing this property, the other action groups of Carlos Felipe lack this characteristic. What seems to hold the people together (in both peer and patron-client groups) is not *common* interest and *common* resources but rather *complementary* interests and resources. By pooling complementary resources the individuals who control them seek to achieve their individual goals. The philosophies and long-range goals of the participants may differ profoundly (for example, that of the Peronist movement, the Peronist intendente, and the large landowners). In terms of short-range goals, however, and in terms of meeting immediate problems and responsibilities, the complementarity of the resources seems to be a greater determinant than long-range goals, at least as overtly stated in terms of an explicit personal philosophy. The fact that such groups are focused upon individuals and resources is reflected in their fluid membership. This contrasts strongly with the family. I do not mean to imply that the family could not have broken apart, given the problems that the Felipes faced, but the constraints—social, customary, and emotional—on the family make it a far more difficult group to withdraw from than a patron-client set or a peer group. The gains to be achieved by withdrawing from the family and its resources (including emotional ones) must be far greater before its members will break with it than the kinds of advantages that would motivate one to withdraw from the other action groups discussed here.

The question still remains whether, and to what degree, the peer groups and the patron-client networks differ from each other. Certainly from a structural viewpoint they do (Wolf 1966a). Patron-client relations are usually considered to be those that cross class lines; action groups consisting of peers tapping different sectors of the economy and polity for related goals have been considered as distinct (Wolf 1966a;

Mintz and Wolf 1950; Leeds 1964). From the structural-functionalist viewpoint and the Marxist one as well, the function of the patron-client relationship is to provide links across social class boundaries and, it has been argued, to minimize the development of social class solidarity in the lower classes.

Though these "functions" may, in fact, be the unanticipated consequences of such relations, it hardly seems likely that this is the goal sought by the participants in these groups. Rather, the actors are seeking to achieve specific goals. In order to achieve these goals they usually must be able to harness resources that complement those they already control. Similarly, others may wish *their* resources for still other ends and the two (or three, or four, or more) make up a mutually advantageous "package." This is as true for a cowhand wishing to become a capataz as for a businessman seeking entrée to a rancher's land for contracting; as true for a ranch owner seeking a dependable labor force as for a cattle buyer seeking a secure source of livestock.

The structural characteristics of these two kinds of groups, I would argue, are epiphenomena of (1) the specific goals of the participants, and (2) the *de facto* distribution of resources, powers, and personnel in the society. Carlos Felipe establishes patron-client relations with his cowhands not in order to establish a relationship across class lines but because this is the only way to ensure himself a dependable labor force. People who control the resource of dependable labor are, by the nature of the society, Carlos's socioeconomic subordinates; a relationship with a contractor or cattle dealer involves him with a class peer.

I have elsewhere (Strickon 1965) described a change in cultural-ecological patterns that also involved a wholesale shift of one particular type of relationship in this locality away from patron-client relations between ranch owners and sharecroppers and tenant farmers, to the peer relationship with contractors. This move is comprehensible in terms of a persisting goal, the advantages of mixing agriculture and livestock ranching, operating in a changing context of economic and political variables. What seemed a structural discontinuity was, from the point of view taken here, a processual continuity.

One of the questions raised in this analysis is whether the actor or the society should be the focus of social science analysis (or at least a kind of social science analysis). Addressing this question, however, leads us beyond the problem set at the beginning of this paper and beyond the relations of Carlos Felipe to his family, friends, and employees. At this point I would merely like to note that Margaret Mead (1953) once pointed out that any member of a society is a representative informant on that society if we are able to specify his place within it. I would add that a member of a society may also give us not only data on the society but also insights into its operation and, equally important, tests of social science concepts and theories about the nature of society and the actors within it.

NOTES

1. The name Carlos Felipe is, of course, a pseudonym, as are some of the other names used. Other minor details have been changed in order to protect Sr. "Felipe's" privacy, but I do not believe that the changes affect the presentation of the case or the analysis. If any reader has a need to know, I will provide the names of the real persons and places.

The research upon which this paper is based was carried out in 1958 and 1959 under a grant of the Grace and Henry Doherty Foundation and in 1967 under a grant by the National Science Foundation. Analysis of the materials was aided by summer research salary support by the University of Wisconsin Research Committee.

2. Carlos Felipe's daughter, a university graduate and lawyer married to a factory manager, once asked me what I thought of her family's furniture. I said it was beautifully made. "Yes," she answered, "but would you furnish your home with it?" I had to admit that I wouldn't. "As you can see," she smiled, indicating the Scandinavian modern furnishings of her apartment, "neither will we."

3. The characteristics of the "cowboy" job market in Argentina may generate a more than passing feeling of déjà vu in an academic audience.

4. The foreman's holdings would not be considered as an *estancia* locally, but as a *chacra de ganado* or *chacra mixta* (cattle farm or mixed farm). An even better translation would be the term "family spread" of the northern U.S. plains.

5. Before World War II, agricultural work on the ranches in the zone was done primarily by resident sharecroppers and tenant farmers and their households who lived and worked on the ranch. For the transition to the present arrangement see Strickon (1965).

6. Rural policemen are assigned to a particular area through similar arrangements. In this case, however, the constraints imposed by national and provincial criteria are less flexible. Ties to others in the same social class as the policeman in the countryside are usually not present, unless he marries locally after his assignment. Similar arrangements, though operating at a higher level, may also be involved in the assignment of doctors and nurses as visitors to public clinics in the rural areas.

4

Charwomen, Cesspools, and Road Building: An Examination of Patronage, Clientage, and Political Power in Southeastern Minas Gerais

SIDNEY M. GREENFIELD

Departments of Sociology and Anthropology
The University of Wisconsin, Milwaukee

In the following pages I shall relate and analyze three incidents that occurred in the mid-1960s while I was conducting fieldwork in the *municípios* of Paraízo and Boa Vista [1] in the Zona da Mata [2] of the Brazilian state of Minas Gerais. The three incidents were very different from each other, and their importance—to the participants, to other residents of the community, and to members of the larger society—varied considerably. However, all three illustrate at different levels, and enable us to extend our understanding of, the broad system of patron-client relationships and linked patronage networks that permeate the social structure of this part of Brazil.

THE SITUATIONS

The Charwoman

The first situation arose shortly after I began my work in *Paraízo*. It was precipitated by the appointment of a *servente* (charwoman) to fill a civil service post at the elementary school in the *sede* (seat) of the *município*. The job was to clean and mop floors in the school buildings, which were part of the state educational facilities.[3]

No sooner did notice of this particular appointment become public than a storm burst upon the local scene. Before the air cleared, four members of the *câmara municipal* (municipal council) had submitted their resignations, impeachment proceedings had been instituted against the *prefeito* (mayor), and the citizenry was in open conflict.

The woman appointed to the post, whom we shall call Maria, was the sister of the mayor's wife. She was married to the owner and cultivator of a small piece of property, who was a member—by descent—of one of the largest and most influential and respected families of the *município*.

The couple had moved back to Paraízo from another *município*, where they had gone to live after their marriage, only a year or two earlier, when the husband had inherited the land he now worked. In the town where they had formerly lived, less than fifty kilometers from Paraízo, Maria had developed a reputation for "running around with men." According to reliable informants, she had not even tried to hide her escapades. Since her return to her husband's home, however, very little had been said about her, and no affairs with men of Paraízo were rumored.

As soon as her appointment as charwoman became public, however, her former reputation was aired by a number of local citizens. Characterizing themselves as "civic minded" and "concerned," although few of them had children of school age, they asked: How can a woman with such a reputation be permitted to work in the school? How can she be allowed to be in such close contact with the children of the town? Would she not be a bad influence?

The mayor took the brunt of the reaction. The first charge was nepotism, since Maria was his wife's sister. (This is a common practice and an equally common charge to raise against a political opponent.) Soon, however, the talk was that the mayor had arranged the job for her because they were having an affair—right under the nose of the innocent wife.[4]

Maria had been given the post in preference to an equally qualified applicant who was generally considered more deserving. The other woman, Lourdes, was in her mid-forties and a spinster with a widowed mother to support, whereas Maria had a husband to provide for her.

Furthermore, Lourdes had an impeccable reputation. Some indignant citizens never let this be forgotten, even though Lourdes, almost immediately after the appointment of Maria, obtained a better position (at a higher salary) caring for an orphan home in the state of Guanabara.

Immediately after Maria's appointment, and in direct reaction to it, the president of the municipal council, who was a member of the Partido Social Democrático (PSD)—the opposition to the mayor, who was of the Partido Republicano (PR)[5]—called a meeting of the council. The council members instituted impeachment proceedings in an effort to oust the mayor. The effort failed when one of the members of the PR faction, which held a five-to-four majority in the nine-man body, joined the PSD councilmen to defeat the motion. Then the four PR members who had voted for the impeachment asked to be relieved from serving on the council. This left the young PR mayor with a council composed of four members of the opposition and one representative of his own party. It also left the PSD president of the council with a total working membership that was the bare minimum needed for a quorum. All the lone PR member had to do was stay away from meetings and no business could be conducted.

In reaction to the appointment of a charwoman, then, the political machinery of the *município* ground to a halt.

The Cesspool

The second incident occurred in the neighboring *município* of Boa Vista (from which Paraízo had attained its independence only about a decade before my first visit to the region). Sometime in 1964, there had been a landslide at the edge of the city. Several buildings and considerable amounts of land had broken loose and fallen into the major stream that traverses the city and provides most of its water and sewage facilities. The slide had been the direct fault of no specific person or group, but was the result of years of soil erosion characteristic of the region. The virgin forest cover of the land had been removed, as almost all of the virgin timbers in the region had been, to plant coffee. Without the complex root system to hold the soil, and with the coffee planted in a manner that actually enhanced leaching, the annual rains eroded the soils, washing much of it down into the streams and *corregos*.

The stream in question entered the city as fresh water from the northeast and flowed to the southwest, collecting sewage and waste along the way. The debris from the 1964 landslide stopped the flow of water at a point after the stream had passed through most of the city but before it flowed out into the hinterland. During the dry season that followed the slide, the waste-filled water lay stagnant within the city. The stench soon became offensive. More serious than the smell, however, was the epidemic disease potential in the waste-filled water, still being added to daily because no alternate sewage facilities were available to a large segment of the city's population.

Immediate responsibility for doing something about this unfortunate state of affairs rested with the municipal authorities, the *prefeito* and the *câmara municipal*. When pressed by irritated residents for an explanation of their inaction after several months during which the smell grew stronger and more offensive, the *prefeito* explained that the city did not have the resources—neither equipment nor revenue—to repair the damage. Bulldozers and other heavy equipment were needed to push loose the debris and open up the flow of the stream; the banks would have to be widened and reinforced and the stream itself made deeper.

The *prefeito* revealed that he had gone to the state capital and had requested assistance from the appropriate departments of the state government but had been turned down. He turned next to the agricultural university, located within the *município* but on land not subject to its jurisdiction. The university, which had been attempting to fashion itself on the model of the American land grant system, proclaiming the theme of research, teaching, and extension, was supported by state and federal funds. In addition, it had been receiving support for its programs from USAID and the Ford Foundation and had a reciprocal arrangement with a major American land grant university. When approached by the *prefeito*, its administrators maintained that the campus was not located within the *município*, since neither it nor its lands were subject to local jurisdiction. Although they sympathized with the *prefeito*, they said, they could assume no responsibility for what was in fact *his* problem. They explained that they were having difficulty obtaining the funds for their own building and development programs, and that whatever equipment they had was being used to construct the plant necessary to house a truly first-rate university—which, when completed, would make the municipal residents proud indeed. The university had its own water and sewage facilities; although they said they would be happy to provide the local administration with technical specialists at any time, they were unfortunately unable to help at that time with the repair of the cesspool.

The mayor then turned to the city hospital and to local doctors and other medical personnel. To them he emphasized the hazards to the health of the entire population should the cesspool not be repaired soon. In response they offered to innoculate the population against the diseases that most probably would result if the mess were not cleaned up. Help with the repairs they asserted to be beyond their ability—in spite of the fact that individually and collectively they represented a sizable segment of the community's wealth, and wielded political influence in all of the major parties.

Other leading citizens sought out by the city officials, in case after case, made it clear to the mayor that, although they were concerned, they could not help him with what was *his* problem.

It is important to point out that at the same time the cesspool stood creating a clear and increasing threat to the municipality and its inhabitants, the *prefeito* had been able to organize and finance a project to renovate the *praça municipal* (town square). Beautiful old shade trees in the public gardens were cut down, and the entire *praça* was done over with tiled sidewalks and footpaths, benches, and statues. A large sign in front of the square made it quite explicit that the renovation had been the mayor's own project, and that no state or federal funds had been used in his contribution to the improvement and beautification of the municipality.

The cesspool, however, remained, with the *prefeito* unable to obtain the resources for its repair.

The rains came as usual in the fall, and the level of water in the streams throughout the region rose; however, the debris trapped in the stream in Boa Vista was not to be dislodged. Instead, the water carried in more waste and stirred up that which already was trapped. When the rains stopped and the dry season followed the cesspool was worse than ever. As the water drained and the land gradually became parched, the waste remained. Part of it was absorbed in the soil at the sides of the stream, but an offensive and dangerous mess persisted, the smell of which had driven at least some residents to move.

As the first anniversary of the cesspool passed, no epidemics or other calamities had been reported. But no one quite knew what to expect

75

as the second rainy season approached. Most residents appeared to have become used to the condition. The threat to their health seemed remote. The doctors, the faculty of the university (most of whom lived in the town), and other citizens, educated and not, ignored the problem and went about their daily lives as if the cesspool were not there.

Finally, at the end of the second dry season, less than a month before the rains would start again, the mayor announced that he had obtained a *verba* (grant) from the department of epidemic diseases of the federal government to have the cesspool cleaned up. Before the work could begin, a period of time had to be set aside for private firms to submit bids; the lowest bidder would receive the contract. Within two months or so (by which time the rains would have begun—and most such work is stopped until the heavy rains subside), the work could start.

After a year and a half of inactivity, while everyone talked about the cesspool and no one did anything, the repairs were to begin.

The Road

The third incident relates to the construction of a road that would have linked Paraízo to a regional center in the valley below. The regional center was about a ten-minute drive from the Rio-Bahia highway and, from there, about a four-hour drive from Rio de Janeiro. The new road would have placed Paraízo within five hours' travel from the former federal district.

The existing route from Paraízo to Rio de Janeiro went north and west to Boa Vista and then southwest in a circuitous route that eventually came back to the Rio-Bahia highway at the same point as the intended road, but only after first passing through yet a third regional center to the southwest. The trip to the highway junction, on an unpaved road that was impassable during much of the rainy season, took four hours. The entire trip from Paraízo to Rio de Janeiro, a distance of 125 kilometers as the crow flies, took eight hours.

The road was of considerable economic importance for the residents of Paraízo. The region of which the *município* was a part was in transition. Cattle—beef and dairy products—gradually were replacing coffee and other forms of agriculture as the economic mainstay.[6] The primary market for the beef and dairy products of Paraízo was Rio de Janeiro, but the eight hours required for transport placed local producers at a competitive disadvantage.

The road connecting Paraízo to the regional center, which had been a prime topic of conversation from the time of my arrival, first had been projected by the state highway commission in the early 1950s. For more than a decade it had been shown as completed on road maps of the region. Construction actually had begun in the 1950s, and the signs of the work are to be found to the south of the municipal center. They disappear, however, at a precipice, to reappear four kilometers away at the bottom of the serra. In more than a decade the four kilometers needed to complete the road had not been finished. Then in 1965 the moribund issue of the road was revived.

A commission from Paraízo went to see the governor. While in the state capital they also met with the man the governor was supporting to succeed him in the forthcoming election, scheduled for October 1965.[7] Both interviews were reported to have gone well, and the group returned home with renewed optimism.

The commission, and the rebirth of interest in the road, had been organized by a single individual, Antonio Vierra da Sousa, a state deputy (member of the legislative assembly) who also was a professor at the rural university at Boa Vista.[8] As representative for the region including Paraízo—where he had received considerable support in his previous campaign, and where he hoped for even greater support in the elections of the following year—he had decided that the residents should have the road, and that he, Antonio, was going to get it for them.

After a second meeting with the governor and his candidate, Antonio sent a telegram to his compadre, Athos—who was the owner of the only bakery in town, one of his *cabos eleitorais* (mobilizers of votes), and a political leader in the *município*—which implied that he had the word of the candidate (and that meant the word of the governor) that equipment would be sent to begin work on the road the following week.

Instead of reporting the news to the party leaders as he had been instructed, Athos posted the telegram in the bar for everyone to see. The federal tax collector, a leader of the opposition, offered to wager one hundred thousand cruzeiros that no machines would arrive the following week. Antonio Vierra da Sousa, he declared, did not have the *pistolão* (connections) needed to get the road completed.

77

Athos the baker countered that his compadre did not lie: If he said the machines would be there, they would. If the tax collector chose to doubt it, Athos would write a check for a million cruzeiros that the other could cover if he had the courage.

After much discussion, with partisans on both sides becoming quite vocal in their support or criticism of Antonio, the tax collector chose not to accept the wager.

That weekend, in the guise of helping me to organize a study of transportation facilities, Antonio suggested to a group of partisans (assembled by him to provide me with assistance) that they appoint a commission to visit on Monday Sr. Nelson Morreira, the regional director of the Departmento de Estradas de Rodagem (Department of Roads and Highways). Antonio, *prefeito* João Resende (the mayor who had appointed the charwoman), Padre Dico, the priest, and Marta, my research assistant, were selected. Later, state tax collector Francisco da Rocha and Athos the baker were added to the group.

Antonio also had suggested to the group that a small celebration be planned to mark the arrival of the machinery. But while they were at the regional office of the DER on Monday, a young boy in Paraízo was celebrating his birthday, and as is the custom, fireworks were set off in honor of the occasion. Hearing the noise, Doña Maria Helena, João Resende's mother (in her own right a supporter of Antonio) and several friends and other partisans ran into the street shouting that the machines had arrived. The streets soon were filled with people looking for machines that were not there. The disappointment of the partisans was made even worse by events at the regional office of the DER.

Sr. Morreira told the delegation that he had received no orders from the highway commissioner in the state capital to resume work on the road in Paraízo. First, he claimed that the *município* was not within the area of his jurisdiction. When reminded that it was, he claimed that all machinery in his jurisdiction was committed to other projects, and that without direct orders from the central office he could not even schedule the work.

Antonio, humiliated before his supporters, immediately radioed the capital, only to learn that the machines could not be released at that time. Marta, the only female in the group, was sent home by car, while the rest of the group went off to the capital to see the candidate and the highway commissioner. Antonio also called on a friend and fellow professor of sociology who was a federal senator and the state president of the governor's political party.[9]

By the end of the day they had learned that, while the road was agreed to be worthwhile, before work could start a study would have to be made, bids taken, and a contract awarded. Only after a period of some months—after the election—could the job be done. They were promised, however, that the project would be given top priority.

The group returned home dejected and disappointed. Antonio remained in the capital for the week, while his supporters were exposed to the ridicule of the opposition. When he returned home for the weekend, however, he received a call from the federal senator saying that the project was in the works, and that Antonio should expect a visit from Sr. Morreira to discuss the timetable.

Antonio invited the individuals who had formed the commission, plus another compadre and political aide, to lunch at his home. Later that afternoon Sr. Morreira, a young engineer, arrived with his assistant. Sr. Morreira, whose father was a wealthy landowner who had supported the governor in the last election, had been appointed to his job just after finishing school. His future was politics; he planned to run for a seat in the federal congress the following year. He viewed the DER, and the building of roads, as a means by which to attain this goal.

After lunch and a lengthy discussion, the group went out with the engineer to inspect the area where work on the road remained to be done. It took three vehicles to transport them. Sr. Morreira and his assistant took the lead in a new Ford pickup truck that bore the emblem of the Alliance for Progress. The others followed in Volkswagens.

Before going to the site in Paraízo Sr. Morreira took the group to see several other projects. At each one they stopped, left their vehicles, and talked. By the time they arrived at the site of the projected road, an understanding had been reached.

Just before arriving at the site, Antonio took the lead and directed the procession to a fazenda house where he stopped. There an elderly fazendeiro, the president of the PR in Paraízo and a former *prefeito*, was added to the group. The procession, led by the new pickup truck with the Alliance for Progress symbol, made quite an impression as the party drove through Paraízo (which had only ten registered vehicles). Antonio and his followers were being redeemed for their previous humiliation. Even the federal tax collector was impressed. He confided that everyone really wanted the road, but that he had not thought that Antonio, after all these years, could get it done; but perhaps his visit to the United States and the connections he had established there had been the key. After all, Sr. Morreira was driving a vehicle donated by the Alliance for Progress, and an American professor had returned with Antonio and was working in the *município*.

When Sr. Morreira left, he told the group that the first machines would come the following week. They would only clear the parts of the road that had been cut previously; after more than a dozen years, this had to be done before any new work could be started. In the meantime, he said, the officials would request bids for the completion of the road.

The following week the machines did arrive, and a celebration (without fireworks) took place. However, the candidate for governor lost the election, and when I returned to the *município* in 1968, the road still had not been completed.

BACKGROUND

Some background on the development of Brazilian society, economy, and politics is necessary before analyzing these cases.

Administrative Changes

For almost all of her history Brazil was a primarily rural society, dominated by an agrarian system that produced export crops for overseas markets. Until 1930, political control was in the hands of the landowners. The Old Republic itself represented the high point of this political hierarchy. It was established in 1889 with the objective of decentralizing the administrative machinery the emperor had created several decades before in his efforts to transform the colony into an independent nation. As the primary producers of wealth in the society of his time, the landowners had been taxed to raise the revenues needed to build and run the nation. In 1889, in coalition with other sectors of the population, they succeeded in sending the declining Dom Pedro II into exile and establishing a new form of government. Jurisdiction, under a new constitution, was given to the states (the former provinces of the colony and the empire), which were controlled indirectly by the landowners through a system of political-electoral exchange referred to as *coronelismo* and the politics of the governors (Nunes Leal 1948; Petterson 1964). During the Republican period Brazil actually was more a group of federated states—dominated by the larger and richer ones—than a unified nation.

In 1930 Getúlio Vargas was made president by the military, in spite of his having lost the election the preceding year. The coup marked the end of the old Republic and signaled the beginning of the second phase of nation building in Brazilian history. Under Vargas's leadership, a national administrative apparatus was constructed that through yet another constitution reestablished the primacy of the central government.

As the land declined following the Great Depression, the power and influence of the landowners also declined. A sizable segment of the population, formerly wedded to the land for its livelihood, began to migrate to the towns and cities. Brazil was in the process of urbanizing.

It is important to note that the administrative machinery Vargas created in his effort to establish a strong and viable central government was located primarily in the growing urban centers and incorporated the burgeoning population of the cities. The hinterland that had been dominated by the landowners of the Old Republic remained, for the most part, outside the framework of the nation.

As the administrative transformation progressed, the economic crisis was coming to a head. For the second time in less than two decades the external markets upon which Brazil depended for both the sale of her export crops and the purchase of manufactured and other products were closed, this time due to the advent of World War II. With Brazil unable to sell her products or to obtain needed goods, the highly centralized government of Getúlio Vargas reached the inescapable conclusion that she should industrialize. Industrialization was therefore not the spontaneous result of the entrepreneurial activities of private investors but the result of a conscious decision by a highly centralized, authoritarian administration.

Industrialization and Development

The vehicle by which a respectable industrial capacity was quickly developed was the administrative bureaucracy of the state. Under Vargas's leadership agencies sprang up within the government, charged with tasks ranging from planning to arranging capital to actually constructing and operating industrial plants.

Industry was to provide the formerly imported material commodities for the rapidly growing, increasingly urban population. This population, however, also needed other goods and services, which neither industry nor the metropolitan centers to which they were flocking could provide. Housing, schools, water and sewage facilities, electricity and other forms of power, transportation, and much more were needed if Brazil was to become a truly modern industrial nation able to provide a decent life for its expanding population. Thus the government created additional agencies charged with planning, producing, distributing, and administering the goods and services required (Graham 1968).

The Vargas government's vision of an industrialized society included more than industry and basic services. The "welfare" of the people, in the qualitative sense so much discussed in intellectual circles in the 1930s, also was to be provided for. Again the government became the means by which these needs were to be satisfied. New agencies were to provide welfare benefits such as health and medical services and social security and retirement benefits. Labor unions were also created by the government and administered through the new Ministry of Labor.

The outbreak of World War II delayed the Vargas timetable for the creation of "the new Brazil." By the late 1930s, the initial plans had been established and the process of transformation set in motion. But before he could return to the task of completing the Estado Nôvo (New State), Vargas was forced to step aside in response to the wave of democratic enthusiasm that followed the victory of the democratic powers on whose side Brazil had fought.

In 1945 a new government, based on yet another new constitution, replaced the Estado Nôvo. Although the means by which government office was to be filled were changed to popular elections, the goals and objectives (in the dominant economic sphere) of the new system essentially were those of the dictatorship (Leff 1968). Industrialization, modernization, and the development of an economically strong and productive national society were the primary objectives of the new regime. As under Vargas, the strong central government was to effect the transformation to the new Brazil. Beginning in 1945, a series of administrations established agency after agency (at both federal and state levels) within the government bureaucracy to build the plants and produce and distribute the goods and services for the new society.

By the time Vargas was elected to the presidency in 1950, a major change had taken place in the national economy. In contrast with the pre-1930 situation, when the primary source of wealth came from the land in the form of export crops, now the primary sources of goods, services, and wealth were the industrial-service-welfare agencies created and administered by the state. Prior to 1930 the key to the control of resources and wealth had been the control of land; after 1945, to an ever-increasing degree, it became control over positions of authority—at the directorship level—in the industrial-service-welfare agencies created by the state.

Patrimonial Authority

The concept of patrimonial authority must be introduced at this point in order to make clear the developments that occurred in the postwar period. "Patrimonialism" is a form of authority that has been associated by Max Weber with "traditional societies." Its essence is that the head of a group or organization, whose position is legitimized by tradition, exercises authority as a personal prerogative. Authority, writes Weber (1947:347), "is primarily oriented to tradition but in its exercise makes the claim to full personal powers. . . ." Or, as Parsons (1947:63) put it, "The position of authority . . . is still traditionally legitimized, but not the detailed structure of carrying it out which is . . . a 'right' of the chief to do what he will within his sphere of personal prerogative."

In brief, patrimonialism is a form of authority in which the head of a group or organization exercises that authority as a personal prerogative in the sense of having full power to use the group or organization, and its resources, at his personal discretion.

Weber associated patrimonialism with traditional systems of authority, which he opposed to modern, bureaucratic forms. As Brazil industrialized and became transformed in the modernization process by means of state-created "bureaucratic" agencies, patrimonialism, the form of authority that had been implanted by the Portuguese at the beginnings of colonization and had characterized Brazilian society for more than four centuries,[10] rather than disappearing, was incorporated—implicitly—as the form of authority to be practiced in the organizations created by the government.[11]

Along with the establishment of the numerous state agencies that were to transform Brazil into a modern industrial nation came the creation of countless new job categories, the vast majority of which were incorporated into an expanding civil service (Graham 1968). Those positions at the level of director, however, where decisions were made, were not made part of the civil service. Here, where patrimonial authority was to be exercised, positions were to be filled by means of appointment and for limited tenure. Those empowered to make appointments to these positions of authority were to be the heads of state, now to be chosen by popular election.

Politics and the Distribution of Resources—1945–64

What developed in the period from 1945 to 1964 was almost predictable. As successive governments expanded their efforts to industrialize and develop the society by creating more and more agencies and organizations to produce and distribute goods and services, more and more positions vested with patrimonial authority came into being. The means of obtaining those positions, and the associated control over most of the wealth of the society, was appointment by the government. But the government was to be elected, so a competition for the eligible electorate ensued.

The political parties created by law in 1945 never really developed significant ideological foundations. They stood for winning elections, and they did what was necessary to achieve this end. Material commodities, therefore, the basis of worth and value, came to be exchanged for votes. Votes, the key to office and control of the primary sources of wealth in the society, were bought, bartered, secured by whatever means possible. With enough votes to assure election—no matter how they had been obtained—the major productive plant of the society could be secured. Once elected, the victor had the right to appoint those who had helped him to the positions of authority in the wealth-producing and -distributing industrial-service-welfare agencies.

Given the nature of patrimonial authority, people appointed to directorships in the state agencies could employ the resources of those agencies in a number of ways. The resources could be used, where possible, to satisfy directly the material needs of the position holder. To secure and prolong tenure, which was at the pleasure of the government, they could be used to "reciprocate" for the appointment; that is, the resources of an agency could be made available to the elected officials who had appointed the director.

Maximum tenure, however, was for the duration of the administration, a period of four years or less. Reelection could mean reappointment. Even though individuals could not succeed themselves to executive office—and the executive was the key to the political system in Brazil—they could make "arrangements" with others to secure succession, if everyone could be "satisfied." Elections required votes; votes were available for material considerations. By exercising their patrimonial authority, the directors of the agencies that had been created to provide goods and services for the entire population could make those commodities available, on a selective basis, only to those who had supported the candidate "suggested" by the director. In brief, the resources of the agencies could be used in exchange for voting support. Instead of all citizens receiving the welfare benefits and services disbursed by the public agencies, in accord with need or some universal standards, only those who paid the price (in loyalty, support, and votes) generally obtained them.

As the massive patronage-exchange systems developed that harnessed the new sources of wealth to the open electoral system, large numbers of people, spread over great distances, had to be drawn in. The agencies were primarily in the cities. The population, though concentrated in the cities, was dispersed throughout the nation. A system of networks developed through which the goods and services of the industrial-service-welfare agencies moved in exchanges for electoral support.

Since this was an open system, aspirants to office were able to combine previous prestations with promises of "payment," after election, in building networks and voting bases; once in office, they could reward loyal supporters. Those out of office and therefore without access to the wealth-producing sector of the society had two options. Prior to elections (or sometimes after, to secure a voting majority in the legislative bodies), they could negotiate their votes to the government in exchange for a specified number of appointments or other considerations. Alternatively, however, they could establish themselves as an opposition and

85

contest the election. To pay for the votes they would need, they could promise the resources of the industrial-service-welfare agencies that they would control if they were successful. With the stakes so high, the opposition often offered more to potential voters, specifically to those persons (*cabos eleitorais*) who controlled blocs of votes, than those in office. In fact, it was not uncommon for frustrated and anxious members of the opposition to promise more than they ever would have to distribute should they succeed. Winning was the first hurdle; time enough afterward to worry about distributing the spoils.

It did not take long for competition among factions to become intense. The voters, especially the *cabos eleitorais*, were able to play off one political group against another, negotiating and supposedly making bargains with several simultaneously. As a result, neither incumbents nor their opponents could ever be quite sure of their support and the size of their vote. The only hope was to outbid the competition. The regular entry of new voters during the two decades of the postwar era intensified the insecurity and heightened the competition.[12]

Besides goods and services, the agencies of government also had as resources to be distributed the remainder of the jobs in the industrial-service-welfare complex, most of which had been incorporated into the civil service system. In this period of great insecurity, with life becoming a game of Russian roulette for those participating in the opportunities for upward mobility, the civil service positions offered about the only security anywhere, thanks to the erroneous effort to develop an "efficient" American style of public administration (Graham 1968). Even the most active "careerists" or players in the game for riches and success also desired some public service position (*emprego público*) as a hedge against failure.

Careers

A Brazilian career, as Leeds (1964:387) summarizes it,

> . . . consists of a continual branching out into new activities—
> sometimes multiplications of old ones, sometimes in new situses.
> The main problem is to establish the first step, to create a *trampolim*
> or springboard, as they say. The variety of techniques for this is
> numerous and sometimes used singly or in combination. I mention
> only a few, such as notable activity in university student associa-

tions, especially in the law schools; flamboyantly joining Communist or Fascist groups; making public stands in favor of policies not in favor with the entrenched powers; marrying rich girls; being helped by one's godparents; being helped by a *pistolão* ("a friend in the right place or position to give a hand"); journalism; making a name in sports; entering into politics in lower level political positions; entering into a small bureaucratic office from which upward and outward ties can be established.

The significant thing about each of these connections, as the careerist ideal-typically uses them, is that none of them is intrinsic to the career's end as such, but rather to the creation of a *nome* (name), the beginning of *uma promoção* ("a self-promotion"), the eliciting of *projeção* ("a presence growing in time").

The end of the careerist dynamic was the acquisition of wealth and power. The primary means in the period 1945–64 was to obtain a position of authority in one of the industrial-service-welfare agencies controlled by the state. This required a close association with elected government officials. How was an individual to make himself an "associate" of those holding public office? The answer lay in votes and their control. But given the size of the electorate and the vast distances over which they were distributed, it was impossible for either officeholders or hopefuls to know all the people they would need. Reputation—the *nome* referred to by Leeds—became crucial. Anyone who could build a reputation for being able to control a bloc of votes was to be reckoned with. People constantly were striving to project themselves as having greater influence over the electorate than they actually had. Given the complexity of the situation, officeholders and aspirants had to be alert to all possible "associates."

The careerist typically parleyed one opportunity into another, using the rewards from one as a springboard for the next. Almost anyone, regardless of background or formal education, who controlled some minimal good or service (with the latter becoming progressively more important as the system matured) could enter and begin a *promoção*. With only a little luck, he might be viewed by some enterprising incumbent or aspirant as a "comer." A small reward like a job might be arranged as the beginning of a potentially long-term relationship of asymmetrical exchange between the newcomer and the established party. The nature of the job or reward was secondary; it was a start in a career.

In the course of most careers, individuals moved from field to field and from specialty to specialty. In contrast to the North American and western European definition of a career, in which the individual progresses upward in the area for which he has been trained, a Brazilian trained in medicine, let us say, might find himself with an appointment in an educational, banking, or construction agency. Someone trained in engineering might find himself starting in hospital administration and moving to agriculture or commerce. Others without formal training of any kind might find themselves in the same bank as a man trained in law or philosophy. Then, upon demonstration of ability (that is, as one who could deliver votes), the person with a position in construction might be rewarded with a bank post. The first position would not necessarily be relinquished; third, fourth, and even fifth positions might be added as the career advanced. Not only would the positions most probably be in different fields, but one would be added to the next so that the mobile careerist became what Leeds refers to as a *cabide de emprego* ("coathanger of jobs").

The important thing was for the careerist to use each new job to extend his contacts, thereby increasing the number of votes he could control or at least speak for in negotiations. To do this, he usually approached other, often younger and less successful careerists, launching them in exchange for their dependence and the votes he believed they controlled.

In time, the successful would establish a *nome*, the reputation of a man able to deliver support when needed. Political aspirants other than the careerist's patron might then begin to bid for his support, and such bids could be used to negotiate larger rewards from those with whom the careerist had been associated in the past. If not satisfied (with jobs, appointments, and access to resources), the careerist could shift his allegiance (and his votes) to people willing and able to better reward "loyalty."

Although he might not be a politician (that is, a candidate for office) himself, the success of any careerist was related directly to his ability to secure, control, and deliver votes. At times a career could best be promoted by associating with other careerists in groups referred to by Leeds (1965) as *panelinhas* ("little sauce pans"), or as *rodas* ("spokes") in the Zona da Mata. Such groups, strictly voluntary, continued as long as the participants believed that their individual careers were being best served by the joint endeavor. Some groups rose to the top together;

others split apart as the members found other associations to be more advantageous.[13]

In the course of a career, each new appointment or other reward represented increased access to resources to be used primarily in securing additional dependents and hence more votes. These in turn were bartered to aspirants and officeholders in exchange for additional appointments and access to the wealth-producing and -distributing agencies and their directorships. With a large enough dependency base, the careerist could negotiate for a directorship of one of the many industrial-service-welfare agencies of the state. The very successful were able to obtain appointments in several agencies.

THE ANALYSIS

Given this background we now may turn to the analysis of the three situations presented earlier. We shall take them in the reverse order from the way they were presented since a more comprehensive understanding of the social system is to be obtained in this way.

The Road

The road to link Paraízo to the regional center ten minutes from the Rio-Bahia highway was to be built under the authority and jurisdiction of the DER, an agency of the Minas Gerais state government that had been created explicitly for the purpose of building and maintaining roads. In theory, the road was to be for the benefit of the inhabitants of the *município* and the region, and ultimately the whole nation. However, as we have seen, in addition to the manifest ends of Brazilian institutions are their latent goals. In the context of Brazilian politics in the period 1945–64, the DER also existed to help elect to office people in the party and network of its directors and to advance the careers of people who held its positions of authority.

In 1965 the DER was being asked to build a road in Paraízo. The immediate initiative had been taken by Deputy Antonio Vierra da Sousa, whose primary interest was in being reelected the following year. He had approached the governor, who was campaigning at the time for his chosen successor, and also had appealed to the highway commissioner, an appointee of the governor. Since the road already had been planned and approved, the decision to complete it—after a delay of fifteen years—was an executive one.

Antonio, nominally at least, was a part of a coalition of political groups and parties that controlled both the governor's palace and the legislative assembly. When he went before the governor—and the candidate—to request completion of the road, he stated explicitly that compliance with his request would be "good politics" for all concerned: his party, the PR, which was supporting the governor's candidate, would be solidified and its people shown once more that loyalty was rewarded; their vote, as guided by Antonio and Mayor João Resende, would go to the governor's candidate. Antonio was playing *cabo eleitoral*; he was exchanging the votes he controlled for access to resources.

Sr. Nelson Morreira, the regional director of the DER, however, was not at first a party to the exchanges. True, he was supporting the incumbent governor's candidate, since he was indebted to the governor for the appointment to his present post (which he had been given because his father had supported the governor with money and votes in the previous election). But he planned to run for the federal congress the following year; he had to use the projects of the DER under his jurisdiction to build his own voting support. If the project at hand could not do this for him, it would not be in his interest to see it completed.

When the group from Paraízo first appeared in his office, Nelson had not been advised of the exchanges taking place. His first response was to stall. When informed of the details by a member of the governor's staff, however, he was able to work out a way of participating that would benefit him.

The coalition of interests and offices that were being mobilized around the road comprised: (1) the governorship, for which the campaign was being waged; (2) a seat in the state assembly, for which Antonio sought election the following year; (3) a seat in the federal congress, for which Nelson planned to run the following year; (4) a seat in the federal senate, which the incumbent professor of sociology would try to retain a few years hence; and (5) the office of *prefeito* of Paraízo, which João Resende wished to retain.

As soon as Nelson was convinced that a place had been made for him in the exchanges surrounding the road, a meeting was arranged to discuss the timetable for construction. What took place was typical of the negotiations by means of which networks were formed, candidates elected, and goods and services distributed during this period in Brazilian history.

When the group (Antonio, João, and the half-dozen *cabos eleitorais* from Paraízo) was taken to inspect other projects under construction before going to the road site, Nelson subtly yet clearly indicated that he would agree to proceed with the road if those present would provide support for his candidacy. The several stops were taken up by negotiations ending in the understanding that, if work commenced on the road, all present would provide electoral support for the candidate for governor that year and votes for Nelson and Antonio the following year. In return for the promise of votes given by the *cabos eleitorais* from Paraízo, Nelson agreed to do what, in theory, had long since been planned for the good of the people of the state and the nation.

Once the understanding was reached, Antonio then led the group to the home of Pedro da Silva, an old fazendeiro,[14] president of the PR in Paraízo, whose support was needed to complete the deal. At his home the agreement was repeated. Pedro, who had been unable to make the early part of the trip, rode with Antonio and João into Paraízo to show that the group had united to pool their influence in obtaining the road.

Soon after the agreements had been reached, work on the road was begun. Unfortunately for the allies of the governor, Antonio and João, the DER was unable to complete the remaining four kilometers. The best it could do was to clear, clean, and refinish the sections of the road on which work had been started years before.[15] The new section, like all new public works construction, required special procedures.

There were two ways to administer construction projects financed by agencies of the state and federal government. The more common one, used at times other than before elections, was through the Secretaria de Viação e Obras (the Secretary of Public Works), who maintained a permanent staff of engineers and construction workers. The second and more desired means was to have the project administered through the local *prefeitura* in one of two methods, both of which provided opportunities for the mayor to dispense patronage and make a profit. In the first, private firms submitted public bids, and the contract was awarded to the lowest bidder. The firm awarded the contract always left some room for the local officials to share in the profits. The officials also could recommend unskilled laborers—thereby giving the mayor and his group control over jobs in an economy where employment was scarce.

In the second, the mayor himself appointed someone to organize the work and disburse the funds of the financing agency. In practice, a mayor would select a kinsman or a compadre, who then mobilized their mutual dependents, provided them with jobs and income, and pocketed a profit by using cheap—often defective—materials.

Federal and state agencies funding projects at the local level generally preferred to have them administered by the Ministry or Secretary of Public Works. In election years, however, for the purpose of gaining electoral support, projects funded by agencies of the state and federal governments often were approved for local administration. The new section of the road in Paraízo was such a case; a public auction was to be held and a contract awarded.[16]

The road from Paraízo to the Rio-Bahia highway has never been completed. The network that had been mobilized was on the losing side. The governor's candidate lost the election. The new state administration appointed a new highway commissioner, a new regional director of the DER, and others in the relevant secretaries. All had their own debts to repay. They proceeded to use the resources of the state to reciprocate for the support that had elected them to office.

The Cesspool

The case of the cesspool in Boa Vista illustrates the rule that one never does locally what can be obtained as patronage from an agency or an individual at a higher level. There was no reason the local community could not have completed the work on the four kilometers of road; the benefits far outweighed the costs. There was no reason the citizens of Boa Vista could not have cleared the blockage themselves and done away with the cesspool. Brazilians would not do these things primarily because of the expectation that such things *ought* to be done by the state or by some other agency outside the local community. The local population turned a deaf ear to the mayor; it was up to him to arrange for the needed resources. In effect, this was a test of his ability to manipulate his patronage network and secure resources; success would enhance his prestige, and failure would make his reelection doubtful.

The *município* administration obviously could have mustered the resources for repairing the cesspool if it had chosen to. The funds that went to redo the *praça*—which did not need redoing—would have been more than enough to handle the emergency. However, the repair of a defect (no matter whose fault) cannot be used for self-promotion as can an impressive material structure such as a *praça*. The mayor could say that he gave the people a *praça*. This would highlight him as a patron and also establish an open obligation for the citizens to reciprocate, perhaps at some future date. The mundane repair of a defect was not at all the same thing.[17]

Since it was not in the *prefeito's* interest to use the limited funds at his disposal to repair the cesspool, he went to the state capital to ask for the resources in the name of the community's health. An understanding of what happened requires some background on the local political-electoral scene.

Boa Vista had been the home of a former president of the Brazilian Old Republic. His personal influence has been important in the political development of the region ever since. His son, who also became a politician, capitalized on his father's prestige and rose to become a federal senator in addition to assuming the presidency of his father's party, the PR, when the aging politician retired. The son was an important man, with prestige and influence at the state and national levels; he also retained control in his home territory.

The *prefeito* of Boa Vista had been a member of the PR. He was the head of a Lebanese family that had become rich as coffee merchants in the years when coffee still was bringing wealth to the region. He had been vice mayor of the PR ticket between 1958 and 1962. In 1962, on the grounds that his family there would support the party, he asked the PR congressman to arrange for postponement, until after the elections, of the independence of a district that was to become an independent *município*. Then he switched allegiance, betraying the congressman and the rest of the PR network. With the aid of his family, which was concentrated in the district that was to become independent (which they now control), he won election as mayor on the PSD ticket.

The congressman, a kinsman of the former president of the republic and a close confidant of his son, lost his bid for reelection. All was not lost for the old forces, however. After the UDN candidate for governor (the same governor referred to in the case of Paraízo's road) won the election over his PSD rival, the PR, through its leader, the son of the former president, switched its allegiance. It ended its coalition with the PSD and entered into one with the UDN governor, providing him with the majority needed in the legislative assembly to pass his legislative program. The *prefeito* had become the opposition, both locally—since the local PR opposed him for leaving the party—and on the state level.

When the *prefeito* of the *município* of Boa Vista went to the state capital in search of funds to repair the cesspool, the son of the former president went to the governor and made sure that the mayor would receive a very cool reception. For a year and a half the *prefeito* was in the embarrassing position of being unable to secure funds. The objective of the head of the PR was to discredit him, to expose him as a man without influence, unable to secure the resources, dispensed as patronage, needed to repair the cesspool. The fact that a danger existed to the entire community (most of whose residents were kinsmen or dependents of the former president and his son) was not regarded as relevant. The mayor was responsible; as the local citizens constantly reminded him, the cesspool was his problem. His political opponents would do nothing to help him even if their inaction placed an entire community composed of their people in physical danger.

Fortunately for the mayor and the community, some influential members of the PSD with whom he had made his deal to switch support had moved from the state to the national government. Through them, the grant to repair the cesspool was finally arranged. Although it had taken time, the *prefeito* was redeemed. He had arranged for the funds, and in a way that gave him administration of the repairs. With the work to be done by a private firm instead of the Ministry of Public Works, the mayor would obtain a profit and would be able to give out jobs to his people.[18]

The Charwoman

The case of the charwoman requires a different level of analysis. In the preceding cases, resources were being sought—and dispensed—from an agency of the state, to be used in the local community. The patron-client exchanges, and their extensions into networks in the electoral arena, were the means by which such resources were obtained, and also the means by which candidates for the offices that controlled the sources of patronage secured electoral support. The case of the charwoman expands the picture to show how jobs came to be included as part of the resources exchanged as patronage for political support.

Charwomen, Cesspools, and Road Building

The job of charwoman carried little if any prestige and also paid relatively little. The appointment of anyone to the position would not appear to be of sufficient import to generate the kind of reaction described earlier. But the job was of greater value than would seem to be the case at first glance. The position held civil service status; in addition to salary, its holder was entitled to benefits such as free medical service, retirement pay, and maternity leaves with pay. Furthermore, the job carried life tenure, which added security to the other benefits in a society where insecurity is common.

To obtain any civil service position an applicant had to take and pass a competitive examination or *concurso*. Then his name would be placed on the list from which nominations for appointment were made. Authority for nominations was vested in the executive officer of the appropriate level of government; at the state level, the governor had final authority for all appointments. In practice, however, he delegated this authority to subordinates for their use in making exchanges for political support. A state deputy, for example, in return for having his dependents support the governor or governor's candidates, and for his own support of the governor's legislative program, would receive control over nominations for appointments to jobs in the district of his greatest electoral strength. There, in turn, he would offer control over nominations to the appropriate leaders and *cabos eleitorais* for their continuing support of his candidacy and that of others he might suggest.

The charwoman in Paraízo had obtained her nomination through Antonio and João Resende, referred to in the discussion of the road. The problem was the result of a split in the faction that controlled the local PR.

João had been a compromise candidate proposed by Antonio—in an effort to consolidate his support—and accepted only reluctantly by the senior group that controlled the party in the *município*. Soon after his election, to the dismay of the old guard, João began to make decisions without consulting them first.

Just prior to the appointment of the charwoman he had gone to the state capital to arrange for a change in the local police detail. Policemen were permanent state employees assigned on a rotating basis to duty in the municipalities. Locally they were under the jurisdiction of a sheriff, appointed by the state government in agreement with the local leadership.[19] In practice this meant that the group in power locally selected one of its trusted members and, as part of a general series of exchanges with state groups in office, had him appointed sheriff. The old guard leadership of the PR had had one of its own group appointed to the position before João could exercise the prerogatives of his office. Soon he found himself to be opposed to the sheriff, and went to the capital to see if he could have one of his own supporters as a replacement. His senior associates got word of his plans and sent their own delegation to the state capital; the sheriff was not replaced.

The appointment of the charwoman, which generated minor popular reaction because of Maria's reputation, was then seized as an issue with which to impeach João and replace him with the vice mayor—a solid member of the old guard. Even if he could not be unseated, his independence might be broken. The actors involved in the drama really did not care who became charwoman, although both candidates for the post were related to influential members of the contending factions. All the participants knew that neither candidate actually would lift a mop to clean the school.[20] The issue was who would get the plum and thus demonstrate the strength of their influence and connections. João won this time. A total split was avoided, however, thanks to the road. In spite of the problems and the eventual failure, the mobilization of efforts to secure the road served to reunite a local network that had been badly split.

NOTES

1. Paraízo (literally, Paradise) and Boa Vista (Beautiful View), of course, are not the real names of the *municipios* studied. All names of persons and places have been changed to protect the many citizens of Brazil who were kind enough to cooperate with and assist me while I was conducting the fieldwork. My appreciation also is expressed to the Social Science Research Council, The Graduate School of the University of Wisconsin, and the Agency for International Development for the financial support that made the fieldwork in Minas Gerais possible. All views, interpretations, and conclusions herein contained are those of the author and not necessarily those of the supporting organizations.

2. The Zona da Mata (literally, Zone of Woods) is the name of a geographical region in the southeastern part of the state of Minas Gerais, which borders on the neighboring states of Rio de Janeiro and Espirito Santo. The region—ecologically an extension of the Paraíba Valley—was given its name because of the dense forest that covered its hilly surface when the Portuguese first settled there. In the years since intensive settlement began, the forest cover has been systematically cleared from the hills. No longer applicable, the name is still used to refer to the region.

3. As an aside I might mention that, in my experience, maintenance generally has been very poor in this area. On several visits to the region between 1960 and 1968, I was always surprised to find school buildings that had been built since a previous visit looking old and in need of repairs only a year or so after completion. The *serventes*, along with other members of the maintenance staff, were supposed to keep the building clean, but in general they did not. Dirt and filth were common in most schools, whether or not charwomen and other maintenance people were appointed and actually paid to care for them.

4. My research assistant, who had been a *professora* at the school before taking a leave of absence to work with me, was asked to spy on Maria and report on the visits made by the young mayor; he lived across the street from the house Maria shared with her husband (who walked to and from the town daily to tend his fields).

5. The Partido Republicano had formed a coalition with the UDN (União Democrático Nacional), which controlled the governor's palace and therefore was the party in power on both the state and local levels.

6. For a discussion of this transition see chapter 6, by Robert Shirley.

7. At the time, Brazilian executives—the president, governors, and so on—were prohibited by the constitution from succeeding themselves in office. To project their influence and to extend their power, incumbents invariably selected from within their party someone to be their successor. Gubernatorial elections were held in October 1965. They were the first major elections to be held after the military coup of April 1964. The governor of Minas Gerais had been one of the leaders of the coup that brought Marshall Castelo Branco and the Brazilian military to power. He selected the candidate, who then received the support of the state government as well as that of the military regime in Brazilia. The fact that the candidate, Sr. Resende, lost the election to his opponent, who was a last-minute replacement for the original opposition candidate (disqualified by a military court only a month before the election), is not relevant to later events related to the road.

8. He also had been a visiting professor and colleague in my department in Milwaukee the semester before the fieldwork began and had served as my research associate during the early stages of the work in Paraízo. He left for the state capital when called to the legislative assembly as a replacement for a member of his party.

9. The esteemed gentleman held the chair in sociology at the federal university of the state, located in Belo Horizonte. Although he had not occupied the post for more than a decade, while holding various political offices, the chair and its benefits remained his. In his absence he appointed assistants and friends to give lectures and direct things in his name.

10. Perhaps the best single exponent of the importance of patrimonial authority in Brazilian society is Gilberto Freyre (1946, 1963a, 1963b, 1970). Although he uses the term "patriarchialism," his numerous works indicate clearly and lucidly that he is talking about what Weber, writing in terms of a broader and more comparative framework, referred to as "patrimonialism." Freyre demonstrates quite clearly the importance and the tenacity of the form in Brazilian society and culture.

11. In a sense it may be argued that Vargas's Estado Nôvo was a case of the exercise of patrimonial authority, with the president-dictator exercising that almost

unrestricted personal power in the centralization of the administrative machinery of government and in the transformation of the productive and distributive sectors of the society.

12. By Brazilian law all persons 18 or over who could read and write were eligible to become registered voters. The literacy requirements, however, disqualified most people who otherwise would have been eligible, since the majority of the population was illiterate. Massive literacy and voter registration campaigns, stimulated primarily by politicians or would-be politicians, increased the number of registered voters from some 7.5 million in 1945 (for the presidential election) to more than 15.5 million in 1960 (for another presidential election) and 18.5 million in 1962 (for the legislative elections). The 7.5 million voters in 1945 represented just over 16 percent of the population; the 18.5 million voters in 1962 represented about 25 percent. Because approximately half of the population 18 or over (which was less than half of the total population) was illiterate, by 1962 just about all eligible voters had been registered. Competition for the increasing number of new voters, combined with efforts to gain the support of those in search of greater rewards, was to be the key to social mobility during the period.

13. *Panelinhas* or *rodas* were based upon exchange relationships of the type Foster (1961, 1963) referred to as "colleague contracts." A number of relative equals aspiring to common ends that could best be attained jointly entered into an agreement to exchange and share their differing skills and access to diverse segments of the power system for their mutual benefit. Such associations were qualitatively different from those of the patron-client type otherwise entered into by careerists.

14. There an incident occurred—unrelated to the road, but illustrative of the local system of patronage exchanges—which will be elaborated in the analysis of the case of the charwoman. When he entered, Antonio was asked by Pedro's wife if her daughter had been to see him. He responded in the affirmative, saying that everything had been taken care of. The daughter had just graduated from the local normal school and was seeking a position as teacher in the state-supported school in Boa Vista. She had passed her examinations and had qualified in the competition for positions, but had to be appointed before she could be assigned to the school and become eligible for the benefits (in addition to salary) that went with the civil service position. Appointments to all civil service positions were made by the governor from the lists of persons who passed the open competitive exams.

The governor, however, delegated such matters to the appropriate secretaries, whose heads exchanged appointments for support—for the governor, his selections, and themselves. Antonio had obtained an appointment for the daughter. This had further solidified his reciprocities with Pedro, whose support he needed for reelection.

15. While its crews were doing this, they also cleared and repaired private roads on the lands belonging to João Resende and his supporters. Roads on the lands of the opposition, of course, were left untouched.

16. Those interested in obtaining the contract began to court Mayor Resende as soon as word of the project was released, offering him numerous benefits in return for the contract.

17. A *praça*, a road, a school, a bus station, a church, etc., makes a very visible sign of the magnanimity and importance of the person or persons who can claim to have been its donor. The maintenance and repair of such a structure, however, especially when it has been built through the effort of someone who has already used it for the promotion of his own career and is gone from the local scene, adds nothing to the prestige of a party not associated with its original construction. Therefore maintenance and repair work in general tends to be neglected. The result is that new *praças*, schools, churches, bus stations, water and sewage systems, hydroelectric facilities, etc., are built but not necessarily maintained. Between the poor quality of the materials used in construction—so as to increase profits and provide a share for the appropriate officials—and the inadequate maintenance, many projects fall into a state of disrepair shortly after completion. This enables some new party to arrange for the building of a new structure with which his name will be associated, and which will promote his career.

18. The behavior of Antonio Vierra da Sousa, who was an actor in the case of the road, is also of interest in the case of the cesspool. His home happened to be within a few hundred yards of the cesspool. When the slide occurred he was in the United States, where he expressed repeated concern for both his family in Boa Vista and the entire community. Combining his sociological training with his previous experience, however, he was able to analyze the situation and predict the sequence of events quite accurately. When he returned home he first tried to assist the *prefeito*—a political enemy—in repairing the cesspool. Soon, however, he was devoting his energies almost exclusively to securing his own reelection, which would mean that his family could leave Boa Vista—and the cesspool—and move to the state capital.

Antonio also was a distant relative of the former president, but he was associated with the Young Turks in the party who were seeking to oust the son of his kinsman as the party leader. The former president's son therefore opposed Antonio, undercutting him in his first bid for election and intervening to frustrate him on several occasions in the matter of the road. He would have preferred to oppose the completion of the road, so as to discredit his kinsman, whom he saw as a threat. Luckily for Antonio, the political situation was such that the governor and the UDN needed all the support they could get. In the end the road was supported, although never completed.

19. Control of the sheriff's office can be very important to the local residents. Those on his side, and hence on that of the police, are never bothered by the law. Those in factions opposed to the sheriff can be repeated victims, punished for violating numerous laws, generally unenforced, that appear to be kept on the books primarily so that those in power can pressure and intimidate their opposition.

20. In Boa Vista, for example, a fairly well-to-do woman was appointed charwoman in a rural school, some distance from her home, that was part of the state school system. She had obtained the nomination and appointment through the intermediacy of the state deputy, who was closely associated with and a relative of the son of the former president mentioned above. She and her large family had supported the deputy in his successful campaign against Antonio (both members of the PR). Once appointed, the woman appeared at the school only to collect her pay. When teachers and school inspectors complained because the building was filthy and beginning to deteriorate, she said openly that mopping

floors and cleaning latrines was not for the likes of her. In her own home she had an *empregada* ("maid") to do such work. She took the job, she maintained, only to get money to buy clothes for her daughters and to send them through school, and because the medical and retirement benefits would be helpful. The school authorities had no way to coerce her into doing what, in theory, she had been employed to do. She had been nominated through the intermediacy of the state deputy, who had the support of the governor and the son of the former president of the republic. She was well protected and secure with her life tenure. She could continue to collect her pay and receive her benefits. Whether or not she performed the job had nothing to do with it.

5

New Patrons for Old:
Changing Patron-Client Relationships
in the Bolivian Yungas

DWIGHT B. HEATH

Department of Anthropology
Brown University

The Aymara campesinos of the yungas region of Bolivia are proud beneficiaries of the only social revolution in twentieth-century South America. Although they took no part in the fighting [1] that brought the Nationalist Revolutionary Movement (MNR) to power in 1952, they are still militant in support of the party that they say "gave [them] the conquests of the revolution, namely: agrarian reform, universal suffrage, nationalization of the mines, and educational reform." [2] Perhaps the most telling indication of the quality of change since the overthrow of the traditional quasi-feudal system is the depth of feeling with which campesinos assert, "Now we are becoming human beings!" [3]

It is difficult for those affected—as either beneficiaries or "victims"—to do other than overestimate the pervasiveness of change in such a revolutionary setting. As a social scientist who never suffered the pain and humiliation of serfdom nor the anguish and discomfort of losing land and laborers, I discern marked continuity in terms of functions, in spite of appreciable formal change, in analyzing what has become of patronage, clientage, and power structures in the yungas region of Bolivia.[4]

THE SETTING

Among the many and immensely varied ecological niches in Bolivia, the yungas are so distinctive that their Aymara name has come into universal geographic usage. They are areas of rugged montaine jungle in the eastern range of the Andes—semitropical in climate and as spectacular as they are tortuous, with mountain peaks 10,000 feet high towering over snow-fed rivers that rush through narrow valleys sometimes as little as 2,000 feet above sea level. The steep slopes (sometimes of grades as great as 80 percent) are covered with dense vegetation where they have not been cleared for the cultivation of coffee or, more striking, coca ranged in narrow terraces that follow the contours of the hills.

Scattered through the yungas are small-scale farmers, most of them freeholders since the large haciendas that used to predominate were divided among former serfs as a result of the agrarian reform enacted in 1953. The farmers are mostly Aymara-speaking campesinos,[5] although there are a few settlements where Negroes predominate;[6] my discussion will focus on the Aymara in the province of Nor Yungas.[7] Their residence patterns are diverse: perhaps a third of them live in scattered homesteads, with roughly equal numbers living in towns (old commercial and administrative centers, dominated by whites and mestizos,[8] with total populations under 2,500), and in hamlets (with populations under 150, including few noncampesinos).

There has been no archaeological work in the area, but apparently the horticultural Lecos were driven northward when groups of Aymaras came from the altiplano as *mitimaes* (forcibly relocated communities) during the latter years of the Inca Empire. The cultivation of coca has been important ever since, providing a labor-intensive crop easily transported to the markets in the densely populated altiplano (about sixty miles west, across the mountains). Only one community in the region claims to have been chartered by the Crown as a *comunidad indígena* ("indigenous community," with special collective rights); most of the rest of the area was divided into haciendas where the traditional quasi-feudal system of *colonato* prevailed until the MNR revolution.

Haciendas in the yungas were not as large as in many less mountainous areas,[9] and the beneficent climate was such that many of the hacendados (hacienda owners) made their homes there, in contrast with the predominant pattern of absentee landlords in other areas of *colonato*.

A few scattered gold mines in the area were worked briefly during the colonial period, but only one is still active. Lumbering is carried on in a few isolated camps, which, like the mine, employ mostly mestizos from other areas. Hunting and fishing play no role in the local economy, and animal husbandry consists of a few pigs and chickens that scavenge unattended [10] and mules that are used for transport from throughout the region to the single road that provides a perilous connection with the rest of the country.

In contrast to the altiplano and temperate valley regions, there were no peasant uprisings in the yungas throughout the colonial and republican periods. The sporadic sieges, massacres, and other violent activities that served as periodic outbursts against intercaste oppression elsewhere were unknown.

Many of the most vocal and active *patriotas* (anti-Royalists) in the War of Independence were from the yungas, and the area served as a refuge for beleaguered guerrillas during the seesaw fighting that raged on the altiplano for fourteen years before the Republic of Bolivia was established in 1825.

From the Inca period to the present, the yungas contributed little to the rest of the country except coca—and the ever-increasing taxes derived from it—and got little in return.[11] A railroad intended to link La Paz, the *de facto* capital of the country and also the major commercial center, with the cattle-rich department of Beni in the eastern lowlands was to have passed through the yungas, but the project was abandoned decades ago before work had progressed that far.

One of the few material achievements of the Chaco War in the 1930s was construction, by Paraguayan prisoners of war, of a road connecting the yungas with La Paz.[12] Nevertheless, the people of the yungas are like Bolivians everywhere in decrying that wasteful war that left both countries bankrupt politically and economically. However much they may deplore it, Bolivians also recognize the Chaco War as a critical event in their history that somehow laid the groundwork for the revolution of 1952; although few have thought it through in such detail, most would probably agree with the perceptive analyses of Patch (1960) and Klein (1968) on this subject.[13]

One cannot understand any revolution except in historical context. Peasant revolts had flared sporadically throughout the Andes all during the colonial period, and they continued in the republican period. They were characteristically violent, but they were usually in reaction to specific local grievances, and were quickly and ruthlessly suppressed. There was little communication and less community of interest among the peasants, so that a successful revolution on the part of the Indians was out of the question.

There were others who felt oppressed in a very different manner from the Indian peasants. The traditional coalition of landed gentry and the military shared a monopoly of political power, in an oligarchic context where few others had any access to wealth.[14] With commercial and administrative expansion came a growing middle class with rising aspirations. They became especially restive when the Chaco War clearly demonstrated that the traditional leadership was weak, and that the old values did not fit with modern problems. The 1940s saw Bolivia opened as never before to influences from without. The Allies wanted her rubber and tin, and the Axis spoke of the altiplano as "an unsinkable aircraft carrier." Foreigners also brought ideas; the Trotskyite Revolutionary Workers' Party (Partido Obrero Revolucionario) was founded at that time, as were the Marxist Party of the Revolutionary Left (Partido de la Izquierda Revolucionaria) and the eclectic Nationalist Revolutionary Movement (Movimiento Nacionalista Revolucionario).

This last party, the MNR, emerged as a loose coalition of people with a wide range of outlooks toward the left of the political spectrum. Their first practical experience came in the mid-1940s when Victor Paz Estenssoro and other MNR activists served in the cabinet of Major Gualberto Villarroel and proposed a variety of progressive social legislation. Trade unions were readily established among the miners, and the Interamerican Indigenist Institute was invited to hold its congress in Bolivia. In connection with the latter meeting, the first National Indian Congress was called, at which four decrees were issued that would have undermined *colonato* if they had not been generally ignored throughout nearly all of the country.[15]

When Villarroel's government fell to revolution a year later, Victor Paz went into exile in Argentina. Virtually all Bolivians were surprised when, still in exile, he gained a plurality in the presidential election of 1951, but the decision was referred to Congress because he did not have a true majority of the votes. A military junta intervened, but was deposed when the MNR finally came to power in a bloody revolution in the capital city, April 9–11, 1952.

The accession to power of this party did not represent, as had many of Bolivia's previous so-called revolutions, a mere changing of the palace guard and transfer of political incumbency from one upper class clique to another. The revolution of 1952 was the basis of a real social revolution. It significantly altered the status of the former elite and resulted in immediate and far-reaching modifications of political life and government policy that were subsequently codified in constitutional changes. The formal organization of government continued much the same as before, although the locus of effective power was greatly altered. The oligarchy (locally called *rosca*) were generally exiled, impoverished, or otherwise rendered ineffectual. The army was emasculated, its career officers forced into retirement and its weapons distributed to miners and peasants, who formed popular militias. Clearly the bases of the old quasi-feudal order were broken, and popular support for the revolutionary regime was assured when Paz enacted universal suffrage, enfranchising the Indian masses who had previously had no voice or vote.

The new government strove quickly and remarkably effectively to overcome the serious problem of how to incorporate the numerically predominant but hitherto passive Indians actively into a more open social system. A Ministry of Campesino Affairs (Asuntos Campesinos) was established and given the task of defending the campesinos and planning the fundamental reforms in their economic, social, and political positions that had been promised by the MNR. The very name of the new ministry reflects the zealous reformism of MNR officials, who expunged the word *indio* (literally, "Indian," but with deprecatory connotations) from Bolivian Spanish, and substituted *campesino* ("peasant"), which is far less emotionally charged.

Campesinos

Many Bolivians viewed Indians as subhuman beings, and there was little communication at a meaningful level between the tiny but totally dominant upper class and the enormous but silent mass of peasantry. Even an ardent *indigenista* who rhapsodized about his country's Inca heritage, and who served as minister of education to a populace of whom fewer than one-half speak Spanish, confessed that he could not deal with an Indian as an individual: "The Indian is a sphinx. He inhabits a hermetic world, inaccessible to the white and the mestizo. We don't understand his forms of life, nor his mental mechanism. . . . We speak of the Indian as a mass factor in the nation; in truth we are ignorant of his individual psyche and his collective drama. The Indian lives. The Indian acts and produces. The Indian does not allow himself to be understood, he doesn't desire communication. Retiring, silent, immutable, he inhabits a closed world. The Indian is an enigma" (Díez de Medina 1956:253). In such an ambience, it is little wonder that hacendados made no pretense of understanding their *colonos*.

Unfortunately, no studies were made in the yungas by social scientists during the prerevolutionary period,[16] and fragmentary documentary evidence is a scanty supplement to the oral tradition for purposes of historical reconstruction.

A number of distinguishing features set the Aymara peasantry of the yungas apart from the local gentry and the dominant national culture of Bolivia. In some cases the distinctions were clear and objective; in others, they were situationally relative, so that an outsider might not have agreed with locally accepted criteria. Complete lack of familiarity with Spanish was an insurmountable barrier to many campesinos, and almost none of those who achieved some fluency was able to overcome the distinctive Aymara accent. The generalized *indio* physique still exists as an important stereotype, despite the fact that some adult Indians have been able to "become" mestizos for decades. Until the 1940s the campesinos of this area also had a distinctive manner of dress: a heavy broad-brimmed hat with tiny round crown, short tight trousers of homespun wool and a tight waistcoat of the same material, bare feet and a bowl-shaped haircut are generally agreed on by campesinos and townsmen alike as having been identifying features.

Furthermore, Indians normally lived in small thatched huts of adobe or wattle and daub, scattered through the countryside. They were generally thought to be "ignorant," and this was attributed as much to "Indian blood" as to the absence of schools. Nominally Catholic, they were still strongly influenced by their indigenous religion. The fiesta complex provided an occasional frenetic contrast with workaday drudgery, but it was not integrated with a socioreligious hierarchy as was the case among the highland Aymara. Class differences were constantly reinforced by the quasi-feudal policy; a peasant of any age could be called *yocalla* ("boy," in a demeaning, condescending sense) and sent on an errand by anyone of the landholding group; they in turn were addressed by peasants, with hat in hand, as *tata* ("father").

Kin ties among campesinos were important, featuring patrilineal descent, monogamy, systematic respect for elders, a preference for patrilocal residence. Because virtually all surnames were names of animals and natural objects, it might be tempting to speculate about these as possible survivals of a pre-Columbian system of totemic patrilineages, but there is no indication that the ayllu, so important on the altiplano, was a meaningful social unit in this region in the twentieth century.

Division of labor by sex was marked, with women's only agricultural contribution being collaboration in the coca and coffee harvests. Virtually all Aymara were farmers; a few skilled *yatiris* (approximately, "medicine men") served as diviners and curers, combining herbal and magical techniques; other Aymara learned rudimentary masonry, carpentry, or tinsmithing, but few other occupational opportunities were open to them.

In short, the Aymara-speaking campesinos participated in a distinctive local sociocultural system that provided no direct access to regional or national institutions of education, government, or commerce. Most of the contacts of Indians prior to the revolution were with others on the hacienda; the rare dealings they had with the world beyond were almost invariably mediated by the hacendado as both broker and patron.[17] In retrospect, this combined brokerage and patronage role is justified by the gentry as a benevolent paternalism; it is roundly condemned by the campesinos as having been a systematic limitation of their horizons.

Hacendados

Until relatively recently, both local and national governments were content to leave management of the campesinos almost entirely in the hands of hacendados. In the yungas area (as opposed to the altiplano), most hacendados actually lived on their properties, and many took an active part in dealing with their *colonos:* settling disputes, administering first aid, sanctioning marriages and divorces, and so on. The relative autonomy of the hacienda could be attributed in part to problems of transportation and communication, but perhaps more to the point were indifference of officials toward Indians on the one hand and respect for the traditional autarchy of hacendados on the other.

The hacienda comprised a community in most senses, and the Indians had little recourse to domains beyond. For certain limited purposes, they dealt with institutions elsewhere in the province, but such dealings were always mediated by the hacendado. The power of the hacendado was virtually absolute on his own property, and the hacendados formed a bloc whose wealth and political connections allowed them to effectively manipulate other levels.[18]

Among the services that hacendados exacted from *colonos* were not only tenant farming, but also *faena* and *pongueaje*, rather more feudal in nature. *Faena* refers to group work projects on hacienda property— maintaining roads and trails, repairing walls, caring for grounds, and so forth. *Pongueaje* was the periodic in-house service rendered, by turns, by all *colonos*—women serving as cooks and maids and men as busboys, a week at a time in the house of the hacendado. Similarly there were various obligations such as providing eggs, collecting firewood, driving the mules to the altiplano, or drying or baling coca—a variety of periodic tasks without pay.

Proud of their "white" heritage,[19] hacendados took their dominant positions to be not only "right" but even "natural," in view of the supposed inherent inferiority of Indians. Few were sadistically abusive, but most enjoyed a degree of leisure and comfort that cost dearly in terms of labor on the part of *colonos*. Indians were considered "like children," so many hacendados provided first aid for their *colonos* and rudimentary schooling for a few chosen individuals and even spoke on their behalf on those rare occasions when a *colono* had to deal with anyone beyond the hacienda community (for example, if more sophisticated medical aid were needed, the hacendado would take his *colono* to the government clinic or to a pharmacist in the provincial capital; if the police charged a *colono*, the hacendado would intermediate; and so forth). In each such instance, the hacendado would serve as patron and broker for his *colono*, who in turn was his client. Clientage was generalized whereas patronage was selective. The hacendado had power over the *colono* and could choose those realms in which he wished to serve as patron. The hacendado-as-gatekeeper could be restrictive as well as facilitating, and the *colono* had virtually no way of seeking other patrons, even for limited purposes.

Even when the social reformers of the MNR acceded to power in 1952, no one would have been so bold as to predict the degree to which the sociocultural system of the campesinos (ex-*colonos*) was to be opened, and the pervasiveness of change in ways of thinking and acting that have in fact occurred. It is a truism that most of this change was also felt by the ex-hacendados as well (although the effects of such changes were obviously restricting rather than facilitating for that formerly dominant group).

POSTREVOLUTIONARY
SOCIAL ORGANIZATION

The cardinal purpose of this paper is to illustrate how some major realignments of patronage-clientage networks have occurred as old roles have been redefined and new ones created in the aftermath of the MNR revolution.

Probably the most important changes in social organization are three that took place at the level of the individual hacienda community. First, the *colonos* (tenant farmers in an almost feudal serfdom) became *ex-colonos* (independent freeholders) at the same time that they traded the demeaning label *indio* for the more egalitarian *campesino*. Second, the hacendados (quasi-feudal landlords) were generally forced off the land and lost all claim to the services of campesinos; most ex-hacendados moved to the provincial capital and established small businesses there. Third, virtually all *ex-colonos* joined to form a *sindicato* (peasant league), a corporate entity to represent all who had been colonos (or *arrenderos* [20]) on a single hacienda.

The change in status of former *colonos* is the basis for the enormous psychological impact of the revolution, and campesinos cherish what they call their "liberation from slavery." They look back on their obligations to the hacendado as having been extremely burdensome, and their status as having been degrading, even in those instances where hacendados were not physically abusive or sexually exploitative.

The change of status of former hacendados has been, by contrast, a harsh deprivation that they strongly resent. They consider that their property (often household goods as well as the land) was "stolen" and that the Indians, supported by the opportunistic MNR, have unjustly and systematically persecuted them for no other reason than covetousness, rationalized by a few aspiring politicians with the slogan "class warfare."

The formation of *sindicatos* has been a potent force (probably the crucial one) in providing political socialization for campesinos. On most former haciendas, the *sindicato* provides both a sense of participation in the community and a channel for brokerage with respect to nearly all of an individual *ex-colono*'s contacts with the world beyond.

From Colono to Ex-Colono

The point has been made before, but it deserves to be underscored: the cardinal significance of the revolution from the point of view of the individual who had been a *colono* was that he was no longer an "Indian" and a serf but rather a "campesino" and a freeholder. Emancipation from labor obligations to the hacendado means more in terms of their "becoming human beings" than does even the title to land—holdings that are often actually smaller than those to which they previously earned usufruct privileges by labor.

Freedom, however, always entails some responsibility. The *ex-colonos* were confronted with the need to budget time and resources, to make decisions, and to market produce, all of which had been done by the hacendado or mayordomo before the revolution. Even the most authoritarian hacendado had performed many crucial roles as patron to his *colono* clients, and the *ex-colono* was not well equipped to do many of the things that had been done for him.

Ill equipped by language, training, and experience to act independently in the world beyond the ex-hacienda, the *ex-colonos* have not readily abandoned the pattern of personalistic clientage, but have sought some new patrons, and established new relationships with some old ones.

From Hacendado to Ex-Hacendado

Hardest hit by the revolution were the hacendados who lost their properties and their privileged social standing and economic base. The properties that they lost were not merely tracts of land; they were estates that had often been in the family for generations, and sometimes even houses and their contents were abandoned.

A few of these men who were truly wealthy left Bolivia altogether and will probably never return. A few who had skills or capital went to La Paz and found jobs in business or government or established commercial enterprises on their own. The majority had never done anything but manage a farm, were neither wealthy (in terms of liquid assets) nor cosmopolitan to begin with, and did not want to venture far beyond the provincial capital. One became a carpenter (and was sheriff during my stay); one ran a pharmacy (where he diagnosed and treated more patients than did the physician in the government clinic up the street); one ran a bar; another was named mayor of the town but earned more from the freight hauled by a truck he owned. A number of small general stores were run by ex-hacendados, as were a bakery, a pool hall, and occasional cockfights. Many of these same individuals have also been able to capitalize on their experience in selling produce and now serve as middlemen in marketing the coca, coffee, and citrus fruit raised by *ex-colonos* on land that used to be theirs.

It is noteworthy that many of them still serve as patrons to their former *colonos*, with respect to selected realms of activity, although their status within the social system has changed in many significant respects.

The Sindicato: A New Institution

In order to effect anything approaching pervasive reform in a quasi-feudal system, it is necessary to create new social institutions. After the revolution, the campesinos on a given ex-hacienda were often linked to each other only as distant neighbors and as former co-workers of a dispossessed employer. The ex-hacendado and former mayordomo who had been the coordinators, decisionmakers, and brokers usually left the community, so that leadership and organization were minimal until the *sindicatos* emerged as effective institutions, based on new kinds of authority and explicitly oriented toward a new set of goals that could be subsumed under the novel rubric of campesino welfare.

The *sindicatos* were unlike anything seen by most yungas campesinos before, but their organizational structure is very similar to that of the miners' unions. It appears that it was primarily representatives of MNR, under the auspices of the party and the newly created Ministry of Campesino Affairs, who toured the area in the early 1950s and laid the groundwork for sindical organization that has become almost universal.[21]

Many of these changes at the local level are integrally related to other changes at the provincial, departmental, and national levels. New administrative institutions were created and some old ones were ignored or bypassed; *sindicalismo* quickly became a potent movement with local *sindicatos* organized into provincial federations, which in turn were organized into departmental federations, with all of those comprising a national confederation of campesino *sindicatos* (see figure 1).

The legislative basis for such *sindicatos* was not spelled out in the agrarian reform act (Bolivia 1953) or in related decrees. What happened in practice was that the former *colonos* of an hacienda would constitute a *sindicato*—following guidelines of the organizers from La Paz—and that the first enterprise of such a *sindicato* would be for the secretary general to file with the local agrarian judge a *demanda* ("petition") for reallocation of land. Provision was made for latifundia to be expropriated and reallocated, with communal plots, commons for grazing livestock, school areas, and other details to be worked out on an *ad hoc* basis by the agrarian judge and topographer on the site. The result was that specifications for the disposition of each ex-hacienda were unique, and subject to revision at several stages in the progress of the claim.

Although the *sindicatos* were constituted primarily as means of securing title to land, they gradually came to serve other functions as well. They were effective organizations for political socialization and indoctrination by a small cadre skilled in demagoguery and able to channel small-scale patronage.

What the clients in this relationship had to offer was occasional support for MNR by participating in political demonstrations, both locally and in the national capital. Because of the difficulty of transportation, campesinos in the yungas were rallied less often than those nearer the larger cities, but when they was a threat to MNR incumbency (real or supposed), they would crowd into trucks when summoned and race to La Paz, where their militant shouts of "Viva!" reinforced by their weapons and sheer numbers, often intimidated the opposition. On such occasions, the leader would be reimbursed for the truck rental and given a standard sum (usually Bs. 12,000, or U.S. $1) per man; about one-half of the head fee would be passed on to the individual campesino demonstrator as per diem, but many complained (confidentially, not publicly) about the unreimbursed cost to them in terms of lost work time. Local demonstrations included occasional shows of force, parades, guerrilla raids on Falangist or supposedly Communist groups, and so forth.

The activities of the *sindicatos* are varied, and include much more than land claims and political demonstrations. Often the activities overlap with the jurisdiction of preexisting formal institutions. For example, the *sindicatos*, not the courts, have supplanted the hacendado in resolving conflicts between campesinos: not only informal accusations of petty theft, minor assault, and so forth, but even such institutionalized differences as divorce. Such conflict resolutions do not have the legal force of orthodox court procedures, but they are often respected locally. The *sindicatos* also mediate in some cases of inheritance, land exchange, and so forth, despite the fact that they have had no official legal jurisdiction since dissolution of the Juntas Rurales, short-lived rural land courts of the mid-1950s. It is well known, even to campesinos, that formally structured courts in the provincial capital are already supplemented by a chief of police and a *subprefecto* (*cf.* sheriff in U.S.A.); campesinos believe, however, that within the formal official system "justice belongs to the rich." They rarely subject themselves to its costs and delays, and hesitate to lay themselves open to the indignities and abuses that they still frequently suffer from white and mestizo townsmen, including judges and other public officials. More often they seek to resolve their conflicts within the extraofficial and relatively informal system of the *sindicato*.

Another important kind of sindical activity is public works. For example, on many of the ex-haciendas *ex-colonos* pooled their labor to build schools, and often they even went on to hire teachers paid by special assessments (*cuotas*) when the authorities declined to assign government-paid teachers. The self-conscious concern with education is deep and pervasive in contemporary campesino life. Other public works projects include the installation of water systems, the building and maintenance of roads, bridges, and trails, the construction of football fields or of plazas, occasionally the construction of a first aid station (*puesta sanitaria*), and so forth, for which campesinos usually provide both funds and labor but seek technical assistance and material through higher level campesino organizations.

Sindicatos are involved not only in law, education, and public works but also in economics. One of the most popular and inaccurate myths concerning Indians in highland Latin America is their supposed predilection for communal cooperation. Urban nationals seem to have accepted this myth as uncritically as have foreigners, and many ambitious development plans have failed because they were based on it. This is not to say that the Aymara of the yungas are totally uncooperative. The aini, the traditional pattern of reciprocal labor exchange that used to be restricted to the extended family, now sometimes involves most of the members of a *sindicato*. Similarly, cooperation of other kinds has been taught as a crucial tool in effecting the common goals of the *ex-colonos*, both within the local community and beyond it. They early learned, from their organizers and from the dramatic example of miners and other unionized workers, that there is power in united numbers. One of the most dramatic illustrations of this power, without official authority, is the case of the twenty-five-pound arroba in which they agreed to force coffee buyers to pay them on the basis of a twenty-five-pound unit (rather than a thirty-two-pound one), and succeeded after a brief sellers' strike (Heath 1966).

A variety of other apolitical activities take place among the campesino *sindicatos*. One of the most widespread is soccer, with frequent intersindical competition enjoyed as a spectator sport. In a few *sindicatos*, teachers offer night courses in Spanish and literacy; such courses are well attended, by women as well as men. Occasionally, a first aid kit and some medicine are kept for use, at cost, by members. Although there is no formal program of social security (orphans and the aged are usually cared for by kinsmen), in at least some instances when there were no relatives on the ex-hacienda needy individuals were informally adopted by neighbors within the *sindicato*. Occasionally, an imaginative and energetic agricultural extension agent takes advantage of the sindical organization in order to reach *ex-colonos* more efficiently with demonstrations, films, and other educational services.

Other means by which campesino *sindicatos* could serve their members are often discussed, more by leaders than by the rank and file. For example, it is not only outsiders who talk about the potential value of cooperatives. A highly publicized aspect of MNR policy was to foster cooperatives, both by exhortation and by preferential taxation. Sindical leaders throughout the yungas agree that the economic situation of *ex-colonos* could be strengthened by the introduction of cooperatives for buying staple goods and necessities and for selling agricultural produce. In no instance, however, had this ideal been translated into action.

The elected secretary general of a *sindicato* clearly has power in many domains, but it is by no means unlimited. In sharp contrast with the stereotype held by townsmen, only a few campesino leaders have become caciques—despotic autocrats. On the contrary, major decisions are usually submitted to the rank and file, although support is often achieved through demagogic oratory rather than studied debate.

In some instances, a secretary general also plays an important political role beyond the local *sindicato*. In the yungas, campesinos have not been elected or appointed to public office as have a few *ex-colonos* from other regions. Nevertheless, a secretary general may also be head of the local cell of MNR and have influential contacts in the party and in various ministries.[22] Usually he is also an officer in a larger regional association of *sindicatos*, and an enterprising man can make political capital out of the fact that he can muster a large number of men—and an even larger number of votes!

Quite apart from representing the *sindicato* elsewhere, the secretary general also has considerable responsibility on the ex-hacienda. It is he who oversees public works projects, such as the preparation of a soccer field or building of a school. He keeps track of those who have fulfilled their obligations (called *faena*) and serves as foreman throughout the work. Not only does a man in this status serve as a spokesman for his *sindicato* vis-à-vis other groups and administrators, but he must also provide hospitality to visiting secretaries general and any other distinguished visitors. By the same token, any outsider attempting to gain effective entrée into the ex-hacienda community would be unwise not to explain his mission first to the secretary general, whose local authority, like that of the hacendado before the revolution, is manifold and rarely disputed.

In short, the status of secretary general is *primus inter pares*; as a cultural broker he plays a crucial role as intermediary between his constituents and other sociocultural systems. Ideally, therefore, he should speak Spanish; most of those in the yungas do. He should also be a fairly articulate and dynamic person; many of them are.

The channels through which the secretary general acts on behalf of his neighbors and fellow members are often those established by the Ministry of Campesino Affairs in an affiliated sindical bureaucracy. Figure 1 depicts the hierarchy of sindical organization, which links each *ex-colono* of ex-hacienda Minachi with the president of the Republic. It also depicts the discrepancy between the formal table of organization and the real organization as it was constituted in 1964–65.

Each individual who had been a *colono* on hacienda Minachi has become an *ex-colono*, member of Sindicato Minachi. Those who had been *arrenderos* have similarly become members of the *sindicato* and have gained social and political equality with *ex-colonos* (although they received smaller land grants when the ex-hacienda was expropriated and reapportioned). This and two neighboring *sindicatos* are unusual in that they more often meet jointly (as the subcentral of Cruz Loma, and often as the central of Cruz Loma) than they do independently. The physical proximity and smallness of these three ex-haciendas contrasts with the situation elsewhere in Nor Yungas, and they often ignore other *sindicatos* that are nominally affiliated with the central. Furthermore, a dynamic and politically ambitious campesino early convinced the *ex-colonos* there of the advantages to be gained from collaboration; results have included the building of a school and a number of houses around a newly made common plaza at Cruz Loma, which may soon become one of the "new towns" that are an unforeseen product of the MNR revolution (Preston 1969, 1970). This central, another central, and three unaffiliated subcentrals (comprising altogether some thirty-six local *sindicatos*) send representatives to the Provincial Federation of Nor Yungas. That organization, together with federations representing each of the fourteen other provinces that make up the department, are in turn administered by the Departmental Federation of La Paz. During the period of research, however, there was a power play at the departmental level with three leaders each claiming to speak for the federation; representatives of provincial federations were not constant in their support of these men, and the National Confederation (comprising this and the federation from each of the eight other departments) officially recognized only one faction, although the other two were occasionally able to get the ear of people in the confederation. The National Confederation is the highest organization of campesino *sindicatos*. However, its informal support of the minister of campesino affairs is sufficiently strong that he often acts as their representative within the cabinet, and lobbies on their behalf with the president of the Republic.

The MNR has attempted in many ways over the years to inculcate the view of "the peasantry" as a unified bloc. The diversity of the

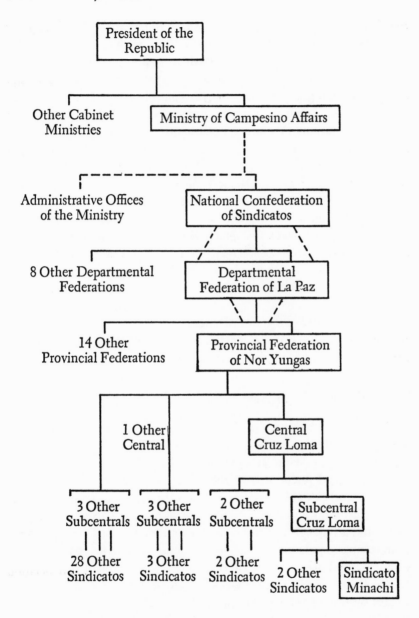

FIGURE 1. HIERARCHY OF CAMPESINO SINDICAL ORGANIZATION

Bolivian population remains a real obstacle to national unity. Linguistic and cultural differences between speakers of Quechua and Aymara are best known and most striking, but there is also appreciable regional variation within each of these groups. Furthermore, there are several other campesino groups throughout the country; even those who do not have distinctive languages and cultures are often intensely regionalistic in their orientations. At the level of rhetoric, there is general consensus that "the peasantry must stand united in defending the accomplishments of the [1952] revolution"; at the level of overt action, there is little effective collaboration beyond the level of the provincial federation which, in the yungas, has been a fairly effective coalition.

Class antagonism was explicit in the MNR revolution and remains important both in theory and practice; because the dominant socioeconomic class were virtually all mestizos and whites, and the oppressed peasantry were mostly Indians, the interclass antagonism is sometimes also phrased in racial terms, with the *misti* ("white man") cast as the villain by the Aymara.

"The authorities" are allies or enemies, more on the basis of party affiliation than any realistic evaluation of the attitudes or behavior of the individual persons in positions of authority.

Old Patrons in New Roles

This tendency to deal with blocs or classes of people is balanced by occasional establishment of particularistic relations with specific individuals, sometimes even in violation of the stereotyped relations. For example, general resentment of the *misti* does not necessarily interfere with a peasant's establishing ties of compadrazgo (co-parenthood) with a townsman who is not only white, but also an ex-hacendado, a merchant, and a Falangist. Such cases are commonplace and reflect a fairly clear compartmentalization between relationships based on economic advantage, and others where affect plays a more dominant role. In fact, despite their cherished new freedom, many *ex-colonos* retain ties with ex-hacendados who are strikingly paternalistic in ways reminiscent of the classic prerevolution patron-client relationship, particularly with respect to commercial agriculture.

The yungas region is unusual in Bolivia in that agriculture has long been commercial as well as subsistence. Coca and coffee, the predominant crops, are still produced for the market, but new channels of distribution have had to be established. Hacendados used to sell the produce from their haciendas to wholesalers and exporters in La Paz; *ex-colonos* who have lately virtually monopolized production do not have either the personal contacts or the quantity of goods that would be meaningful to those merchants. It is not surprising, therefore, to find campesinos selling their produce to middlemen in the provincial towns, and to find that many of these middlemen are, in fact, ex-hacendados, who call the economic differential between their buying and selling prices "interest" rather than "profit." There is some justification for this because a middleman often lends money to his campesino suppliers during the lean months between harvests, and so gets the option to buy their produce but deducts only the value of the loan, without added interest, when the goods are delivered. Middlemen also serve as compadres to their clients, with the understanding that, when a campesino comes to town, his compadre should provide the hospitality of food and a place to sleep; the campesino, in turn, should reciprocate by bringing a few eggs, some fresh fruit, or a similar token gift. Occasionally, too, the townsman will provide counsel, first aid, or some other assistance if a campesino runs afoul of the law.

In sum, the relationship between an *ex-colono* and his middleman is strikingly consistent with the pattern of patronage-clientage that was the ideal in prerevolutionary days, when a "good" hacendado did the same things for a "good" *colono*. It should be no surprise to find that, in many instances, *ex-colonos* are happy to continue in such a dependent (and secure) relationship with their own former hacendados; others, of course, have sought to establish a similar relationship with other merchants or even other ex-hacendados. The fundamental point in this connection is that, in this respect, there is remarkable continuity in social organization (in terms of the roles, or functions of relationships), in spite of considerable change in social structure (in terms of the form of status networks within the social system).

New Patrons in Old Roles

In like manner, my discussion of the range of sindical activities may have emphasized social innovations, but I feel it important also to consider some of them in terms of new forms serving old functions, or as possible survivals of previous patterns under the jurisdiction of a new institution.

For example, when the secretary of justice or the secretary general takes the law into his own hands in adjudicating a case between members of a *sindicato*, he is not significantly encroaching on the sphere of influence of the sheriff, the police, or the courts, none of which ever really had effective jurisdiction on the haciendas even in prereform days. Rather, he is filling the role of the hacendado, who used to do the same thing, with no more regard for the formal legal institutions of the nation-state.

By the same token, public works projects undertaken in the name of the *sindicato* are more than analogous to the prereform *faena*; they are often virtually identical, called by the same name and performed jointly on Sunday mornings, but now on behalf of the *sindicato* rather than the hacienda.

For that matter, the secretary general acts very like a prereform mayordomo when he oversees the *faena*, or work on the collectively held property. Furthermore, he acts like a benevolent prereform hacendado when he serves as broker for his constituents in lobbying for a teacher, a sanitarian, or some other form of patronage.

In rare instances a powerful secretary general has institutionalized a labor draft whereby members of the *sindicato* take turns cultivating his crops while he is away, ostensibly on sindical business. Such a pattern of mandatory labor in the fields of another is reminiscent of that *colonos'* obligation to the hacendado which was the primary target of agrarian reform. A little less compelling in its similarity to the prereform situation, but still related, is the more common pattern whereby a few members of a *sindicato* help in the secretary's agricultural work on a voluntary basis.

When sindical leaders speculate enthusiastically about the potential value of instituting buying cooperatives, they cite the very advantages that *colonos* used to enjoy in many hacienda commissaries.

There is no clear-cut survival of *pongueaje*, the housekeeping obligation of *colonos*, but the role of members' wives in cooking for and serving "visiting firemen" on sindical business is required and unremunerated as was similar work performed for the hacendado in prereform days.

CASE STUDIES IN CHANGING
PATRONAGE-CLIENTAGE
NETWORKS

In short, despite sweeping reforms in the forms of social structure instituted by the MNR revolution, there are many instances in the yungas in which aspects of the *patrón-peón* type of patron-client relationship persist virtually unchanged, in functional terms, between former hacendados and the campesinos who had been their *colonos*. There are also many instances in which a new *patrón-peón* type of patron-client functional relationship has been established, with a new form, the *sindicato* or the secretary general, assuming the dominant paternalistic status formerly held by the hacendado, and the campesino continuing in a relatively dependent servile status.

But it would be grossly inaccurate to view the *sindicatos* as nothing but new names for haciendas, with absentee landlords (ex-hacendados) now living in the towns as middlemen, or with secretaries general acting as Aymara-speaking hacendados.

Continuity in function, with dramatic change in form, is only one aspect of the role of *sindicatos*. Another aspect of the role of these new institutions is their serving new functions, some of which are not only discontinuous with prereform patterns but are distinctively and dramatically inimical to the old order. It is noteworthy, for example, that political socialization is by no means limited to the few dynamic secretaries general who are effective lobbyists for their own interests and those of their constituents. Awareness of and concern for the active role of citizenship has pervaded the *sindicatos*, reshaping the outlook and the lives of many members as well as those of the leaders. At periodic meetings of the *sindicatos*, occasional special open forums, political rallies, and on other occasions, campesinos are outspoken in a way that no one would have predicted on the basis of the prereform stereotype of the Aymara.

In one sense, this entire paper can be considered a case study in patronage, clientage, and power structures. It is clear that the networks of social, economic, and political interdependence in which the Aymara of the Bolivian yungas participate are unique and complex; it is also clear that there has been change—sometimes dramatic and extensive—with respect to those networks through time.

In another sense, however, my description of patron-client relations has been in general terms, and it seems appropriate now to focus on those networks that are used for particular purposes. This should help us to achieve a fuller appreciation of both continuity and change, of status and role, of form and function, of ideal and real, and of other kinds of variation that are significant in any system of patronage and clientage.

In attempting to understand changing patron-client relationships it seems appropriate to examine the ways in which individuals seek access to a few selected goods and services. With respect to the Aymara of the yungas, a variety of important points can be made by comparing pre-revolution with postrevolution [23] patronage-clientage networks for curing, land, justice, public works, and the sale of produce.

Curing

One of the few realms of culture in which the 1952 revolution has wrought little change is curing, and yet the ways in which clients seek access to it illustrate the nature and type of changes even within the same provincial setting (figure 2).[24]

Before the revolution, colonos usually sought remedies directly from the yatiri; although resident on an hacienda (level A), he also served a clientele throughout the province (level B). The sole alternative (somewhat less popular) was to ask the hacendado for help. On those occasions when the hacendado's first aid ministrations were insufficient, he referred colonos to the government clinic in the provincial capital or (almost as often) to the pharmacist there. Colonos virtually never went elsewhere for treatment.

Since the revolution, the yatiri retains his dual clientele, including not only ex-colonos on the same hacienda but also those from other haciendas throughout the province. The ex-hacendado has been effectively banished from the local community, but is still visited in the provincial capital by a few ex-colonos seeking help. A similar number of the ex-colonos seek help directly from the pharmacist, and a very few go directly to the clinic, but many more apply to the sindicato, where some get first aid and others are referred to the pharmacist. The ex-hacendado

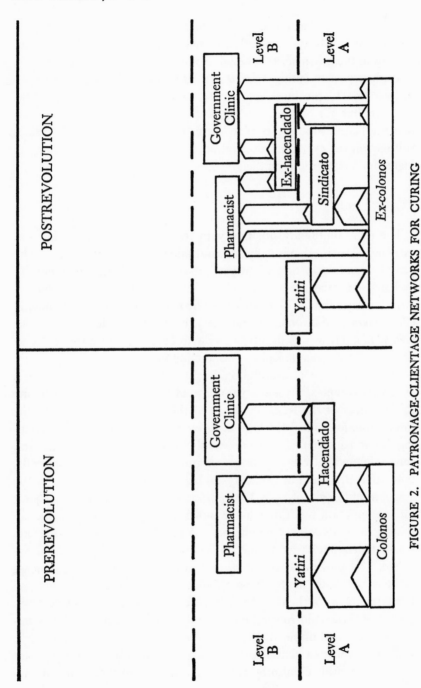

FIGURE 2. PATRONAGE-CLIENTAGE NETWORKS FOR CURING

does no more curing but continues to refer faithful *ex-colonos* to the pharmacist and to the clinic. The clinic, in turn, occasionally refers *ex-colonos* to the pharmacist, but he does not reciprocate.

With respect to curing, then, it is clear that the campesinos still tend to look first to the local community, and then elsewhere within the province, but not beyond. The *sindicato* has assumed some of the roles that the hacendado used to play in this network, but some campesinos still rely on the ex-hacendado, and others take the initiative in going to higher level institutions on their own.

Land

The prerevolutionary situation with respect to agricultural land was extremely restricted, virtually all controlled by the hacendados, who provided usufruct privileges on portions of their holdings to *colonos* in exchange for labor (figure 3). On a few haciendas, a small group of *arrenderos* got the use of smaller plots by helping *colonos* (becoming, in effect, *colonos*-of-*colonos*; see note 20), or by offering less labor to the hacendado. There was no other access to land, and no one outside of the individual hacienda had any jurisdiction there.

By contrast, the postrevolutionary situation with respect to land is extremely complex, involving patronage at each level to and including the president of the Republic. Most of the former *arrenderos*, like the former *colonos*, joined the local *sindicato* primarily as a means of securing title to land that they had previously worked. The *sindicato*, in turn, submitted and actively supported a claim for portions of the hacienda, both collectively and individually, on behalf of its members. Under the agrarian reform act of 1953, the appropriate channel for such a request for expropriation was through the provincial agrarian reform judge, although many *ex-colonos* sought support for their claims from the provincial federation of campesino *sindicatos*, as did the officers of the *sindicato*. The provincial federation did, in many instances, speak or act on behalf of those clients, trying to influence the agrarian judge and also to enlist support of the departmental federation of campesino *sindicatos*.

The ex-hacendado found himself in direct competition with his former *colonos*, and often tried to defend his holdings from expropriation. The law stipulated that his defense against the claims of *ex-colonos* should be considered also by the provincial agrarian judge; in some in-

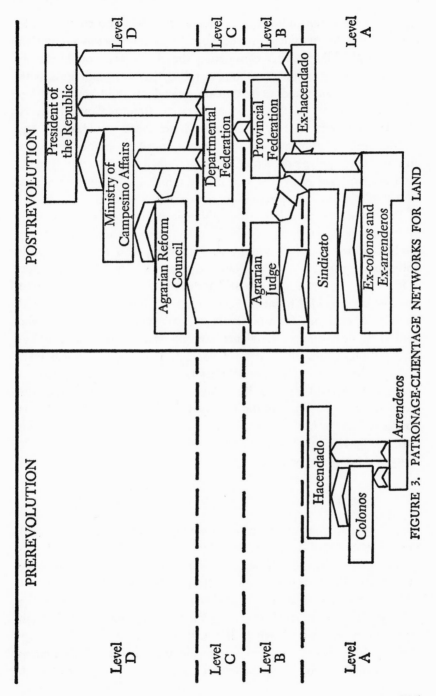

FIGURE 3. PATRONAGE-CLIENTAGE NETWORKS FOR LAND

stances, however, an influential ex-hacendado would also communicate directly with the president in the hope of getting special exemption for his landholdings. After considering the claims and counterclaims, the agrarian judge made a preliminary ruling that was binding on both *ex-colono* claimants and ex-hacendado defendants, and routinely forwarded the dossier to the National Agrarian Reform Council. Every case was reviewed at this level, so ex-hacendados would often try, through personal influence and other means, to get the council to reverse an unfavorable judge's decision. After the council had passed judgment, each case still had to be reviewed by the minister of campesino affairs, who regularly received appeals from departmental federations on behalf of their constituencies. Even the cabinet-level decision was not final; every case (even those in which there had been no reversal of lower level decisions) was reviewed by the president, who received appeals both from departmental federations and from individual ex-hacendados.

In marked contrast with the still restricted network for curing, that for land has expanded to include every level within the nation-state, and there is no continuity from prerevolution patterns. The hacendado who used to be the patron par excellence, controlling access to all agricultural land, no longer provides land for anyone; on the contrary, he has been cast as a client seeking bureaucratic patrons who might grant some land to him. A specially devised hierarchy of agrarian courts is, like the hierarchy of syndical organizations, affiliated with but not integral to the postrevolutionary Ministry of Campesino Affairs, and ex-hacendados have not been happy having to deal with bureaucrats whose ostensible concern is campesino welfare.

Justice

The quest for justice (by which I mean simply conflict resolution) in the event of civil or criminal problems at the level of the local community reflects the recently expanded horizons of campesinos, and one of the many functions of the new syndical organization.

Before the revolution, nearly all such conflicts were settled on the hacienda: most were resolved among the *colonos* themselves, although some thorny ones were taken to the mayordomo for him to settle (figure 4). Those that the mayordomo found problematic, he referred to the hacendado, who was unchallenged as judge with respect to the af-

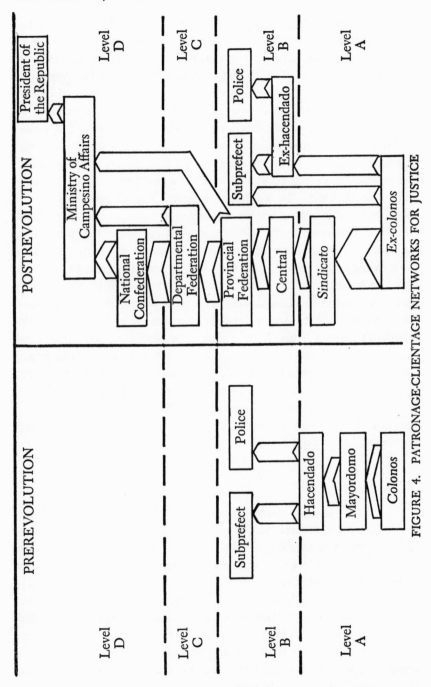

FIGURE 4. PATRONAGE-CLIENTAGE NETWORKS FOR JUSTICE

fairs of everyone within the hacienda community. On those rare occasions when *colonos* got into trouble with anyone beyond the hacienda, they asked (usually through the mayordomo) for the hacendado to intervene on their behalf with the concerned officials at the provincial level, the police (for criminal cases) or the subprefect (for civil cases).

Since the revolution, *ex-colonos* generally discuss their differences in the *sindicato*, which serves as a kind of community forum. The ex-hacendado has no further authority on the hacienda, but some *ex-colonos* still ask him, just as before, to intervene on their behalf with the police and subprefect in the provincial capital; a few now have confidence enough to deal with the subprefect directly. Not all problems are resolved in the *sindicato;* a few are then referred to the central (a regional alliance of *sindicatos* found within some, but not all, of the provinces), but more are elevated to the provincial federation of campesino *sindicatos.* Most of the conflicts that are not settled there are, in turn, referred to the departmental federation of *sindicatos;* those that remain unresolved go to the national confederation of *sindicatos,* which passes a few important ones to the minister of campesino affairs, a member of the president's cabinet whose help is sought by officials of most provincial and departmental federations. In those rare instances when both principals are wealthy or politically ambitious, a final judgment may be sought from the president himself (for such a case, see Heath 1969a).

In theory, campesinos still have access to the formal system of courts, as they did before the revolution; in practice they very rarely have used the courts, recently or in previous years.

Public Works

Campesinos laid no claim to roads, water systems, or other public works before the revolution. Hacendados, however, often sought such concrete forms of patronage from the subprefect, chief official within the province (figure 5). If unsuccessful there, they would sometimes make the same request to the prefect (chief official in each department), to the ministry of public works, or to the president of the Republic. These alternatives were often tried successively, although an influential hacendado would occasionally leapfrog lower officials and initially approach those at higher levels. Even when the minister of public works approved a request, extreme centralization of fiscal authority demanded that presidential approval be sought.

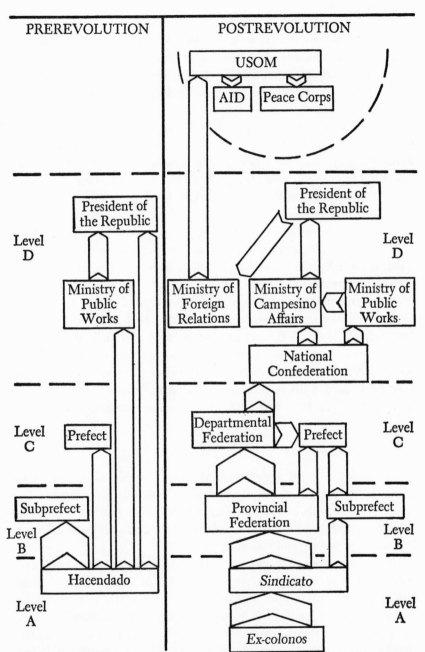

FIGURE 5.   PATRONAGE-CLIENTAGE NETWORKS FOR PUBLIC WORKS
(ROADS, WATER, ETC.)

In the postrevolutionary years, by contrast, the ex-hacendado plays no role whatsoever, and requests for such services are usually initiated by those who never did so before, the *ex-colonos*. Requests are formalized in the local *sindicato*, which serves as corporate petitioner on behalf of its members with the provincial federation of campesino *sindicatos* and sometimes with the subprefect (who has almost no funds, so usually relays requests to the prefect). Pressures are exerted on the subprefect by each individual *sindicato*, and by the provincial federation; in similar manner, the several provincial federations join the departmental federation in trying to enlist the prefect's aid. Very few projects are supported at the departmental level or below; most are referred upward to the national confederation of *sindicatos*, which may appeal to the minister of campesino affairs, or to the minister of public works (who nowadays routinely relays any such request to Campesino Affairs). If a project is deemed worthwhile but too ambitious to be handled by that ministry, the president may be advised and he, through his minister of foreign relations, can usually enlist the aid of the United States Operations Mission. By having recourse to an institution that is patently outside "the national system", the actual work is often eventually done in the local community by Peace Corps or the Agency for International Development, entities that were unheard of before the revolution but that have introduced skills, funds, and equipment that are not available at any level within the entire range of Bolivian patronage networks.

Selling Produce

In a market-oriented agricultural economy, the sale of produce is of crucial importance. Notably, the relevant social network comprises the same few individuals before and after the revolution, and yet the altered statuses and roles of those individuals make for a very different network in terms of patronage and clientage (figure 6).

The hacendado used to enjoy a virtual monopoly on agricultural surplus; a little was "sold" to *colonos* in a system of contrived and hereditary debt-bondage. He sold most of the produce directly to a wholesaler in the national capital who in turn supplied both regional markets within the country and international markets. The rest went to a merchant in the provincial capital, who sold some to local townspeople but who shipped the bulk of his purchases (amassed from various hacen-

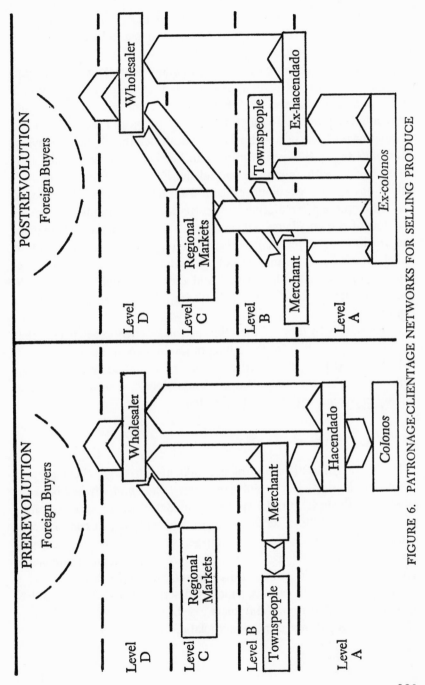

FIGURE 6. PATRONAGE-CLIENTAGE NETWORKS FOR SELLING PRODUCE

131

dados within the province) to the same national and international wholesalers; he was able to charge more than hacendados by waiting until the harvest-glut had subsided.

Nowadays, it is the *ex-colonos* who generally control agricultural production. In a dramatic reversal of roles, they sell some of their surplus to the ex-hacendado, who has left the hacienda and now serves as middleman in the provincial capital, still selling produce to the national and international wholesalers with whom he dealt before. (Sometimes, when *ex-colonos* resent the man who used to be their own hacendado, they prefer to deal with another ex-hacendado. For this reason, the individuals in any specific *ex-colono*–ex-hacendado relationship as diagrammed may differ in the prerevolution and postrevolution situations.)

A few of the *ex-colonos* sell some goods in local markets throughout the province, or in regional markets, but most of the produce goes to merchants (who sometimes go out on buying trips from the provincial capital to individual ex-haciendas) and then to regional markets or to the wholesalers in La Paz, the nation's *de facto* capital and center for export.

In contrast with most of the other patronage-clientage networks that we have analyzed, that for the selling of produce comprises no new individuals or institutions since the revolution. It is also one of the few realms of activity in which the *sindicato* does not serve as a broker linking *ex-colonos* with higher level systems.

CONCLUSIONS

In the foregoing discussion of networks of patronage, clientage, and power relationships in the Bolivian yungas, the emphasis has been on two major themes: (1) the specificity of networks for various realms of concern (or fields of action, or aspects of culture), in contrast with the generalized brokerage (or "patronage," or "hinge," or "gatekeeper") status so often characterized in the literature on this topic; (2) changes (sometimes dramatic and extensive) in such networks through time.

The main purpose of this paper is descriptive; nevertheless a few striking conclusions from the Aymara case bear on the conceptualization and analysis of patronage and power relations in broader terms.

The Local Situation

Despite sweeping changes in the forms of social structure instituted by the revolution, there are many instances in which the traditional paternalistic relationship persists virtually unchanged, in functional terms.

A new patron-client type of functional relationship has been established with a new form, the *sindicato* (or, sometimes, its secretary general), assuming the dominant paternalistic status formerly held by the hacendado, and with the *ex-colono* in a relatively dependent and servile status.

At the same time it is noteworthy that, for certain limited purposes, *ex-colonos* are happy to retain the old patron-client relationship that linked them as dependents to specific ex-hacendados, despite resentment of their years of "slavery" and their rallying around the slogan of "class warfare."

Some General Propositions

It is obvious from these case studies that different individuals are often patrons for different purposes. On the one hand, there is real value in looking at crucial individuals (or, more accurately, crucial statuses), when one is attempting to characterize in general terms the channels of communication, distribution, and other linkages between a given local community and the broader society. On the other hand, it is also necessary to look at various individuals (and various statuses) in attempting to characterize in any detail the quality of communication, distribution, and other linkages between individuals in a given local community and individuals and institutions in the broader society. In short, patronage/brokerage can be role-specific—and perhaps most often is so.

It also is clear that patronage-clientage networks for different purposes change in different ways and at different rates. The phenomenon of change in patronage-clientage networks is neither unique nor unexpected. The value of having analyzed this particular situation in some detail lies in the clear demonstration that changes in patronage/brokerage for one realm of concern are not necessarily similar to those in patronage/brokerage for another realm. (For example, the immensely increased complexity of the patronage-clientage network concerning land is not at all reflected in the slightly altered network concerning curing.) In short, power and change can also be role-specific—and perhaps most often are so.

Lastly, many relationships that appear, in structural terms, to be impersonal and universalistic are, in functional terms, personalistic relationships of patronage and clientage.

N O T E S

1. For that matter, none of Bolivia's Indians fought to topple the old oligarchy, although many (including the Aymara of the yungas) later formed peasant militias to defend the MNR from counterrevolutionaries (see Heath 1966, 1969b).

2. The "conquests of the revolution [of 1952]" have survived the overthrow of the MNR by a military junta in 1964 and six other subsequent changes of government. The list of "conquests of the revolution" is a litany in which each catchphrase is pregnant with meaning. "Agrarian reform" refers primarily to the fractionation of large haciendas and abolition of the quasi-feudal *colonato* system, whereby campesinos worked without pay in exchange for usufruct privileges to small plots that have since been allotted to them. "Universal suffrage" refers to dropping the combined literacy and property-holding requirements, so that the electorate was promptly increased by more than 1,200 percent, and the formerly disenfranchised Indian majority won a voice in politics. "Nationalization of the mines" refers to the holdings of Hochschild, Aramayo, and Patiño enterprises, each of which used to have an annual budget larger than that of the Republic of Bolivia; operation of the mines by a government entity has been economically disastrous but immensely popular. "Educational reform" refers to the fostering of formal schooling for campesinos; as limited as it is now, it is symbolically important to people who were previously denied access to schools.

3. Anthropologists have often remarked that they find it difficult to reconcile the somewhat wistful quality of my favorite Aymara quotation—"Now we are becoming human beings"—with the harsh and despicable image that has been generally drawn of the Aymara. It is not at all unusual in Latin America to find that the dominant white-mestizo population views the Indians as subhuman beings, with *indio* or *indiobruto* as an epithet for those who are not *civilizados*. It *is* unusual, however, to find that anthropologists and travelers from different cultural backgrounds concur in characterizing a people in wholly negative terms, as was long the case with the Aymara. For nearly a century, consistently disparaging adjectives were applied by virtually all those who tried to know them, adding up to a dismal thesaurus on Aymara character: "anxious," "apprehensive," "doubtful," "drunken," "dull," "fearful," "filthy," "gloomy," "hostile," "ignorant," "insecure," "irresponsible," "jealous," "malevolent," "malicious," "melancholic," "morose," "negative," "pessimistic," "pugnacious," "quarrelsome," "rancorous," "reticent," "sad," "silent," "sinister," "slovenly," "stolid," "sullen," "suspicious," "tense," "thieving," "treacherous," "truculent," "uncommunicative," "unimaginative," "unsmiling," "untrustworthy," "violent," and "vindictive" (Forbes 1870;

Squier 1877; Bandelier 1910; Romero 1928; La Barre 1948, 1950; Tschopik 1951). The pattern was so consistent, despite the diversity of the observers, that La Barre and Tschopik took considerable pains to "account for" such a negative "basic personality structure." Anthropologists who have worked with the Aymara during the past two decades, however, have generally found them to be at least somewhat sympathetic (Buechler 1966; Buechler and Buechler 1970; Carter 1964; Hickman 1963; Heath 1966; Plummer 1966). Different field methods and approaches to the Aymara may in large part account for these differences in evaluation; it is also conceivable that the heady "liberation" experienced by the Aymara as a result of the 1952 revolution is reflected in their changed actions and attitudes.

4. This chapter is based on fieldwork conducted in Bolivia in 1964–65 under United States government contract PC(W)-397, administered by Research Institute for the Study of Man.

5. *Campesino* is used in Bolivian Spanish in a dual sense—not only meaning "peasant" (as it does in Spanish elsewhere, and in English in recent years) but also as a postrevolutionary euphemism for *indio* (Indian), which carried an immense burden of negative connotations. The ironic result of an MNR attempt to effect cultural change by semantic fiat is that they can now boast, "there are no more Indians in Bolivia," while more than half of the adult population are campesinos who still speak only indigenous languages.

6. The Negroes are descended from African slaves brought to the area in colonial times. Living apart in a half-dozen hamlets, their dress and workaday activities are like those of the Aymara, but they speak Spanish and rarely intermarry with either Indians or whites. Those in Nor Yungas have only been briefly visited (see Newman 1966; Preston ms.); Barbara and William Léons studied a Negro community in nearby Sud Yungas in 1969.

7. The *provincia* (roughly comparable to a county in the U.S.A.) of Nor Yungas is an area of approximately 2,000 square miles, within the *departamento* (similar to our state) of La Paz. While studying social and political organization in the provincial capital (Coroico, a declining colonial town of about 2,200 population), epidemiological studies in the outlying areas provided an entrée that I systematically used from August 1964 through July 1965 in order to get ample ethnographic data on the Aymara campesinos throughout the province. Although I never achieved easy fluency in Aymara, I enjoyed the advantage of working through a skillful interpreter who had for years lived with the campesinos and was well known and liked by them.

8. Despite the social and historical importance of the distinction between "whites" and "mestizos," it seems appropriate to phrase this discussion in terms of the single distinction that is overwhelmingly important from the point of view of the local population: that between those called "campesinos" and all others.

9. The majority were smaller than 200 acres, although a few exceeded 1,000 acres.

10. Two chicken farms have recently been established near Coroico, both owned and operated by mestizos from other parts of the country.

11. Like so many regional historians, Morales (1929) on the yungas is intensively chauvinistic in tone, but he provides a fairly accurate body of data.

12. The one-lane road is often cut by landslides, and trucks that carry both freight and passengers still frequently plunge into the canyons, but it is an im-

provement over the mule trails that used to require a two-day trek from the sub-tropical yungas through a cold pass at more than 13,000 feet.

13. Although both Bolivia and Paraguay suffered enormous losses in wealth and manpower, Bolivia was especially traumatized by the realization that her political and military leaders were equally inept and by the implication that Indians, having been drafted to defend the nation, might claim some rights as citizens.

14. The Catholic church is usually linked with the landed gentry and the military as constituting the dominant institutional triumvirate in countries where *colonato* prevails. Although the church was indeed wealthy and powerful during the colonial period, it did not play a particularly important role in Bolivia after independence.

15. It is impossible to document the compelling hunch that these decrees may have been issued as little more than window dressing to impress visiting dignitaries at a time when Bolivia was being called a Fascist country. The decrees (*Decretos leyes* 00318–00321 of May 15, 1945) abolished *pongueaje* (the compulsary un-remunerated labor that *colonos* had traditionally owed to their *hacendados*), called for the establishment of schools on haciendas, and spelled out mutual obligations of landlords and tenant-farmers. It is noteworthy that the Aymara of the yungas seem to be unaware of this event or these laws. There is no evidence that hacendados anywhere obeyed the letter of the laws, but a nod in the direction of their spirit may have been the reduction of unremunerated labor requirements (from four days weekly to three), a change that is generally remembered but un-explained by older campesinos in the area.

16. For that matter, there have been few studies since the revolution either. La Barre (1948, 1950) offered little more than the affirmation that the Aymara of the yungas were markedly different (in unspecified ways) from their relatives on the plateau around Lake Titicaca where he did more extensive and intensive research; Carter did exceptionally detailed work at Irpa Chico (1963) and comparative work among Aymara on the altiplano, but explicitly denies familiarity with the situation in the yungas (1964:6). In the mid-1950s Isabel Kelly worked in the same area where I did a decade later, but she has not yet written anything on her findings. Buechler conducted a survey of land tenure patterns in the yungas (1969), and has also dealt with the continuing migration of Aymara to that area from the altiplano (1966). The Léonses studied sindical organization (M. Léons 1966, 1970: W. Léons 1970), and land reform (M. Léons 1967; M. & W. Léons 1971) in a campesino community that is physically nearby but culturally different (the extent and depth of variation among Aymara communities within a small region deserve detailed study). McEwen (1969) compiled a fairly accurate account of life in the provincial capital using field notes collected by me and several assis-tants. I have analyzed selected aspects of campesino life elsewhere: politics (Heath 1966), sindicalism (1969b), and interethnic relations (1971). A cultural geographer has offered brief but incisive commentaries on changing ecology (Preston 1969, 1970) and a sociologist has outlined the history of sindicates (Muratorio 1969).

17. I use the term *broker* in the same sense as Wolf (1956:1076), to designate one who mediates between different levels of integration of the same society, and *patron* in the same sense as Foster (1963:1282), to designate one who combines status, power, influence, and authority to help someone else defend himself.

18. The most powerful manifestation of hacendado unity was the Sociedad de Propietarios de Yungas, which maintained the road, lobbied in Congress, and in many other ways defended their interests.

19. See note 8.

20. The few *arrenderos* on prereform haciendas were *colonos*-of-*colonos*; that is, they served a few *colonos* in much the same way that the *colonos* themselves served the hacendado. In return, they got usufruct of a portion of the land that the hacendado had relegated to the *colonos*. In such instances, the *colono* was almost wholly powerful as patron over his *arrendero* client(s), although he in turn was almost wholly dominated by the hacendado. Vestiges of this pattern persist in the institution of *utawawa*, landless campesinos treated as virtual slaves or stepchildren within the households of a few *ex-colonos*.

21. The emergence and multiple functions of campesino *sindicatos* in this region have been described by Heath, the Léonses, and Muratorio (see note 16). It is clear that they did not follow the pattern of Ucureña, which is historically important but atypical (cf. Patch 1960; Dandler 1969).

22. A few influential MNR members were able to stay in responsible positions in the administration even in 1965, after René Barrientos's "Revolution of Restoration" had driven Paz into exile in Peru. It is too early to judge the effect of the revolution of August 1971, which returned the MNR to power (in coalition with FSB).

23. The "revolution" referred to is the MNR victory in April 1952, the major impact of which was felt in the yungas considerably later. Although news of the takeover arrived within a day, changes in specific realms of behavior took place only gradually, with *sindicatos* and expropriation of haciendas not being begun until 1954.

24. Figures 2–6 obviously do not portray specific behavioral data. Each is a crude graphic representation embodying no less than 85 percent of the specific observed behavior sequences in relation to that particular good or service.

In the diagrams, the party at the base of each arrow—the client—seeks patronage from the party at its tip—the patron—with the width of the arrow between them roughly indicating the volume of such requests. (Note that attempts to establish patron-client relations do not always follow "through channels" of bureaucratic organization (e.g., fig. 3), and that upper level clients occasionally seek patronage at lower levels (e.g., fig. 6).

Although I do not discuss in detail the kinds of exchanges and expectations that obtain between specific pairs of patrons and clients as diagrammed, it should be clear that the flow charts do imply such reciprocity, with each patron expecting some *quid pro quo* in the event that he helps a client.

In simplest terms, I have tried to represent graphically some of the complexity of the functioning social organization, which is *not* congruent with the formal social structure. And it is obviously in the dynamic aspect of the linkages in such a network that the idiom (comprising values, orientations, covert patterns) shapes specific cases. That order of analysis, however, is beyond the scope of this descriptive paper.

6
Patronage and Cooperation: An Analysis from São Paulo State

ROBERT W. SHIRLEY

Department of Anthropology
The University of Toronto

The patterns of patronage in Southern Brazil, most notably São Paulo State and south, may be seen in part as an effort by the holders of important positions to maintain these positions in the face of an increasingly complex social and economic environment. The "styles" of politics proposed by Alberto Guerreiro Ramos (1961)—clan, oligarchical, populist, pressure group, ideological—may be examined as a kind of sequential development reflecting these continued efforts.

Patronage has always played a vital role in Brazilian social structure. The Portuguese term *fazendeiro* is used to describe one of the key positions in the Brazilian patronage networks: the commercial planter, the central figure of rural Brazilian social life. It is he who has the commercial ties through which the products of his dependents and sharecroppers are marketed, and this position gives him local control over almost all aspects of the monetary economy and the goods involved. Through his commercial ties with the towns and cities of the country he has effective monopoly control over the products of industry on his lands and to an extent within his sphere of influence. He thus in addition is in a position to buy political power either by hiring his own "enforcers" or by influencing local political leaders. At times in the past, and in many regions still, in Brazil, where the land and its products were the economic base, the great fazendeiros, and their families, the clans, dominated the scene.

The fazendeiro's resources were his commercial links, which gave him access to, among other things, weapons, clothing, and medicine for himself and his dependents. In the past and in many areas today these individuals had virtual independent sovereignty over their lands because of their isolation and the weakness of Brazilian administrative systems.[1]

A more complex situation develops when governmental agencies, local, state, or federal, become a significant factor in a region—when police or legal institutions move in, for example, or the government attempts to build roads and schools to "develop" an area (Shirley 1970). Under such conditions, for the fazendeiro to maintain his dominant position in the society he must somehow gain control over the resources represented by these agencies. In some cases, especially where important commercial interests are involved, the economic power of the great clans may be such that they can dominate local (and sometimes even state) administration effortlessly. In other regions, especially in the interior of Brazil, the mechanisms of what has been called the "cartorial" state have developed (Jaguaribe 1968:144 f.), wherein the planters exchange the votes of their dependents in return for local autonomy and control of the governmental resources and apparatus (see chapter 4). This is the general pattern of Guerriero Ramos's "oligarchical style" of politics, "most appropriate for the periods between 1822 and 1930 and centering on regional political 'bosses'" (quoted in Graham 1968:95).

The interior of Brazil was made up of hundreds of these little autocracies, protected by extensive patronage networks that were capable of controlling state governments and until 1930 even the national government. The fazendeiro and his allies combined many potential roles into an extensive redistributive pattern with local monopolistic control. These huge patronage hierarchies largely dominated and even replaced other systems of administration and distribution.

Brazil, however, has not stood still. Industrialization has taken place at a substantial rate in the major cities, especially in the south. This, together with the extensive demographic changes brought about by the growth of the industrial cities, has brought about many new demands and pressures on Brazilian social institutions as well as many new resources and opportunities. The Brazilian elite and the patronage patterns have again shifted to meet the new complexities.

The cooperative movement in São Paulo illustrates many of these changes. As an idiom and an ideology the cooperative movement began largely as an effort on the part of the poorer members of society to help one another as a class. It was linked with early socialist movements in England and other parts of Europe, an effort to reform the entire industrial system for the elimination of private profit in favor of the consumers (Webb and Webb 1921). In Europe, moreover, these small early self-help movements found support and ideological integration from members of the elite itself, including, in some of the Scandinavian countries, support from the landed aristocracy.

Ideologically, patronage and cooperation seem at first glance antithetical to one another. Patronage implies sharp class differences and great inequalities in power relationships, so that advancement and protection of the poorer clients occur only through the support and aid of the powerful patrons. "There can, by definition, never be a client/client relationship," says Kenney (1960:23) about patronage in Spain. It would seem, therefore, that in rural Brazil, where patronage is extremely important and the vertical structuring of society is very strong, the cooperative movement would stand very little chance.

But the real situation reveals many complexities. The Brazilian cooperative movement, if one includes all those institutions called *cooperativas* under Brazilian law, is a very extensive affair. It includes huge production organizations worth millions of dollars and tiny consumers' cooperatives that are little more than general stores. It has its own intellectuals, its own political leaders, its own journals, and its own elite. *Cooperativas* produce more than half the milk supplies of the major Brazilian cities, nearly a quarter of the coffee of São Paulo State, and a fair proportion of the food consumed by the urban populations, including nearly all fresh produce.[2] Clearly there are important forces at work in the situation, and I contend that this involves shifts in the resources and idiom of the patronage patterns and, equally, changes in the technological base of the region.

Brazil has had, in fact, a long history of populist self-help movements, most of which developed with the sufferance and sometimes even the encouragement of the elite. Religious brotherhoods existed in the eighteenth century, formed by former slaves to purchase the freedom of others (Alba 1968:225). Mutual aid groups and societies, the *mutirão*, are a basic institution in the peasant culture of southern Brazil (Caldeira 1956). Even this, however, frequently involves the elite, who may themselves "give" the *mutirão* by donating the food and especially the drink by which the day's work traditionally should end in considerable festivities. One large landowner in São Paulo State when asked about *mutirões* on his land replied that during the past year he had given fourteen and thought that his people had given another dozen or so. Housebuilding was and is traditionally a time of intense mutual aid.

The cooperative movement in the formal sense, however, did not reach Brazil until 1908 and 1909 in the states of Rio de Janeiro and Rio Grande do Sul (Alba 1968:195–96). The ideological norm of the movement is the same in Brazil as it is worldwide. It is borrowed from England and is largely derived from the constitution of the Rochdale Equitable Pioneers Society Limited, which established certain basic principles that are supposed to distinguish a cooperative from a private corporation: (1) open membership; (2) democratic control—one member, one vote; (3) profits distributed on a basis of the number of transactions of the members; (4) limited returns on capital (Pinho 1962:186; U.S. Department of Agriculture 1958).

The populist, egalitarian, and horizontal ideology of the cooperative movement, however, contrasted sharply with the Brazilian political structure, which was firmly based upon vertical patterns of patronage wherein the elite's privileges and power were firmly protected by the mechanisms of the cartorial state. With some exceptions (in the cities and in the south of Brazil), the movement made little headway during the first three decades of this century. It was weakened not only by the opposition of the fazendeiros but also by the widespread mistrust that the poorer Brazilians hold toward any kind of official organization. The intellectuals in the movement repeat this theme again and again; Brazilians don't cooperate easily, since they simply don't trust one another. This mistrust is reflected in the organization of current Brazilian cooperatives, which demands that all three of the top officials of the cooperative be present before major business can be transacted, a factor that severely hinders the efficiency of their operation.

An Analysis from São Paulo State

The cooperatives, especially consumers' cooperatives, did make some headway in the larger Brazilian cities. Here they were able to find some articulate and influential defenders among the *bacharéis*, the professional classes, so that they were protected by urban law. From the *bacharéis* of the cities come the intellectuals and ideologues of the movement. Here are the real idealists and theorists of cooperation, honest and outspoken, though often distant from the harsh realities of Brazilian rural politics. Their support, however, has meant that a number of quite genuine cooperatives have been established in the cities, frequently consumers' cooperatives selling food and other goods at reduced prices to its members.

Even these cooperatives, however, do not to any great extent help the really poor. For the most part they tend to attract the people who have some, though not extensive, resources and usually a fair degree of formal education: the middle to lower middle classes, schoolteachers, civil servants, some factory workers, and the like. One may well argue that the average poor Brazilians' mistrust of formal organizations in a country such as Brazil is well based, but it has also meant that even the most idealistically run cooperatives, and there are many, do not as a general rule reach the very people that the cooperative ideal was designed to help (Soares 1966). Even the most important, honest and well-established urban cooperatives, such as the Consumers' Cooperative of Lapa in the City of São Paulo, were founded by Europeans working in Brazil, and the Brazilians themselves were willing to enter only after the institution had proven itself.

Another artifact of the prevailing mistrust is the custom of the "Old Professor," a man of impeccable reputation who is named to the presidency of the cooperative in order to maintain the confidence of the members. This too is related to the Brazilian political culture. Brazilians tend to trust someone important whose reputation they know and respect rather than strangers at roughly the same status level as themselves. The individuals concerned, however, are less patrons or bosses of these cooperatives than sponsors who, for a number of diverse economic and ideological reasons, were willing to help the cooperative movement. They also offered an influential voice in the political protection of the movement in the cities. There are numerous examples. A few of the most notable are Theodoro Henrique Maurer, Jr. (1966), professor *catedrático* of classical languages at the University of São Paulo and

143

founder of the consumers' cooperative in the same city; Dr. Tomás Alberto Whately, founder of the immense coffee cooperative of Mogiana; and Dr. João Rodrigues de Alckmin, known to all as *"O Professor"* or *"seu João,"* president of the Central Dairy Cooperative of São Paulo (Balde Branco 1966:73).

It could well be argued that the landed patriarchate and political bosses of Brazil made no effort to disband the urban cooperatives, even though they could probably have done so, because their basic interests were not at stake. The development of cooperative stores in the cities bore little relation to problems of land and labor in the interior. On the other hand, cooperation was decidedly antagnostic to the fazendeiro's interests in the rural regions and here the movement was firmly excluded for decades. The great rural political oligarchical networks managed this.

In 1932, the greatest *patrón* of all appeared on the scene. In that year Getúlio Vargas broke the national power of the rural aristocracy and set about developing Brazil as a modern centralized and industrial state. He apparently seized upon the concept of cooperatives as both a possible political counterbalance to the elite in the rural zones and a potential way to develop Brazilian agriculture economically without returning power to that elite. The Basic Law of Cooperation was thus set out as a law by decree (*decreto-lei* No. 22, 239) on December 19, 1932 (Padilha 1966:10). The law not only defined the cooperatives but also established several federal and state agencies to regulate them and encourage their development. In addition, they were exempted from taxes. For the first time the Brazilian federal government was willing to support the cooperative movement with real political and economic resources. The cooperatives were thus forged in one blow into Vargas's weapon for bringing various aspects of the Brazilian economy, especially the rural economy, under the control of his corporate state. There is general agreement among the leaders of the movement that the real development of the cooperative movement dates from this time.

The complexity of the problem and the range of Vargas's interests are illustrated by the fact that this law (quoted in full in Moura 1965:23–45) sets out sixteen kinds of cooperatives:

agricultural production
industrial production
work (trade union cooperatives)

product processing
purchases in common
sales in common
consumers'
supply
credit
insurance
public housing
publishing and libraries
schools (educational cooperatives)
mixed
central cooperatives
federations of cooperatives

The Brazilian elite, however, is extremely adept at turning a potential threat into a source of support. Through regional political bosses and the votes of their clients they managed to turn election procedures into a means of maintaining control, and to a large degree the cooperative movement met the same fate in most regions.

In the interior of Brazil the system of clientele politics generally means that most of the administrative resources of a region are devoted to maintaining the system rather than doing actual work. This is why Brazilian bureaucracies and administrative structures are frequently so inefficient; appointments are made for political reasons rather than for ability (Leal 1948:27). It is quite possible, for instance, to find teachers in the interior of Brazil who cannot read, and even in São Paulo State teachers are frequently appointed because they are the wives of fazen-deiros, even if they are not legally qualified to teach because of their poor education. In these cases, the patron, the local political boss, will simply use the resources given to him by the state for education to buy the political support of members of the local landed elite and their dependents.

A similar pattern largely occurred with the cooperatives. Because the federal and state governments were willing to provide some real resources in the way of tax exemptions and at times actual subsidies to encourage the development of rural cooperatives, many of the local oligarchs simply adopted the idiom, that is, set up corporations with the name *cooperativa*, with a local fazendeiro as president and his political dependents as members. He could maintain his position as commercial seller and broker and at the same time obtain tax advantages from the government. Such cooperatives are said to have *donos* (owners) and ignore the principle of democratic control, although as corporations they may be fairly well run. The Brazilian cooperative movement, however, abounds with tales of how presidents of cooperatives misappropriated organization funds, and this is another reason for the general mistrust. This type of structure, according to experts, is especially characteristic of "cooperatives" in Brazil's northeast, although it can be found in the south as well. In recent years many of these "owned" cooperatives have gone out of business, as the government has reduced or eliminated the tax advantages offered to them (especially with regard to the ICM, the circulation of products tax) and the local *dono* no longer finds it to his advantage to maintain the idiom. One government official stated that he did not know how many cooperatives there were in Brazil because many of them had simply closed without official announcement.

Another interesting pattern in southern Brazil is the use of cooperatives by regional political bosses for political rather than economic reasons. In one case in a municipality in São Paulo the local political chief, who at the time was also mayor, set up an agricultural cooperative with himself as president and only his political supporters invited to join. Since under Brazilian law there can be only one agricultural cooperative in each municipality, all of the advantages the cooperative could offer, tax benefits and reduced prices for many kinds of products to consumers, became his to bestow. The cooperative became a series of resources distributed selectively to his political supporters; an important prop in his political apparatus. As a cooperative it apparently was very straightforwardly run, to the benefit of those who belonged, though those excluded complained rather bitterly about how deeply politicized it was.

Given the nature of the clientele networks in Brazil and the power of the elite in many of the rural zones, one might expect that cooperatives as cooperation would be found in very few rural regions, and that such cooperatives as do exist would be either "owned" or co-opted into the political networks, as noted above. There are exceptions, however, and these are important enough to warrant examination in considerable detail, because they reveal a great deal about the changing nature of patronage in São Paulo due to technical changes in the economy.

It should be noted at the outset that agricultural marketing cooperatives are very different from consumers' cooperatives. The cooperative ideal, the Rochdale ideal, comes from European reformist philosophies of a Fabian bent, which hoped eventually to eliminate private profits completely. Marketing cooperatives, on the other hand, are basically capitalistic. In Europe as well as in the United States they are organizations set up by private landowners to increase their profits.

> [Commercial] farmers are essentially capitalistic. Their pride of ownership is strong. . . . Their chief complaint against the established order is that it has not enabled them to be better capitalists —to own more. Their reason for cooperative endeavors, whether buying or selling, is not to eliminate private profit but to get more profit for themselves. They attempt to do this on the one hand by buying supplies cheaper; on the other by getting a greater net return from what they produce. . . . This distinction in ideology is so marked that many European cooperative spokesmen refuse to classify farm cooperation as real cooperation at all. They say it is merely a modified form of capitalism, and as such they do not like it (Gregory 1937:139).

The economic element, then, provides a clue for an explanation of the existence of large marketing cooperatives in Brazil. Simply put, many landowning families benefited from their development. The fazendeiro of Brazil as a commercial producer has always had a marketing problem, in that his production of subsistence crops—corn, beans, hogs, and so on—had relatively little monetary value in the international economy. What income he did have usually came from selling foodstuffs and livestock to local (often mining) towns and administrative centers. The coffee boom in the middle of the last century, which has lasted until the present time, did give the São Paulo planters an extremely valuable crop for international export. The coffee planters became the most important Brazilian elite, a group that dominated the politics of the country until 1932 and still is exceedingly important.

The Brazilian fazendeiro, moreover, has land and manpower at his disposal as resources, but usually only a moderate amount of money. One should not be misled by the style of life of the Brazilian planter; labor for him is very cheap and he can live spectacularly on a cash income that is frequently surprisingly small. Brazilian agriculture is notoriously undercapitalized. The cooperatives develop, therefore, in situations where marketing costs are far greater than the individual fazendeiros can afford. Rather than lose control completely over their links with the industrial economy, and be faced themselves with possible monopoly (monopsony) control of their own markets by urban or international entrepreneurs, the fazendeiros have resorted to cooperative organization among themselves. Local patrons who have considerable political and economic control over their own small regions have adopted cooperation as a defense against being forced, because of the increased costs of selling certain products, into a client position for their own marketing with still bigger metropolitan interests. The pattern becomes clear if we examine briefly the histories of two of the largest cooperatives in São Paulo, which are supported by many old traditional Brazilian elite families—the cooperatives of coffee and milk.

The Cooperativa Central dos Cafeicultores da Mogiana is a coffee-producing cooperative whose various subsidiary branches are located, for the most part, in the region north and slightly east of the city of São Paulo. This area is served by the Mogiana railroad, from which the cooperative's name is derived. Coffee has traditionally been the main cash crop of Brazil, and many of the country's greatest fortunes, especially in São Paulo, have come from this crop. Hence it may seem that a cooperative of coffee growers is a contradiction in terms; but, examined carefully in the national context, it is not.

The Mogiana region was one of the first areas where extensive coffee plantations developed at the end of the last century. Here in 1899, Dr. Francisco Schmidt, the "King of Coffee" reigned over twelve plantations containing 3.5 million coffee trees. Other owners had similar vast holdings. Under Brazilian law, on the death of any landowner, his land must be divided equally among his children. Thus in the following two generations, the great fazendas of the original planters were divided and redivided among numerous children and grandchildren. The coffee trees aged, the soils became exhausted, and the coffee frontier moved farther and farther to the west. Thus the proud coffee-growing families of the Mogiana region found their plantations growing smaller and smaller and their production and profits declining disastrously in competition with the fresher regions to the west.

To rebuild the declining fortunes of the region, the cooperative was founded by the celebrated Tomás Alberto Whately, grandson of Francisco Schmidt (see Martins 1962). From the beginning, there was never any pretense that this was a cooperative of poor peasant farmers. It was and is a pooling of the considerable remaining resources of a once very wealthy area in order to develop new modes of coffee production and, importantly, to try to break into the business of coffee export, a business largely dominated by U.S. and European firms. Such an effort required far more money than any family in this region could raise. The cooperative developed as being, probably, the only way to organize the many moderate-sized producers in the region. Some informants scornfully called it the Cooperativa dos Coronéis (Colonels' Cooperative), but it is a cooperative in many ways even though its leaders and many of its members come from the top rather than the bottom strata of Brazilian society. At the present the cooperative, under pressure from the Brazilian government, is attempting to diversify into the production of other crops to bring about a general modernization of agriculture in the Mogiana region.

The Rochdale idealists in the cooperative movement point to the Cooperativa Central dos Lacticínios do Estado de São Paulo (Central Dairy Cooperative of the State of São Paulo) as the best example of a really large cooperative that keeps the principles of cooperation in active practice. This is true to a great extent; certainly the cooperative and its subsidiary divisions pay more than lip service to the assistance of their least members. Many of the local branches maintain medical, dental, veterinary, and other services free for all members, and the cooperative makes a serious effort to educate its more rustic associates toward modern ranching methods. (It should be said, however, that most big Paulista cooperatives in fact do this.) This cooperative also approaches the egalitarian principle of cooperation better than most big cooperatives, and is extremely open in its operation. It is one of the few cooperatives that freely allowed me to examine its books.

The probable reason for this rather unusual (for Brazil) atmosphere lies in the nature of the cooperative's product, milk, and the corresponding market conditions. Milk is a product with a strong, inelastic, but regular daily demand. Consumption fluctuates little during the year; in fact, in São Paulo the potential demand is probably greater than the supply, as milk consumption increases with the growing prosperity of the population.

Moreover, milk must be marketed by big organizations because it is highly perishable, heavy, and easy to contaminate (Shepherd 1955:359). Simply to sell the product at all in the cities requires a considerable capital outlay. On the other hand, in the milkshed regions of São Paulo and Minas Gerais commercial agriculture either had never extensively developed or had developed once and then declined. The dominant families are frequently land rich but cash poor. In the hilly regions of many of these parts of Brazil, modern agriculture is not feasible, and many landowners, competing on the labor market with the new urban industries, would naturally turn to milk production and cattle ranching, in which labor demands are slight. Since these are relatively poor regions, however, most of the fazendeiros of the milkshed regions would not have enough capital to develop an urban marketing system for fresh whole milk. Cheese production is an alternative with much easier marketing, but the profits are much lower than for fresh milk (Shepherd 1955:362). Although a few large private fazendas in the Paraíba Valley and elsewhere have set up their own transportation and bottling systems,[3] a cooperative was the obvious answer for the many moderate-sized independent ranchers in the region—especially because they hesitated to put themselves at the mercy of a big, urban-based, private marketing firm such as Vigour, which would then have a near monopoly (monopsony) position. The cooperative has protected many smaller landowners from takeover and potential reconsolidation of the latifundia. It is no accident that in many countries, including the United States, dairy products are commonly sold through cooperatives.

The cooperative's intensive effort to recruit and help the small producer of milk can also be explained by market conditions. The city of São Paulo is growing rapidly in size and wealth, and the demand for fresh milk is increasing accordingly. To maintain its dominant position in the Paulista market, therefore,[4] and to prevent possible unfair competition by private firms, the cooperative needs every liter it can get. This is especially true in the winter months (June, July, and August), when the seca—dry season—withers the pastures and milk production, especially in the peripheral areas, falls drastically. Thus the cooperative, as a matter of course, encourages every producer and attempts to improve production in every way it can. Nor should one discount a degree of sincere paternalism on the part of its leaders.

The development of these cooperatives can be seen as an effort on the part of the traditional patrons, the fazendeiros, to maintain their dominant position in the face of increasing scale in the economy and the effects of industrial urbanism. Very few fazendeiros at the present time can dominate decisionmaking in the very large state and national organizations, including the political systems. Even the wealthiest coffee planters complain bitterly about Brazilian government coffee policy. Thus, as Guerreiro Ramos noted, some of the big cooperatives act as pressure groups on the government to protect the interests of the producers.

Recent Brazilian law established three orders of cooperatives: (1) primary Cooperatives, which must be locally controlled and have individual producers as voting members; (2) secondary or central cooperatives, which are cooperatives of the cooperatives, where the voting members are primary cooperatives as units; (3) organizations or alliances of cooperatives. These last are organizations set up to protect the interests of the cooperative movement as a whole or some important industry within it. For example, the União Brasileira das Cooperativas Centrais de Lacticínios (Brazilian Union of Central Dairy Cooperatives) unites the milk cooperatives of Rio de Janeiro, São Paulo, and Belo Horizonte, to promote the general national interests of the industry. Similar unions exist for the coffee and sugar industries.

The cooperatives can be seen as pools of scarce Brazilian capital designed primarily to develop the marketing infrastructure that would enable the fazendeiros to reach urban markets in Brazil and abroad. In a cartorial type of state, however, it should be noted that power and authority are not organized in reliable set patterns but rather are continually renegotiable. Even ownership of property is not automatically defended by a complex and professional legal system, but must be bargained for through the complex networks of patronage. This introduces an important element in the nature of modern urban patronage in Brazil, the system of patronage through which protection from the powers of the state is afforded to commercial entrepreneurs ("pariah entrepreneurs," in the words of Fred Riggs [1964]). The commercial interests then can go about their business of making money without excessive taxation or expropriation by the government.

In the modern capitalist bourgeois-dominated state, such protection is simply taken for granted, is, in fact, seen to be one of the prime roles of the state—the universal protection of property. But it must be noted that until the end of the nineteenth century Brazil was in fact an agrarian empire designed for promoting the welfare of an aristocratic upper class. Thus the Brazilian bureaucracies, including the legal system and the whole apparatus of law enforcement, were in the hands of the agrarian elite. No one can understand the development of modern urban Brazil without remembering that fact.

A new kind of patron thus appeared on the scene, a person whose primary resource is not land or money (though he probably has both) but a strong influence in the political decisionmaking process. His influence can come from many different sources. He may be a politician with control over many votes in the rural zones or populist strength in the cities. He may be a relative or friend of such politicians, especially in the increasingly austere and isolated federal government. His political authority may come from a combination of sources, the important element being that he can influence decisionmaking and offer protection to commercial groups in the cities. His clients may include industrialists, businessmen, and fazendeiros who, however powerful they may be at home, have little influence in the capital city. The relationship differs from the traditional pattern in that the client is asking not simply for local independence in return for political support, but for the permission to carry on business without political harassment. It resembles the usual picture of protection of the landed elite in exchange for political support, but in the urban case the support implies financial and institutional support rather than dependent votes (though there may be an aspect of this as well). A similar pattern can be found throughout São Paulo State, where gradually the politically powerful landed oligarchy is being replaced by a complex "functional" oligarchy (*panelinha*; see Leeds 1964) made up of a number of people with different kinds of authority and power who work together to enhance their positions.

The cooperative movement, especially the production cooperatives, shows these urban patronage patterns very well. This picture is highlighted by a division that took place some years ago when several powerful cooperatives broke with their former patron and went their own way, an action that aroused intense hostility. It can probably be best explained by examining technological change.

To understand the basis of the split, we must examine the history of the great cooperative of Cotia, by a considerable margin the largest cooperative in Brazil and one of the biggest agricultural and marketing organizations in Latin America (Ando 1961; Saito 1964).

In 1927 eighty-three Japanese farmers living in the *município* of Cotia in São Paulo State formed the Sociedade Cooperativa de Responsibilidade Limitada dos Produtores de Batata em Cotia, Sociedade Anônima

(Cooperative Society of Limited Responsibility of Potato Producers of Cotia, Inc.). The several hundred thousand Japanese settlers in Brazil were isolated linguistically and culturally from the larger Brazilian society, yet politically and economically they were wholly dependent on it. They adopted the cooperative pattern as a natural way to advance their group interests. As the colony prospered, so did the cooperatives. The Japanese concentrated on mixed agriculture to feed the growing Paulista cities, and production grew with these cities. The four major central agricultural cooperatives, that is, of mixed agriculture, are all predominantly formed of members of Japanese birth or descent. They are the Cooperativa Central de Cotia, the Cooperativa Central Agrícola de São Paulo, the Cooperativa Central de Sul-Brasil, and the Cooperativa Central Bandeirantes.

Although the Central Agrícola de São Paulo is the largest cooperative in terms of membership—about 30,000, nearly double the size of any of the others—the Cooperative of Cotia overshadows it and all of the others in terms of resources and production. It had a total movement in 1967 of NCr. $438,731,664, or about $150 million, and has branches in several states of Brazil (Cooperativa Agrícola de Cotia 1967). Its success has been due, apparently, to unusually skillful management and a rather ruthless concern for efficient operation, which has led some of the Rochdale idealists in the cooperative movement to condemn it as indifferent toward its poorer members. In fact, a number of experts in the cooperative field insisted that Cotia and Sul-Brasil were not real cooperatives at all, but transplanted Japanese corporations. Whatever the ideology of the situation, Cotia grew, and its success prepared the ground for the greatest division in the history of the cooperative movement.

The main political defense for the production cooperatives in Brazil and the oldest and most important "union" of cooperatives is UNASCO (União Nacional das Associações Cooperativas) and its São Paulo affiliate, UCESP (União das Cooperativas do Estado de São Paulo). These have always been urban patronage institutions of a most complex kind, with powerful rural-based cooperatives such as those of coffee and milk —and their immense political resources in influence, votes, and money— joining other kinds of cooperatives to defend the interests of Brazilian and São Paulo commercial agriculture generally. The president of UCESP especially has always been an exceptionally prominent man, from the most powerful old Paulista families who could offer political defense within the state government in return for political and economic support of himself and his allies. Urban political networks in Brazil often reach Byzantine complexity, with shifting coalitions and combinations of interests, agreeing on some issues and not on others but often staying loosely joined as a general pressure group if their interests are not in direct conflict. For example, the production cooperative unions often support each other in the face of nonagrarian interests.

The Japanese cooperatives were especially vulnerable to political interference; unlike the coffee and dairy cooperatives, they had no previously built political base and no influential family support in the São Paulo government. For many years all of these cooperatives had protectors, Luso-Brazilians with varied and important contacts in the state government, usually from the old São Paulo coffee elite families. Moreover, all of them developed under the broad and powerful wing of UCESP.

Several cooperatives, however, including Cotia, became increasingly restless at enforced dependence on their political patrons. Cotia in fact was becoming one of the major economic institutions in the country. It publishes three journals on agriculture and commerce,[5] does its own market research, and trains its own technicians, some fifty a year, in the United States. It has recently installed a computer system for planning and development. Over the years it has built up a strong support within the federal government not only through its considerable wealth but also by persuading many influential people that Cotia had the key to modernization of Brazilian agriculture. Still another factor in influencing the pro-industrial members of the government, and they for long have dominated Brasilia, is the sheer importance of these cooperatives in feeding the industrial cities. While São Paulo would probably not starve without the Japanese cooperatives, including Cotia, it would certainly have serious food shortages.

The climax came shortly after the Brazilian *coup d'etat* of 1964, when Cotia, confident of its political support within the new government, led more than thirty important cooperatives out of UNASCO and UCESP to found two new organizations, ABCOOP (Aliança Brasileira de Cooperativas) and ACAPESP (Aliança das Cooperativas Agropecuarias do Estado de São Paulo). The separation was both bitter and personal, as it was apparently accompanied with an effort to destroy UNASCO and its leadership politically. The result was a sharp division in the entire cooperative movement. While it is difficult to generalize with complete confidence, it seems that the more pragmatic "capitalistic" leaders of the movement, those who are interested most in the rapid development of modern commercial agricultural methods for Brazil, sided with Cotia. Siding with UNASCO were both the Rochdale idealists and those co-operatives that tended to ally with the traditional state and local political elite rather than the national government, for UNASCO's political connections tend to be within the State of São Paulo. Powerful central cooperatives such as those of coffee and milk stayed with UNASCO; Cotia was joined by organizations tired of playing state politics—its smaller Japanese twin, Sul-Brazil, and Holambra.

Holambra (Lietjens 1964) is a small cooperative founded by Dutch Catholics in 1948. Over the years, despite formidable difficulties, it has prospered and turned square miles of dry interior scrubland into a flourishing agricultural region. Holambra is politically, economically, and ideologically very independent and was one of the leaders in the "revolution" against UCESP; interesting because Holambra is frequently pointed to as the "model" agricultural cooperative in all of Brazil, from the point of view of the basic cooperative principles.

Despite the split, UNASCO and UCESP did not founder. The huge Cooperativa Central Agrícola—also largely Japanese—the important cooperatives of milk and coffee, and another big Japanese cooperative, Bandeirantes, remained in this alliance, and the rebels were unable to break the union's political power and influence in the state. For a while it appeared that a standoff had been reached, but in 1965 the UNASCO forces counterattacked. They pushed a law through the Brazilian legislature that redefined the nature of a cooperative so that a primary cooperative must be restricted to one *município* and those contiguous to it, while a central cooperative could be made up only of primary cooperatives without individuals as members. This legislation apparently was aimed directly at Cotia, a highly centralized primary cooperative which was not only intermunicipal but interstate as well. Cotia was forced in 1966 to undergo expensive and complex reorganization that, together with a widespread fall in agricultural prices, nearly caused the great cooperative to fail. Nevertheless it survived and despite formidable difficulties still leads Brazilian agriculture.

It is my opinion that despite many weaknesses and inconsistencies, cooperation in Brazil, even though far from the Rochdale ideal, has still been reasonably effective in modernizing parts of rural Brazil. The big cooperatives with their powerful political defenses in the metropolitan centers have frequently extended their protection to moderate-sized producers who otherwise might be absorbed into latifundia and "factories in the field." It enables these producers to pool their political and economic resources to develop more modern kinds of agriculture without the problems of monopoly control. While these institutions must still play the complex patronage game in Brazil, they have been able to pool respectable resources for application to economic growth rather than simply maintaining their political position. This is an important factor in the development of São Paulo and this is apparently recognized by some of the "modernizing" elements of the Brazilian elite. The president of Cotia was in fact for a time the federal minister of agriculture.

Nevertheless there are strong counterpressures. All Brazilian cooperatives have had considerable difficulty with the Brazilian tax structure, especially a new consumers' tax, the ICM (Impôsto sôbre à Circulação de mercadorias [CTN 1970:21]), which places a tax on all commercial transactions. Many private commercial firms with their own protection in the patronage network simply fail to collect this tax and often get away with it, whereas the cooperatives with their formal organization must keep careful records, which are easy to examine. Frequently, therefore, the cooperatives pay taxes that some private firms avoid. At a competitive disadvantage, therefore, a number of large and small cooperatives have failed in recent years and many of the "owned" cooperatives in the rural zones have closed. The political influence of the cooperatives has not been sufficient to revoke these taxes, or to develop more generalized and effective fiscal procedures that might protect them from the problems that beset them in the webs of Brazilian clientele politics.[6]

NOTES

1. The idiom, at least in regions where I have worked, is that of considerable paternalism coupled with marked status distinction, a factor reflected in the language. A number of Brazilian novelists such as Jorge Amado, J. J. Veiga, and João Guimarães Rosa, reveal this element in their works.

2. Research of Brazilian production cooperatives in São Paulo was made possible through a grant from the Canada Council in summer of 1968.

3. Interestingly, the only grade A milk produced in Brazil comes from these big private fazendas, not the cooperatives.

4. The Cooperativa Central, with some twenty-two affiliated cooperatives, at the present time sells about 400,000 liters of fresh milk daily in the city of São Paulo under the brand Leite Paulista. It thus supplies slightly over half of the total urban market for fresh milk. The leaders of the cooperative feel that the potential market is much larger than this and are making plans to double the capacity of their present pasteurization and bottling plant.

5. Through its own scientific foundation, Cotia publishes *Coopercotia*, which is largely a trade and technical journal for agriculture; *Lavoura e Cooperativismo* (published in Japanese), a trade journal for the Japanese colony; and *Mundo Economico*, a world economic journal.

6. An extended bibliography on cooperatives in Brazil is Pinho 1963.

7

Ponchos, Weaving, and Patron-Client Relations in Northwest Argentina

ESTHER HERMITTE

Instituto Torcuato Di Tella
Centro de Investigaciones Sociales
Buenos Aires, Argentina

This chapter examines the working of patronage and clientage relationships in Huarco, a small town in western Catamarca province of Argentina. For most of its history (which dates back to the seventeenth century, when the township was founded by a group of "poor and plebian" Spaniards whose leader obtained the land under royal grant), the residents of Huarco have been subsistence farmers working on small holdings. Although they produced some surpluses of cereals that were traded eventually to reach the large metropolitan centers, they remained, for the most part, marginal to the colonial and later national economy.

Toward the end of the eighteenth century the weaving of vicuña and llama ponchos became important in the region. Over the next century and a half, while Argentina was transformed from a Spanish colony to an independent nation and Huarco, like most marginal communities of subsistence farmers in the hinterland, was being incorporated into the national administrative and economic system, the weaving of ponchos gradually (because of the increasing value of the finished product on the national market) came to be the primary source of income, exchange, and wealth in the community.

Weaving in Huarco is an activity performed by women. The domestic group into which the members of the local society are organized is the nuclear family. Within that household group, the traditional division of labor has been that males engage in agriculture, the accepted basis for supporting a family, and females bear, care for, and raise children and manage and run the household. By custom, males are assumed to be responsible for the material support of their women and children. Because few cash crops are raised, however, and there is little surplus above the needs for domestic consumption, most households are subsistence units perennially short of cash. The weaving of ponchos has given the residents of Huarco a much-needed source of cash, and with it access to the world beyond the local community through the national market. However, weaving and commerce in ponchos is "woman's work." In contrast to the norm for Argentina and most of Latin America, some women in Huarco have become the links between the domestic group (and the local community) and the larger, market-oriented, modern world outside the town.

The exchange or sale of ponchos can bring a woman a sizable income. However, the raw materials, vicuña and llama wool, are difficult to obtain locally. In order to obtain them, a woman hoping to earn income from weaving needs contacts that extend far beyond Huarco into the western mountains. Since the markets for the finished products are in the large metropolitan centers like Buenos Aires, she also needs contacts who have access to these markets.

The mobilization of the contacts needed to obtain raw materials and market finished products has produced a system of patronage and clientage in Huarco in which women can be the active participants engaging in transactions that articulate them and their domestic groups with the larger society of the province and the nation. Since the men of Huarco remain primarily subsistence agriculturalists, the system allows women to become the entrepreneurs, patrons, and clients. This fact has had a significant effect on the role of women in the community and on the structure and functioning of the domestic group.

The literature on patron-client relations in Latin America has rarely, if ever, portrayed women holding these positions; the relationship is always presented as being one between men. In Huarco men, of course, do appear in the roles of both patron and client, as will be clear in the course of this presentation. I have chosen, however, to concentrate on women in these relationships in order to see whether this rather unusual form of patronage-clientage can be dealt with in terms of the same variables used in the analysis of the relationships' more orthodox appearances.

THE COMMUNITY

Huarco lies in the valley of the Huarco River and is flanked by mountains to the east and west "notable for their ruggedness and poorness of vegetation as compared with the well-treed alluvial plain. Water supply is a factor which decidedly limits its receptive capacity for new strata of population" (Aparicio 1959:398 ff.). The community is distant from the important cities of the northwest, and transportation and communication are difficult. Of the three most important access routes, two cross slopes that are a severe hindrance to large cargo vehicles and the third is almost impassable during the rainy months. The nearest railroad terminal is ninety kilometers from the town.

The town of Huarco, which goes by the same name as the county (or department), is the county seat and has a population of approximately 6,000. Locally it is called "the Villa," to distinguish it from the department, which contains about thirty-five villages and towns, some of which have fewer than 200 inhabitants. Most of the inhabitants of the Villa are natives of the locality. The most important immigrant ethnic group, with respect to both numbers and impact on local commercial activity, are the Syrio-Lebanese, who began to arrive in the area around 1910. Their descendants, second- and third-generation Argentines, are still referred to as *turcos* ("Turks"). Other nationalities are represented only in very small numbers.

Huarco is not a homogeneous community. It is neither isolated nor self-sufficient. Although most of the individual households are subsistence oriented and marginal to the national and provincial market and political system, the town's status as a county seat means that there are government functionaries and professional men in the population who represent and articulate the local community in the formal institutions of the province and the nation. The extent of the local community's involvement in and dependence upon national and provincial levels of authority in the handling of public affairs is made evident by the fact that as much as 95 percent of the revenues spent on local services are obtained, directly or indirectly, from the provincial and national governments.

By national law, each department in Argentina is required to provide for its residents a series of basic services. The departmental administration of Huarco, headed by an intendente or mayor, however, like most local units of government, is financially unable to provide the required service. Consequently, these services are provided by provincial and national agencies. Their administrators have retained jurisdiction in matters of local importance, which, to the displeasure of the Huarqueños, must be referred to higher levels outside the community for resolution.

Some of the provincial and national agencies that provide and administer services in Huarco are the Dirección Nacional de Agua y Energía (National Water and Power Board), which provides the locality with an irrigation system and an electric power supply; the Obras Sanitarias de la Nación (National Sanitation Board), which supplies drinking water; the Vialidad Nacional (Highway Board), which constructs and supervises the highway system; the Dirección Provincial de Rentas (Provincial Tax Office), which collects taxes; the Dirección Provincial de Catastro (Provincial Land Office), which supervises real estate activities; the Provincial Regional Hospital, which provides medical services; the national and provincial school systems (there are seven primary schools and four secondary schools in Huarco); and the Banco de Catamarca, which is the primary source of credit.

Approximately 60 percent of the budget of the department of Huarco is obtained in the form of subsidies from the provincial government. The province, however, also lacks the resources needed to fulfill its obligations, and something of the order of 60 percent of Catamarca's budget comes as subsidies from the central government.

The supralocal agencies are important to the lives and well-being of the residents of Huarco. Also important to them are the provincial, national, and world markets to which they sell their small surpluses and from which they obtain goods and services not available locally. In addition, the community is a supplier of immigrant labor, specifically to the sugar plantations of northwestern and western Argentina, and of permanent migrants to the larger cities and other areas that require labor; for example, the oil fields of Comodoro Rivadavia in southern Argentina. Huarco therefore may be considered, in Eric Wolf's words (1956:1065), as "the local terminal of a web of group relations which extend through intermediate levels from the level of the community to that of the nation."

Given the importance of outside factors such as agencies, markets, and jobs to the life of Huarco, it must be noted that very few of the individual residents have access to the links that tie the community with the institutions of the larger society. The situation is reminiscent of Wolf's (1956:1073) generalization for agricultural villages:

> Most of the inhabitants of such communities either lack access to new opportunities or are unable to take advantage of such opportunities when offered. Lacking adequate resources in land, water, technical knowledge, and contacts in the market, the majority also lack the instruments which can transform use values into marketable commodities. At the same time their failure to understand the cues for the new patterns of nation-oriented behavior isolate them from the channels of communication between community and nation. Under these circumstances they must cling to the traditional "rejection pattern" of their ancestors, because their narrow economic base sets limits to the introduction of new cultural alternatives. These are all too often nonfunctional for them. The production of sufficient maize for subsistence purpose remains their major goal in life.

AGRICULTURAL PATTERNS

In Huarco the preponderance of minifundia places very real limits on the productive capacity of most agriculturalists (table 1). In fact, the whole community is hemmed into a restricted cultivable zone defined by the relatively fixed flow of irrigation water.

The absence of extended cooperative groups serves to reinforce the limitations created by minifundia. As a production unit, the nuclear and the consanguineal family predominate. The latter represent 22 percent of the total number of families in Huarco, according to a pilot census taken in 1969. Interfamily alliances to maintain property undivided by inheritance are nonexistent (they probably could occur only at higher social levels, as in the case of the few large landowners of the area). The agriculturalist invariably works with the members of his nuclear family, preferably menfolk, although he may employ hired hands for certain jobs. Forms of reciprocal cooperation appear during very short periods of the year; for example, during weed-clearing time (*deshierbe*).

TABLE 1

PLOTS REGISTERED BY THE DEPARTMENT OF IRRIGATION IN HUARCO, 1965

Size of Holding (hectares)	Number
Less than 1	1,312
1 to 5	377
5 to 10	45
10 to 20	10
20 to 30	6
More than 30	1
Total	1,751

The small landholder's adventures into commercial crops such as cuminseed, sweet pepper, and aniseed are timid experiments, and one bad harvest can make him abandon the undertaking. In addition, the market prices for these products fluctuate widely from one year to another, and this fact also discourages the activity. It is interesting to note that the area sown with spices shows notable oscillations from year to year, which is not the case to the same extent for cereals (staples in the local diet) such as wheat and corn. If the farmer used part of his holding for cultivating spices, a shortage of cash may force him to sell his crop as "futures," or in local terms, "at the furrow" (*venta en rastrojo*). This may ease his immediate situation but also plunge him into a deeper crisis should the crop fail, as he will then still have a responsibility to the buyer. Or, if he has grown peppers, for instance, he may have to sell them as soon as they are harvested in order to avoid the cost of grinding.

Even if the farmer obtains satisfactory results, the small marketable surplus does not allow him to travel to the regional markets, not only because the transportation costs would practically cancel the profits but also because he is not equipped to face the impersonal rules of interaction involved in this class of transaction. Although buyers representing commercial firms visit the community, they are mainly interested in large purchases, continued supply, and homogeneous quality. The small argiculturalist is hardly likely to meet all these requirements. Frequently, the solution is to sell the agricultural surpluses to local dealers, storekeepers, or big farmers, who in turn sell to the regional or national markets. This last decision is not so one-sided as it would appear; a many-stranded relationship is set up between farmer and local dealer that includes the performance of mutual services from which both partners benefit.

There is another element in the agriculturalist's situation that contributes to the sense of strict limitation weighing upon him, the seasonal peaks occurring in the agricultural cycle. The interval between these peaks is marked by an exacerbation of the chronic shortage of cash, and it is difficult for him "to wait it out" (*hacer la espera*). At such times there is an increased need for the farmer to buy on credit, obtain loans, or enter into sharecropping arrangements with the person to whom he has sold his small surplus. The relationship thus begun is favorable to the small agriculturalist, but he has the obligation to deliver his produce. If he does not, he risks being unable to obtain help in future crises. Working as a sharecropper or partner of a large producer is a guarantee that the small agriculturalist will not have to deal with marketing problems. Moreover, and this is fundamental, the small producer must live and support his family during the whole period during which he receives no income from the sale of his produce. It is then that the big farmer, by associating the small farmer with his enterprise, guarantees the latter's sustenance throughout the year.

Although the textile craftswoman operates in very different circumstances, her lack of access to certain resources is much the same as the pattern for the small agriculturalist, and the resulting social pattern is similar. In weaving, however, the need for contacts with the extra-local market is most intense, given that the product, unlike agricultural products, is entirely commercialized. Consequently, the woven products have a decisive influence on the economy of Huarco, and the network of interaction created by their production and marketing is more closely knit than in the case of agriculture.

WEAVING

Textile production in Huarco requires certain implements; the *telar* ("loom"), the *huso* ("spindle"), and the *pala* ("rod") for adjusting the weft and the woof are all inexpensive and durable. The raw material is llama wool or vicuña skins. The llama can be sheared every two years; its wool is sold by the kilogram. In the northern part of the country and in other Andean provinces there are large llama herds. The vicuña, however, in which the greater part of the weaving population specializes, is a swift wild animal living in the high mountain ranges. It must be shot. Since the end of the nineteenth century many attempts have been made to prohibit vicuña hunting and prevent its extinction, but the laws have never been strictly enforced. In spite of this, there are restrictions on obtaining the skins. Those skins that have satisfied the legal requirements, called "stamped skins" locally, are almost prohibitively costly. The legal obstacles are circumvented through different channels and the material reaches the hands of the weavers, but since vicuña are not present in the region, the irregular supply of skins presents difficulties. Three vicuña skins are needed to weave a poncho. In 1967 the price of a skin ranged, according to its origin, from three to six thousand pesos (ten to twenty dollars).

Even when these inconveniences are overcome, the technology involved and the composition of the production unit combine to isolate the textile artisans from the channels of communication. The technique used in Huarco, hand-spun thread and weaving on the *criollo* loom (handloom), limits productivity. The spinning of the thread for a vicuña poncho can take as long as a month; the weaving takes around ten days. A llama wool shawl, on the other hand, may take only a few days. There are peaks in the sales of woven products immediately before and during the winter months, when the best prices are obtained; prices decline markedly in the summer.

A critical factor in weaving is that the role of *telera* (very few men are engaged in this activity) overlaps with that of housewife, mother, and occasionally saleswoman of articles that bring cash, such as pastries or home-baked bread. These other activities considerably reduce the time that can be spent at the loom. Weaving is carried on at home. Ideally, all of the women in the domestic group take part in it. The

166

girls are socialized in this activity at an early age, but the boys cannot be asked to cooperate to the same extent. The local cultural pattern, which emphasizes weaving as a purely feminine task, enables the boys of the household to get away to farming or some other odd job. A local saying sums up negative evaluations of the masculine weaver, describing him as a homosexual: "Tejedor, es maricón." Therefore, it is the number of women as a cooperating unit within a household that inclines the balance toward greater or smaller output. A number of circumstances can undermine this potential cooperation, such as the degree of cohesion among the members of the domestic group or the attraction toward other activities implying social mobility (high school education or migration to a big city). The fact that there is no institutionalization of extended cooperative groups reinforces the significance of the household as the productive unit.

The system of reciprocal assistance was traditionally practiced in Huarco. The two best known forms of this reciprocity were the *mingas* of the weavers and the reapers. In the first, a group of women would meet nightly at the house of the weaver who needed to finish a poncho. After the work was finished would come some recreational activity— receiving their men friends, partaking of a meal, or dancing. The group rotated from night to night among the houses of its members. Something similar took place during the wheat harvest, when the men went reaping from farm to farm until all of the participants in the *minga* had harvested their crops. The obligation could last for more than a month.

These forms of complementary reciprocity have not entirely disappeared, although most of the inhabitants regard them as things of the past. But many of the elements of the ritual accompanying these "lend a hand" tasks are lost, and the cooperating units have undergone changes in their membership. The meals, dancing, and musical accompaniments are no longer a feature of the gatherings. The appeal to a large group of neighbors, friends, or compadres to devote some of their time to the cooperation is no longer made. Reciprocal labor persists but it is restricted to a small nucleus of relatives. Stavenhagen (1965:61) explains the disappearance of these forms of cooperation among peasants as coinciding with the introduction of commercial crops and private ownership of the land. It was not until 1945 that the *minga* as an institution began to wane, though land had been privately owned since the end of the nineteenth century; the marketing of spices coincides with the decade of the 1930s.

I believe that, although the two characteristics suggested by Stavenhagen partially explain the disappearance of the traditional forms of cooperation, other and deeper changes must be considered, changes that affected the social structure of the community and were consequences of a new market situation resulting in a greater insertion of the community into the system of regional and even national relationships. Such factors include the exodus of the males to the sugar harvest or to permanent labor markets (the migration to Comodoro Rivadavia began around 1940), the greater demand for textiles in several areas of the country, and the settling of numerous traders in the locality who absorbed production in smaller quantities but more steadily. All these had as one consequence the opportunity for the craftswoman to sell her product individually. The extended groups have lost their function, giving place to a productive unit coinciding with the domestic group.

Returning to the productive potential of the weaver and to the several circumstances that place her in different loci within the system of production and marketing of the ponchos, I suggest the following typology derived from the cases studied.

Type A corresponds to the least privileged position in the two key stages of production and marketing. This is the textile craftswoman who works for others, carrying out one or more of the tasks in the textile process. She lacks access to the raw materials. The problem of marketing does not exist for a weaver of this category; at no time does she own the product.

Type B includes a wide variety of craftswomen and could be divided into various subtypes, but I have grouped them in one because the two principal characteristics selected, production and marketing, show variations that do not introduce substantial changes in the overall situation of the producer. Type B weavers have access to labor within their own domestic group; occasionally, they may also have family contacts outside the community who sporadically help them to obtain raw materials and to distribute the finished product. Nevertheless, the greater part of their production is sold to local dealers from whom credit necessary for continued production is obtained. The variations in productivity and income within this type can be correlated with the number of members of the productive domestic unit and with the contacts, or lack of them, with kin living outside the town.

Type C is a minority that may be classified as "weaver entrepreneurs." Weavers assigned to this type are those who have access to labor outside their own domestic group, often beyond the town limits, as they can hire weavers according to the excellence of their work. As a consequence their output is notably increased and of superior quality, allowing them to compete in the national market and to obtain a steady clientele. Credit possibilities are much greater, not only because certain buyers will advance them money against future deliveries of ponchos, but also because, in view of their level of production, they have easy access to bank credit. The dependence of this type of artisans on local dealers is nonexistent.

The typology is summarized in table 2.

TABLE 2
TYPOLOGY OF WEAVERS

	Access to Resources		
Resource	*Type A*	*Type B*	*Type C*
Labor	Own labor only (labors for a third party)	Limited to own domestic group	Domestic group. Hires labor in and outsde the community
Raw materials	Obtained generally from type C	Buys from local dealers; sporadic remittances from kin living in other areas	Purchases in large volume, generally outside the town
Markets	Virtually nonexistent	Sells to local dealers, occasionally to kin living out of town	Regular customers in the larger cities; travels periodically to regional markets
Credit	Through employer (type C)	Local dealers, Relatives	Cash in advance from regular customers; bank

The boundaries of the types are not absolutely rigid. Upward mobility, although very difficult, can occur over a number of years or when conditions allow for greater production and better marketing. Downward mobility also can take place.

The description of a case is now in order to clarify some of the dynamic aspects in this system of production, such as the importance of the membership of the productive unit, the plurality of needs, the shifts in patrons, and the ups and downs in the fate of the weavers.

The case is that of a consanguineal family for whom weaving was the most important activity. The head of the household was a frail old woman in her nineties, an excellent and incredibly fast spinner who, because of her age, spent her waking hours spinning in the sun. Many of her sleepless nights were occupied with the same task. Her niece, Virginia, also a weaver, was responsible for the weaving and the finishing touches on every woven article. She was a widow of thirty-two with three sons in elementary school. The remaining member of the household was a niece of Virginia, a teenager taking sewing lessons. She contributed little to the textile activities of the other two women. Virginia was in charge of the household chores, and she complained often and bitterly about the refusal of her boys to help in any part of the weaving process.

Support and help from the outside came to the group in five ways. (1) Relatives living in the province of Salta, to whom a vicuña poncho was sent once in a great while for sale, sent remittances of vicuña skins and small amounts of cash. Problems arose when the remittances from Salta were delayed; also, instead of sending the price they had obtained in cash, the relatives sent part of it in skins, which did not fill the family's immediate need for cash. Often, too, the vicuña ponchos did not sell quickly. (2) Virginia sold some of her textile articles to the local Lebanese-owned store where she bought all the supplies for the family. (3) She had a good relationship with a local physician, a man with good connections in the capital of the country, where he had served as a senator years before. He had been instrumental in settling the debts of Virginia's deceased husband. In addition he gave free medicines and treatment to the old woman, who needed them constantly, as well as to the rest of the family. Virginia cleaned the clinic, going very early in the morning for an hour or two. Sometimes the doctor also bought one of the ponchos made by the women. (4) A cousin of Virginia visited them almost every morning before going to work and helped spin some llama wool. (5) Virginia's brother-in-law, a small agriculturalist in Huarco, sent wheat or corn for home consumption, reciprocating for the help given him by the three boys, who loved to do small agricultural tasks in order to escape weaving.

The relationship between Virginia and the store owner became brittle because he refused to give her cash for her woven products and further-more insisted on receiving all of the woven pieces she made. At a time when the situation between them was very tense, an older man ap-peared in the town. He had left Huarco many years before, going to Buenos Aires and becoming a successful weaver-entrepreneur. Upon his return to the community he employed many weavers to accelerate his production for the capital city, to which he made short trips. Virginia started to work for him in her spare time, doing mostly the delicate finishing touches on the ponchos and shawls and receiving cash for her work as well as help in the form of small loans. Simultaneously she acted with great skill to sever her dependence from the store owner; cash in hand, she could buy in other stores. In the meantime, the weaver-entrepreneur increased his demands on Virginia and the old woman, something they accepted gladly because of the independence it meant.

When the old woman died and her contribution to the vital on-going production stopped, Virginia gave up vicuña weaving and de-voted herself to llama wool products. She obtained from the doctor a full-time job in the clinic and worked for the weaver-entrepreneur in the time she had left. Her links with the Salta relatives became very weak.

Obviously a type B weaver, Virginia, with a notably diminished rate of production and without the contacts she had had, would have moved down the ladder, ending as a total dependent of a type C weaver.

With very few exceptions, the agricultural and craft activities yield insufficient income to meet the producer's needs. The fragile economic equilibrium in which most of the small producers live can be upset by unexpected expenses; sickness or death in the family, a wedding, or a baptism is enough to send them looking for loans or force them to sell their products for less than they are worth. They go to the local dealers, especially those who are also store owners; they usually receive part of the sale price in cash and part in kind. The economic balance fre-quently goes against them because of the disparity between their pro-ductive capacity and their needs.

At this point the importance of the credit system in Huarco as the "lubricant which keeps the machinery of production going" (Ward 1960:139) should be discussed. This significant privilege is granted only when there is trust between the parties, and it serves as a basis for strengthening the links with other cultural mechanisms, especially ritual kinship, which helps to ensure a lasting relationship.

Although there are possibilities for obtaining credit in the local branch of the Bank of Catamarca, often the small producer does not have the minimum income required for an advance. He is ignorant of the formalities and fearful of the commitment that the application entails, so he has recourse to those who will lend him money, in smaller amounts perhaps but with less formality and greater frequency than the bank. Stavenhagen, referring to agricultural societies (1965:64), states, "where cheap credit on a large scale and freely available is not to be found . . . local money lenders and traders play an increasingly important part in the community . . . there is an enormous sector of small and large trades people, middlemen and money-lenders who generally absorb the greater part of the regional income."

Those who grant credit in Huarco do not do so haphazardly or without limit, first because in a society such as the one described here person-to-person relations predominate and second because the lender himself has credit obligations to suppliers from outside the community. Ward sums up the situation as follows (1960:138):

> . . . . a large proportion of the everyday commercial transactions . . . produce buying, retailing, paying for services of all kinds, including those of a predominantly "social" nature such as funerals, weddings, etc. . . . [are] carried on by means of some form of credit arrangement. In the vast majority of cases the creditor parties to such arrangements themselves have very little capital, and the number of debtors they can serve is, therefore, closely restricted. Furthermore, these are nearly always arrangements of personal trust made between individuals who are well acquainted with each other, and there is a limit to the number of individuals any one creditor can know well enough to trust in this way, even if he has (as he usually has not) a relatively large stock of capital.

The outstanding characteristic of the credit system in Huarco is the nonsettlement of debts. A monthly payment partially reducing the amount owed is considered a guarantee of the honesty of the debtor. Evidently both parties to the relationship benefit from this system, the debtor because he gets over his cash crisis and the creditor because he assures himself of an inflow of products and eventually of services. It should be noted that most of the stores offer a complete assortment of goods from foodstuffs to clothing. The explanation is not hard to find: the customer must be able to get goods for almost all of his needs in one store, or he will have to shop at various stores, thus weakening the connections that link him to his creditor. Large-scale agriculturalists and local professional men who enter into the same credit arrangements as lenders, although usually they are not providers of goods, can offer land to be worked, indispensable attendance to health problems, loans, and other forms of support.

It is important to note that the nonsettlement of debts is one of the main characteristics of nearly all local arrangements for hiring labor. For instance, farmers who engage workers make a partial payment of the amount due, leaving the balance to ensure the workers' future collaboration.

Partial settlement of the debt, then, is one of the mechanisms that ensure the continuity of interaction. A total settlement would expose the debtor to the risk of having the relationship terminated, ending the series of loans that have alleviated his hardship. Foster says in his work on the dyadic contract (1961:1165):

> A functional requirement of the system is that an exactly even balance between the two partners can never be struck. This would jeopardize the whole relationship, since if all credits and debits somehow could balance off at a point in time, the contract would cease to exist. At the very least a new contract would have to be gotten under way, and this would involve uncertainty and possibly distress if one partner seemed reluctant to continue. The dyadic contract is effective precisely because partners are never quite sure of their relative positions at a given moment. As long as they know that goods and services are flowing both ways in roughly equal amounts over time, they know their relationship is solidly based.

In my opinion the credit system or the partial settlement of the debt do not constitute, in themselves, a perfect guarantee either that the relationship will last or that it will prevent a "competitor" substituting for one of the two participants. Weavers and agriculturalists are numerous in Huarco, but there are also many tradespeople and professional men to make such a substitution possible.

Intensifying of the relationships described above through bonds of ritual kinship is very common in Huarco. It usually begins when a small producer requests the person with whom he already has some economic relationship to be the godfather of his children, but frequently also a creditor may ask to be named godfather. This is explained by certain local criteria regarding prestige, specifically related to politics. "Compadrazgo" between persons of different status (Mintz and Wolf [1950] call it "vertical" to distinguish it from that established between social equals) is characteristic of the community. Individuals who have been outstanding in politics over a number of years have up to 400 godchildren (including those of baptism, confirmation, first communion, and marriage).

The respect and deference that are norms between compadres "formalize certain interpersonal relationships and channel reciprocal behavior modes into customary patterns" (Foster 1953:10). The compadrazgo not only seals a relationship already established but by incorporating the moral ingredient makes the priority of obligations of both participants much more clear.

In view of the absence of groups more extended than the nuclear or consanguineal family and the need of the family to establish relations with people who can give it support and serve as intermediaries, the rules of action prescribed by ritual kinship order and systematize rights and duties. This serves to mediate the interaction between groups whose contact is inevitable. An example of the latter is the fact that the Syrio-Lebanese are among the most conspicuous "godchildren-seekers" in the community. Perceived by everybody as foreigners and store owners actively engaged in buying and selling textile products (all factors that create a negative image), the *turcos* must adjust to the culture by adopting local customs. Compadrazgo is an ideal way to achieve some acceptance, and they benefit from these fictive kinship bonds.

We are dealing, then, with a system of interaction characterized by pervasive patron-client networks in which a large proportion of the small producers are female artisans contributing goods to the other sector, which distributes them, and receiving in exchange necessary materials and services for their subsistence. In Huarco only a very small proportion of these artisans, those of type C, have reached a status that allows them to assume the role of patrons. The other patrons are the merchants, professional men, and a few large landowners of the community.

CONCLUSION

The control by women, because of traditional forms of the division of labor, of a significant skill in the local economy makes them participants in patron-client relations with substantial figures in the community. The roles of client and patron are normally held by men in Latin America, as it is the males who normally control the significant resources. This control over an economically significant skill by women should, theoretically, have an effect on household organization as well as on patron-client relations, and in fact it does.

In addition to nuclear and consanguineal families, there are also in Huarco domestic groups consisting of an unwed mother and her children. If the stable nuclear family were the dominating productive unit in the community, it could be assumed that from the joint effort of the spouses, the farmer-husband providing the staple foods and the weaver-wife contributing cash derived from the sale of *telas*, an economic stability higher than that described here would be assured. In fact, however ephemeral unions are common. Given that weaving is mainly a feminine activity and is the source of cash income, the unwed mother and her children form the nucleus of the household, which is a "regular viable, family unit in a regular, functioning society" (Adams 1960:36). In this unit more or less sporadic presence of the male does not fundamentally alter the maternal dyad. The daughters of women who wish to migrate from Huarco may be incorporated into such matrifocal households.

Even in the homes where the conjugal union is more nearly permanent, the man may not contribute a substantial share of the needed income for the members of the family. Several circumstances explain this. Huarco does not offer a good labor market for men, and some may be unemployed for months at a time and have odd jobs only for short intervals throughout the year. Men such as these, and also many small agriculturalists, often leave the town for seven or eight months of the year in order to work in the sugar areas of the country, hoping to return home with large sums of cash. This expectation is seldom realized, because of the expenses they incur while living outside Huarco and also because they often purchase attractive but expensive and not always useful articles such as radios, phonographs, and watches. Finally, as table 1 indicates, there is an enormous proportion of plots of less than one hectare in size, the produce of which is not enough to feed a family for a whole year.

In Huarco it is not unusual to see a group of women busily engaged in the different steps of the weaving process while the men are sitting around drinking mate (herb tea). The women's description of the "lazy Huarco man" depicts him lying on his back beneath the loom while the woman weaves, his only task being to pick up the thread when it falls to the floor.

The role of the woman weaver as the main economic provider in the home and as the socializing agent of the future weavers grants her greater decisionmaking power within the domestic group. That these privileges, derived from the monopoly of textile crafts, are closely guarded by the women to keep them in feminine hands seems to be demonstrated by the definition of male weavers as homosexuals quoted earlier. Those men who do become weavers and who are homosexuals, or are regarded as such, do not appear to be regarded as competitors by the women. Such men, of course, would seem unlikely to be the heads of normal household units.

Although not all clients in Huarco are women, they make up a significant percentage of those who need the support and mediation of patrons. It is largely the women who have resources that are significant to potential patrons.

This is a peculiar situation in a system of patronage. Traditionally, writers have discussed patronage systems as asymmetrical exchanges of goods and services between males. If we keep in mind the fact that the goods produced by the weavers are extremely valuable (warm, fashionable garments worn in the larger cities and tourist resorts of the country), we can understand the interest a patron might have in helping an artisan. The women also may do useful chores in the house of the patron. Finally, women were given voting rights in the late 1940s, so that having a female following is not to be disregarded. During the Perón era (1943–55), three of the type C *teleras* became active, successful leaders in political campaigns.

Given the organization of the productive units and their connection with the patrons, the patron-client blocks are vertical monoliths through which trust and loyalty move downward and upward. Relations between such blocks are relations between competitors involving a certain amount of distrust. This explains why attempts to create cooperatives for agriculturalists and textile workers could never succeed in Huarco. Attempts to create a local chamber of commerce have failed similarly because of the extreme competition among the upper business spheres of the community.

There are mechanisms, though, that introduce flexibility into this apparently rigid system. A person may change patrons during his life-time or may have more than one patron simultaneously, as in the case of Virginia. Thus the system in Huarco is not only one of dyadic person-to-person relationships but also one that for the potential client, includes all possible occupants of the role of patron. The producer who has to depend on someone else for subsistence must be careful not only to maintain and strengthen his relationship with the present patron but also to maneuver tactically and keep open the possibility of establishing new links.

The need for a client to have more than one patron at a time has come about because of the growing complexity of the town and the parallel increase in the needs of the producer. New requirements, more complex and diverse, for the circulation of goods and services have resulted in new, more specialized patron roles. A single client may need more than one patron in order to gain the services that were formerly provided by a single patron. As a corollary of this change, the strategic positions necessary to play the patron role have been modified, and individuals variously placed in this social system can fill it.

What seemed at first glance, then, to be an unusual form of patron-age-clientage, one in which women rather than men were the clients and sometimes the patrons as well, proves on closer examination to be explicable in terms of the same variables that order more usual forms of the relationship: (1) a significant resource—the ability to weave ponchos, which are a valuable economic commodity; (2) the fact that within the cultural tradition this resource, this skill, is woman's work, which a man can do only at the cost of his standing as a male; (3) the fact that acceptable male activities are so restricted by ecological limitations that they cannot generate resources greater than those of the women, so that the relative distribution of resources does not cor-respond to the cultural expectations of male and female roles in this society; (4) the fact that there are acceptable alternative male activi-ties outside the village, the presence of which may weaken or prevent any redefinition of male versus female activities in the community.

8
Patron-Client Relationships
at the International Level

NANCIE L. GONZALEZ

Department of Anthropology
Boston University

INTRODUCTION

The classical model of patronage in Latin America is based upon *people* as actors or position holders, and poses a dominance-subordinance relationship between the solitary patron and his several clients. However, a closer analysis suggests that a model allowing a greater number of options for both the patron and the client may be more fruitful in understanding certain aspects of social organization in the contemporary world. Furthermore, it may be useful and stimulating to substitute other types of units—such as nations—as position holders. Figure 7 shows the structural characteristics of a patron-client system in which many clients are attached to one patron and in which mobility is limited or nonexistent. It favors the development of mutually exclusive patron-client power blocks, in which any power or potential power inherent in the client group is funneled into and monopolized by the patron who uses it vis-à-vis the society at large, often in competition with other patrons in corresponding positions.

Figure 8, on the other hand, shows what occurs when alternative alliances are possible, that is, when clients look to several patrons for different benefits or resources, *or* when clients may shift from one patron to another even though each participates fully in only one relationship at a time. Wolf (1966a:18) has postulated that this type of patronage exists "where the institutional framework of society is far-flung and solidly entrenched. . . ."

If we accept that in any patron-client relationship both parties derive some benefits from the arrangement, we may be faced with the problem of determining which of the parties is to be labeled the "patron," and which the "client," and just what the two terms actually denote. Pragmatically, one of the two parties is usually bigger and stronger, that is, more powerful, and this one is usually *ipso facto* considered the patron. It is also usually assumed that the patron in any two-way relationship is dominant and ultimately controls the entire situation, and that the rights and obligations involved are *not* symmetrical. This tends to be less so the greater the number of alternative patrons available and the greater the freedom of the client to change his allegiance, as Wolf has pointed out (1966a:18).

Still another distinct problem arises when we attempt an analysis at the sociocultural, rather than at the individual or social-psychological, level. Since individual actors are influenced in their behavior not only by institutional but also by idiosyncratic and casual factors, as well as by the exigencies of the immediate situation, the interrelationships between two individuals acting as representatives of more complex units, in this case nations, may not be congruent with the structure of the interrelationships between the nations themselves. This fact suggests the difficulties inherent in any theoretical framework that assumes a rigid structural definition of the patron-client relationship. "Patrons" may sometimes behave as "clients," and vice versa, depending upon who wishes to accomplish what at the moment. Furthermore, "patron" nations may sometimes prefer their representatives to act as "clients" for diplomatic reasons, and even at the higher level the two parties may reverse their positions on occasion.

In figures 7 and 8, positions a, b, and c may be occupied by persons as well as by corporations or even states. Furthermore, states may sometimes be viewed as patrons by individual clients, and single private individuals have sometimes served as patrons for a state apparatus.

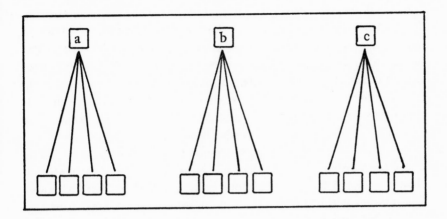

FIGURE 7.   SINGLE-PATRON RELATIONSHIPS LACKING MOBILITY

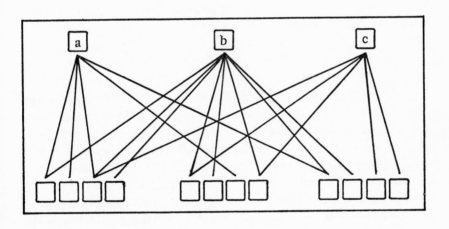

FIGURE 8.   MULTIPLE-PATRON OR MOBILE RELATIONSHIPS

Now, although it makes a difference how one defines such terms as "dependence," "force," "control," dominance," and "power," I would like to argue that the patron is just as dependent upon the continuance of the interrelationship as is the client. Furthermore, in order to preserve the association, either party may resort at times to the use of force, although it is also true that clients may do this effectively only when they band together, as in a strike, riot, or rebellion. Removal of the patron by assassination may also be considered an example of the use of force. Although it might be argued that this destroys the patron-client relationship and thus does not represent a means of control, it should be noted that it is only one particular patron who is removed. His position within the system will almost always be filled very soon by another patron, whose actions, at least in part, will reflect and respond to the wishes of the clients who eliminated his predecessor. "Patron," then, cannot be defined either in terms of dependence or in terms of force. In a smoothly working system, each party is so dependent upon the other that neither can pull out without serious damage to itself. Thus, a balance of power is struck, although the true nature of the ties between the parties may not be apparent to the casual observer; one party may appear to be disproportionately dominant when in fact it is held in check by its very dependence upon the apparently weaker party.

Following Adams (1967), I find it useful to think of power as the ability to control the environment of another party. In any case of true interdependence, each party *by definition* controls certain aspects or dimensions of the other's environment. It is in this context that I would like to explore further those patron-client relationships observable between sociocultural units, in this case, nations.

In order to illustrate my ideas, I will present data from the Dominican Republic to show how patronage-clientage relationships between the United States and that nation have been operating for the past one hundred years. During that century the United States has always been considered capable of exerting more force than has the Dominican Republic, although, as will be shown below, the Dominican Republic has also tried the use of force in an effort to control the United States, with a modicum of success. In the earlier portion of the century under consideration the United States was not so dependent upon the Dominican Republic as it has since become, and I believe I can show

how this fact has made a difference in the foreign policy of the United States government with regard to the Dominican Republic. I will consider two dimensions of interdependence: first, the economic, by which I mean the interchange of goods, services, and capital; and second, the political, by which I mean mutual protection from threats, either real or imagined, posed by outside powers. Starting with rather tenuous ties in 1869, the interdependence of these two nations has been continually reinforced and increased through feedback as each has reacted to strategies of the other. A brief look at the history of the Dominican Republic is necessary in order to put my argument into context.

HISTORICAL SKETCH OF THE DOMINICAN REPUBLIC

The Dominican Republic declared its independence from Spain in 1821, joining the short-lived Republic of Gran Colombia, but enjoyed only a brief moment of freedom before it was invaded, conquered, and occupied by the more powerful neighboring Republic of Haiti in 1822. Finally, after twenty-two years of what Dominicans still look back upon as unbearable oppression, independence was achieved by revolution in 1844; this date marks the *de facto* beginning of the Dominican Republic as a distinct national entity. During the earlier centuries of Spanish colonial rule the Dominican Republic had passed from its early status as the Pearl of the Antilles, a rich source of gold and silver, the location of the first sugar *ingenios* in the West Indies, the spot in which Columbus's son, Diego, chose to build his palace, and the site of the first university in the Americas, to a bedraggled, neglected, and woebegone ruin. Attempts to rebuild the sugar industry in the latter half of the eighteenth century did not restore the early importance and grandeur of Santo Domingo, as the area was known and is still known by many people.[1] During the years of obscurity, the Spanish colony had provided meat and hides to the neighboring rich French sugar colony of St. Dominigue in return for foodstuffs not grown on her own soil. The French slaves' kitchen gardens provided a surplus that was carried across the border in an active commerce. The bulk of economic exchange seems to have taken place with what is now Haiti. Although Dominicans will hotly deny it, many fundamental cultural similarities still persist between the countries at the folk level in such items as foods, agricultural techniques, folklore, religious beliefs, handicrafts, dress, and motor habits.

Following independence in 1844, the Dominican Republic found itself in difficult straits; it had few exportable products and was also incapable of supplying its own foodstuffs and other necessities of life such as clothing and tools. The country had long been informally divided into several sections, generally following natural ecological zones, each of which had been traditionally ruled by a local strongman or petty chief known as a caudillo. The ports of Puerto Plata and Monte Cristi in the north were the principal gateways to the outside world, the capital city of Santo Domingo ranking but third in volume of trade. The predominance of the first two is explained by the fact that they led to the rich Cibao region, which, although poor in an absolute sense, nevertheless has long been the richest agricultural area in the entire country. Tobacco, cacao, and coffee are still important there today, and in the early days of the independence these crops were relatively more important than now because they were virtually the only marketable exports for the nation as a whole, aside from the cattle trade with Haiti. Flowing into the country through these ports were supplies of cotton goods, food items such as flour, rice, and vegetables, and tools, especially iron implements, including machetes, knives, hoes, and saws. Foreign merchants, as well as some Dominicans, flocked to these ports, and there and in Santiago, the primary city of the Cibao region, they became wealthy. Many of the most important contemporary families trace their ancestry from these merchants arriving in the 1820s and afterward from Spain, Venezuela, France, Germany, England, and later Lebanon and other Middle Eastern countries.

The nearness of St. Thomas, a free port in the then-Danish Virgin Islands, contributed to the trade, for European and American goods could be purchased inexpensively from the merchants in that island, smuggled into the Dominican Republic, and sold at high profits. Records show that Santo Domingo (the name then used for the entire country) was one of the primary buyers of goods from Santómas, as this port is frequently termed by natives of the Caribbean.[2]

Although the Dominican government attempted to levy duties on goods imported through its customs houses, there were always difficulties in the actual collection, as well as in the fact that many items were smuggled across the Haitian border. Whoever controlled the customs houses controlled virtually the only source of revenue the entire country had at its disposal, since there were no other taxes of any great importance during the early years of the republic, nor until well into the twentieth century. Thus there were constant struggles over control of the customs houses between those who occupied the offices of the national government in Santo Domingo and the petty chieftains, many of whom are best described as professional revolutionaries, willing to hire themselves out to anyone for the proper price.

The history of the Dominican Republic from 1869 through the military occupation and indeed up to the present time is spotted with tales of smugglers, revolutionaries, bandits, and guerrillas, and the economic and political aspects of these activities have been closely intertwined.

In 1869 the Dominican Republic first issued bonds to secure money to pay its foreign debts and to pay the expenses of the government and maintain the country. In this early period almost all of the bonds were issued to Europeans. As early as 1871 some Dominicans requested annexation by the United States, believing this to be one solution to the country's insecurity and poverty. The proposal was defeated by one vote after a lengthy debate in the United States Senate. After that time, the United States had virtually no economic interests in the Dominican Republic, and apparently felt that annexation would create more problems than advantages by virtue of the country's poverty and its racial composition.[3] In 1888 the Dominicans consolidated all of their debts and secured a major loan through Dutch bankers in order to repay them. It was intended that the customs receipts be utilized to pay their obligations on this debt. However, the situation worsened as new sets of governmental officials took power, took their cuts from the revenues, were then unable to pay their local payrolls, and lost control to a newer set of officials, who repeated the same process. The various European creditors became increasingly more concerned as they failed to secure payment, and their countries put diplomatic pressure upon the Dominican government, some even sending warships as threatening gestures. In 1892 an American company assumed the debt owed to the Dutch, an action that relieved the United States of this particular threat of European intervention in American waters.

In 1877 the first U.S. sugar concern began operating in the Republic. Within a very few years it became apparent that the climate, soils, and labor supply were optimal for the growing and harvesting of cane. Furthermore, if enough labor could not be secured locally, workers could be brought at low wages from the surrounding British, French, and Dutch islands, as well as from Haiti. By 1904, when the United States first seized a Dominican customs house in order to force payments of debts to its citizens, the United States had economic interests in the Republic that could not be discounted, even though they were still minute compared to those to be realized later. Of the enormous sugar interests, 85 to 90 percent were in American hands; there were also a railroad, utility companies, some lumbering, mining, and growing of hemp, and the United Fruit Company had begun a banana plantation on the north coast at Sosua. Furthermore, a U.S. steamship company had a complete monopoly on traffic between the Dominican Republic and the United States and enjoyed benefits in terms of wharfage fees unavailable to other foreign or domestic shipping lines. Local political disturbances were now a distinct threat to U.S. life and property, and as such could not be tolerated. As Theodore Roosevelt said on February 4, 1905, before Congress in a speech submitting a protocol of an agreement between the United States and the Dominican Republic that provided for the disbursement by the United States of the customs revenues of the Dominican Republic:

> The chronic disorders prevailing in Santo Domingo have, moreover, become exceedingly dangerous to the interests of Americans holding property in that country. Constant complaints have been received of the injuries and inconveniences to which they have been subjected. As an evidence of the increasing aggravation of conditions, the fact may be mentioned that about a year ago, the American railway, which had previously been exempt from such attacks was seized, its tracks torn up, and a station destroyed by a revolutionary band (Roosevelt 1910:255).

By the early part of the twentieth century, military and political concerns also loomed large. It is true that the United States, by acquiring control over Cuba and Puerto Rico in 1898, had less interest than formerly in acquiring a coaling station and a naval base in the Dominican Republic. By 1905, however, the United States had discovered that Guantanamo Bay, leased under the Platt Amendment, was neither as big nor as deep as Samana Bay and that the latter controlled the more-frequented Mona passage, lying closer to and facing Europe.

It is clear from State Department documents in the National Archives in Washington that the United States was becoming increasingly concerned about European, especially German, hegemony in the Caribbean. The Panama Canal site had finally been settled upon, and the United States was determined to protect it and keep it out of European hands at all costs. In 1904 the public debt of the Dominican Republic had reached almost $32.3 million, of which about $22 million was owed to European creditors and the rest to U.S. citizens. Because at that time there were no governmental loans or other forms of bilateral assistance between nations, all of these loans had been made by private individuals or corporations.

Roosevelt's move to take over the customs houses in the Dominican Republic was motivated in part by the Venezuelan Affair of 1902 and 1903. Eleven foreign countries to whose citizens Venezuela owed debts became incensed over that country's failure to pay, and finally Germany and Great Britain blockaded the country in order to force the president to come to terms. There was a public outcry in the United States against this blockade by non-American powers, and when in 1904 and 1905 the Dominican Republic fell into similar desperate straits, Roosevelt announced his corollary to the Monroe Doctrine—that the United States should regulate Latin American affairs in relation to Europe.

All of the above are well-known facts of history, but it is not always clear that there were systemic processes in operation by means of which the United States found itself more closely embroiled in a web of interrelationships from which it could no longer extricate itself even if that should have been considered desirable. As Roosevelt himself stated in the same address referred to above, "under the Monroe Doctrine it [the United States] cannot see any European power seize and permanently occupy the territory of one of these republics; and yet such seizure of territory, disguised or undisguised, may eventually offer the only way in which the power in question can collect any debts, unless there is interference on the part of the United States."

In addition to the United States' fear of European aggrandizement in the Americas were the increasing monetary considerations noted above. The two worked together perfectly, in that in order to avoid the Dominican Republic's seeking further European funds, the United States encouraged American investors to put more money into that country. Reciprocally, the more control the U.S. exerted, the more willing were private individuals to invest their funds. And of course, the more money that was invested in the country, the greater the interest of the United States in its internal affairs, and so on.

This leads us to the consideration of another aspect of the situation not commonly referred to in standard U.S. or Dominican histories. I have referred to smuggling as a constant accompaniment of revolutionary activity in the Dominican Republic. Because duties on imports were the only means of securing money to pay government expenses and repay loans, once the United States took over the control of the customs houses it also had to control smuggling, which lowered the revenues. For this purpose the United States developed a Frontier Guard that patrolled the Haitian border and, with the aid of cutters and U.S. war vessels, the northern coastline. This situation was intolerable to the merchants, who then were forced to pay higher duties (or to pay duties for the first time), and especially to the local chieftains and their followers, who had derived their entire way of life either from smuggling itself or from protecting smugglers from government forces.

It should be remembered that any group holding the reins of government tried to put down smuggling in order to secure higher revenues for itself. This meant that the local chieftains were almost continually at war with the central government, changing their loyalties to *individuals* as often as necessary in order to keep up with changes in the Presidential Palace at Santo Domingo. When the United States applied force to prevent smuggling, the local chieftains enlarged their raiding efforts to include U.S. targets. Guerrilla activities were frequently touted as being anti-American, emphasizing their ideological aspect.[4] It is true that they were this, but the underlying economic factors behind these activities seem more relevant for explanation. The constant harassment of Dominican and U.S. government forces, including the assassination of several customs employees, was finally brought under control in the northern part of the country by a concentration of U.S. gunboats and the Frontier Guard. Somewhat later, during the U.S. military occupation of 1916–24, a similar type of raiding occurred in the southern sugar-growing area. Here guerrilla activities were most frequently attributed to "bandits," though it is clear from the records that anti-American feelings were also involved. In fact, it is difficult to separate the patriotic from the economic dimension during either period of guerrilla activity.

188

The continual revolutionary guerrilla warfare eventually led the United States to invade the Dominican Republic and establish a military occupation with the assistance of the U.S. Marine Corps. The American flag flew over the Dominican Republic from 1916 through 1922. From 1922 until 1924 a provisional government, carefully selected and supervised by the United States, was in nominal power. Following a brief six-year term under Horacio Vásquez, a new president, Rafael Leonidas Trujillo Molina, was elected.

State Department documents, including letters from U.S. officials in the Dominican Republic during the period when Trujillo first seized power, reveal that the consular and other diplomatic representatives fully realized the nature of Trujillo's intended rule. Some of the letters specifically warned that he would become a dictator, that his power would be totalitarian, enforced by a reign of blood and terror. Nevertheless, the conclusion is inescapable that the United States felt helpless to do anything but look the other way as Trujillo, trained by U.S. military forces, tailored the fabric of Dominican society to suit his own purposes. His purposes happened to coincide with U.S. purposes and to a large extent with the continued economic development of the country. Even though the United States disliked and disapproved of his methods, it soon became clear that Trujillo could maintain peace and would continue to collect revenues, repay the nation's debts, and protect foreign (especially U.S.) interests.

During the 1930s, as the war in Europe progressed, there was a period during which the United States feared German infiltration in the Dominican Republic. It appears that Trujillo temporarily flirted with the idea of backing Germany, but in the long run he came out clearly and strongly as a partisan of the Allies. This too was in the interest of the United States and fitted in with her short-term and long-range goals.

During the Era of Trujillo the ties were drawn even closer by efforts of the dictator, who paid lobbyists working on his behalf in Washington and lavishly entertained, gave gifts, and paid stipends to American senators, newpapermen, and others who could promote his image in the United States. This situation presents a double patronage-clientage relationship combining the elements discussed earlier. We must consider patronage in relation to the Dominican Republic and the United States at one level and, at another level, Trujillo and various individuals within the United States. American investors were increasingly drawn into the country by its new stability and special inducements in the transfer of profits and exemptions from taxation and import duties on equipment.

At the end of the Era, besides Grace Company, Alcoa, and South Porto Rico Sugar, the Grenada Company, a United Fruit subsidiary, was growing bananas and making plans for citrus. Three foreign banks were operating: the Royal Bank of Canada, the Bank of Nova Scotia, and the First National City Bank of New York. The International Hotels Corporation, a subsidiary of Pan American Airways, had bought two luxury hotels from the government for $9 million (Logan 1968: 192). Only those foreigners of whom Trujillo approved retained their economic interests during his regime. At the time of his downfall he owned all of the formerly foreign-owned sugar mills with the exception of the largest holding in the country, that known as La Romana, a subsidiary of the South Porto Rico Sugar Company, and the three mills owned by the Vicini family, Italian immigrants of the nineteenth century.

By 1961, when Trujillo, who had become the world's most publicized remaining symbol of oppression, was assassinated by some of his own compatriots, the interrelationship between the United States and the Dominican Republic had become so closely interwoven that Trujillo himself no longer mattered to the larger country. The important thing was to maintain the status quo created during the lengthy period dating from before the Customs Receivership (1907) and continuing with little interruption for almost fifty years. Between the United States and the Dominican Republic a patron-client block had been established that served to further and protect the common interests of the Dominican upper classes and the U.S. government.[5] In other words, what was good for the "establishment" in the Dominican Republic was also good for the United States, and succeeding events indicate that U.S. policy has consistently favored the same elements and institutions backed by Trujillo and all other dictators and caudillos before him. As the political scientist Wiarda (1967:6) has said of the period 1965–67, "It is significant that the strongest, most cohesive, and best organized groups in Dominican politics—the armed forces, and the business-professional-landowning elite, and the Church were those sectors which have the longest traditions in the society. . . ."

All accounts of the United States' intervention in the crisis of 1965, regardless of the political stance of the authors, indicate that the United States intervened in order to protect its own political interests. The economic aspect, although still something to be considered, had faded before the spectre of possible increased Soviet influence in this hemisphere. The threat of "another Cuba" with possible ultimate danger to the American mainland itself seems to have been the primary motivating factor. The tiny Dominican Republic, through its strategic position, was able to wield a kind of power over the United States by forcing that country to act. As former ambassador Martin indicated (1966:370), the threat of the Bosch government to secure a loan for internal development in Europe was also a factor, though probably a secondary one, in the 1965 intervention.

A CASE HISTORY OF CONTEMPORARY PATRONAGE RELATIONS

The raw data from which we construct patronage models with nations as units nevertheless stem from observations of people and their actions. This sometimes leads the observer to confuse his levels of analysis, but it need not if one recognizes the problem and is rigorous in its treatment.

During a fourteen-month field session in the Dominican Republic I collected numerous examples of the ways in which the interests of the United States were identified with those of various segments of Dominican society. A more complete analysis of these interrelationships must await a future, and longer, treatise. With a view toward clarifying the nature of the system as it exists today and as I have attempted to describe it in outline form at the international level above, I shall describe one particular concrete structure and how it operates to maintain itself, the status quo of Dominican society, and U.S. interests.

This institution is known locally as the Asociación para el Desarrollo (Development Association). In 1967 it comprised twenty-two prominent business and professional men in Santiago de los Caballeros, the second largest city in the Dominican Republic, long known as the seat of the "oligarchy" and the foremost trading center of the rich Cibao area. The members are bound together by ties of affinity and consanguinity, local affiliation, class consciousness, and mutual interests (figure 9). As in the *panelinha* organization described by Leeds (1964) in Brazil, the members represent different specific economic interests of the country, and because of multiple-faceted careers, one person may often represent several interests. Thus one man is a medical doctor, a farmer, president of a rum factory, and a stockholder in various manufacturing enterprises; another has a degree in engineering, owns some of the most extensive rice lands in the country, and has interests in several factories and other businesses. Commerce is frequently combined with industry, and professional degrees are sought as a symbol of class status and a goal to strive for educationally, even though the profession may never be practiced. All together, the members of the Asociación represent every basic economic pursuit in the Cibao region. They include a bank president, dean of the business school at the local university, a member of the National Monetary Council (Junta Monetaria,) and representatives of the national and private tobacco industries, dairying, rice growing, construction, and rum manufacturing. Most own stock in several enterprises. They are adherents to several different political parties, although their allegiance to the present system of government is unquestioned.

Since the Asociación was formed in 1962 with only twelve members, it has been instrumental in fomenting the establishment of a new Dominican bank, a savings and loan association, and a new university that emphasizes the training of teachers, engineers, nurses, social workers, and businessmen (all nontraditional for Latin American universities). Another Asociación project has been the creation of an agricultural school offering training at the secondary level. Finally, some members of the group, through their contacts both within the Asociación and with its outside associates, have opened a tomato-paste plant, a can factory (to provide cans for the tomato paste), a finance company, and several other smaller enterprises.

One may ask wherein lies the element of patronage, and how this relates to the international sphere of operations. The funds for financing these enterprises have come in part from the pockets of the members of the group itself, all wealthy men. However, these contributions are thought of as "seed money" with which to obtain grants from such foreign or supra-Dominican concerns as the Ford Foundation, AID, the World Bank, and international consortiums such as ADELA.[6] The

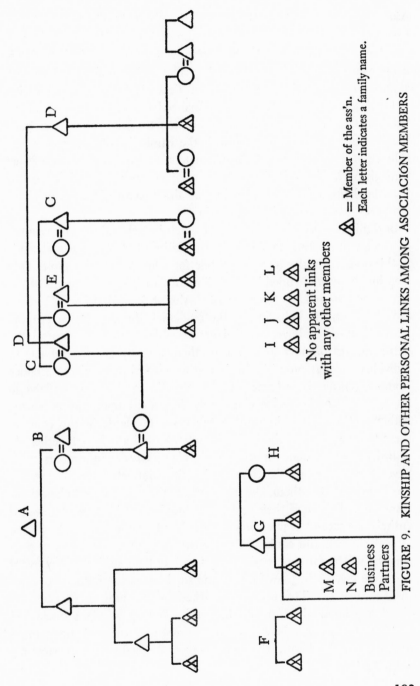

FIGURE 9. KINSHIP AND OTHER PERSONAL LINKS AMONG ASOCIACIÓN MEMBERS

193

Asociación has used the idiom and the social behavior accompanying patronage systems in raising money and moral support [7] for its schemes.

Let us examine one particular enterprise to show some of the inter-relationships of which I am speaking. The agricultural school, at first almost totally staffed by teachers from Texas A & M on contract with AID, also includes a research unit financed by the Ford Foundation. Some of the funds for both the school and the laboratory come from the Dominican government through the Ministries of Agriculture and Education, but these too derive ultimately, at least in part, from loans through AID. All of the funds, from whatever source, are channeled to the school *through* the Asociación, and the director of the school himself never sees any complete accounting.

Beginning in the early 1960s the research branch published a number of studies purporting to show the suitability of the agricultural lands in this northern valley of the Republic for different kinds of crops. One crop highly recommended by the laboratory was the pear tomato of the type used for making tomato paste. Almost immediately AID made available a loan to help finance the modern half-million-dollar canning plant mentioned above. This plant was able virtually to control the entire tomato production of the northern area by giving contracts to individual farmers promising to buy at a specified price all the produce from a given number of acres of land. No other market was available to the growers, so they were completely dependent upon the company. Although there were three other tomato-paste plants in the country, these too operated on the basis of contracts, and all three together absorbed much less than the single large plant. Grower informants could never agree about the bases on which the contracts were awarded. It was apparent to them, however, that those who complained of company policies had their acreages reduced or their contracts revoked entirely the second year of production. The tomatoes had to be picked at peak ripeness and could not be bruised, scarred, or otherwise in poor condition. The farmers were required to buy their seed from the plant and were given schedules for planting so as to space production to the plant's capacity.[8] The tomatoes, packed by the growers in crates of about one hundred pounds each, were picked up by plant trucks and taken to the plant, where they were sorted and weighed; the farmers then were credited with what the company decided was the correct net poundage.

A large part of the total production of tomato paste was destined for the U.S. market, having been contracted for by Stokely Van Camp. The prices paid by that company were determined through competitive nego-tiations, and the Dominican company met this by keeping down the prices they paid for tomatoes while at the same time maintaining local selling prices for paste at almost the same level as the imported product. The company claimed it had to do this in order to stay in business. However, a prospectus made by the company officers showed an ex-pected income of 129 percent over the original investment in the third year of operation. They expected to clear $750,185 in that year and to have recovered the entire original investment. They offered their stock-holders the prospect of dividends of 10 percent on their investment the first year, 20 percent the second year, and 25 percent the third year.[9]

Another project of the research laboratory at the agricultural school was the improvement of locally grown rice. Although rice has been an important crop in this area for about sixty years, the yields first increased and then gradually declined over the last thirty or forty years. A major study financed and carried out through the OAS from 1965 to 1967 showed that the soils in this northwestern part of the Republic had be-come highly saline through improper drainage and poorly maintained irrigation networks. The conclusions were twofold: first, the area desperately needed a revamping of the irrigation system and construc-tion of a series of dams to control the flow of water in the river Yaque del Norte, which together with the Mao feeds the canals in this area; and second, new rice hybrids and more modern methods of cultivation could increase yields even under present circumstances. Through the agricultural school, seed for the new rice was made available for pur-chase by Dominican farmers, and demonstration plots were planted by the school to illustrate its advantages. Most of those participating in the demonstrations were the large farmers, several either members of the Asociación or relatives of its members.

In the early 1970s work began on the first hydroelectric dam in the Dominican Republic, financed by loans from AID and the Inter-national Development Bank. A perusal of the plans clearly showed me that the major benefits will accrue to these same large landholders (Gonzalez: in press).

Finally, the young men being graduated from the agricultural school itself will form a core of trained agrotechnicians. Already they are commanding salaries of $200 to $300 per month, which is far beyond what the average high school graduate can expect to receive in the Dominican Republic. They are currently being employed by the Dominican government and by the larger farmers to act as foremen and managers of their farms. Few of them ever return to farming their own lands or those of their fathers. Some of the better students have gone on to higher education in agronomy at Texas A & M.

It might be expected that the Asociación in some way controls the appointments to the 180 openings for students, all of whom are completely supported for the three-year course. Clearly, these positions would make very useful rewards for favorites of the men in the Asociación. However, according to the director of the school, the high standards of scholarship required for entrance to the school are rigidly upheld. My informant said that in fact senators, prominent businesmen, farmers, and others do come frequently to complain that their sons or relatives or friends did not obtain an appointment. The Asociación refrains from making excuses to these people, leaving the entire matter to the American director. Thus the Asociación members can honestly tell their clients that they themselves have no power over the selection, and the American, since he has no personal obligations to individuals who might be seeking admission, can be severe in upholding the standards. As the director pointed out, should entrance standards slip, the chances for obtaining continued support from Ford and AID might be jeopardized; thus it is important that patronage obligations not be allowed to destroy the system itself.

There is no resident doctor or nurse at the school, but there is a local physician with whom the school board has an arrangement. This man is paid a monthly sum to treat sick students. The physician so employed at a very good fee is one of the two M.D.'s on the Asociación membership roster (the other one is not practicing medicine at all).

A recent movement is urging the expansion of the school to include two collegiate years. The primary instigators are the members of the Asociación; at the time this fieldwork was being done they had secured the interest of the two highest AID officials in the Dominican Republic. According to the director of the school (who was strongly opposed to the new plan), the school was already laboring under the difficulty of obtaining qualified teachers and had too many students for its present facilities, too small a working budget, too little land for demonstration purposes, and so forth. The new proposal would require expansion of the school's physical facilities, meaning further construction, more land, and a larger working budget. Presumably, increased expansion would continue to be handled, as have all other matters, through the Asociación. The sum being mentioned for the expansion was $2 million. According to both the director and my own observations, there were serious deficiencies in the original school construction: after five years many walls were severely cracked, most roofs leaked, the plumbing system was inadequate for the number of persons using it, and so on. The director expressed concern that the original grant of $500,000 for building costs had been misused. However, he said that when he suggested this to the director of AID the latter became angry, declaring that he should not doubt the honesty of the Asociación and its members, from whom AID could not possibly demand an audit without insulting them.

This description would not be complete without mention of the manner in which the school lands were acquired. During the Trujillo regime a local strongman, appointed and backed by Trujillo, confiscated or bought at low prices over 1,000 acres of choice agricultural land just outside the city of Santiago. Upon Trujillo's death a dispute arose between some of the original landowners or their heirs and the strongman himself as to the legal ownership of these lands. According to informants, members of the Asociación made bargains with both sides, agreeing to purchase the lands from the winners once the courts made a decision. Then, through influence in the right places, the case was held up in the courts, and to this day no final decision has been made. In the meantime, the Asociación has used the lands by turning them over to the agricultural school that today stands on the sites. Informants suggest that eventually the lands will simply be deeded to the school when most of the original contenders have died and the public has lost interest in the case.

Thus we see that farming, marketing, industry, and education are all closely united in an interlocking system of relationships. Each of the enterprises and institutions created by or through the influence of the Asociación could be analyzed in a similar fashion, and furthermore, several of these enterprises are themselves interrelated (as is the can company, a subsidiary of American Can Company, with the tomato-paste plant). Other American concerns are experimenting with large-scale industrial agriculture in the same northwestern area, growing pine-apples, cucumbers, sesame seed, and other items almost exclusively destined for U.S. markets.

The patronage system operates at all levels of complexity, but one nucleus of people *through whom* resources and other benefits flow from international sources to Dominican society is clearly the Asociación. I have tried to show these interrelationships in figure 10. This group of men, as *individuals*, but especially as a group, has power both within Dominican society itself and within the larger U.S.–Dominican patron-client bloc.

What are the sources of their power in each of these spheres? Not only do they have tremendous combined financial resources upon which to draw, but they have access to probably every source of information available in the Republic about existing conditions and coming trends. Many of them have influential relatives in the capital and in govern-mental circles. The Dominican ambassador to the United States in 1969 was a brother-in-law of one of the most active members. In rela-tion to the U.S.–Dominican sphere, it should be noted that most of the members speak English fluently, many were educated in the United States, and all engage in a life style thoroughly familiar to representa-tives of U.S. diplomatic and financial interests. That is, they entertain, dress, speak, and relax in an almost-American way, and their wives, also English-speakers, relate well to the U.S. women living in the country. Americans, in short, feel at ease with them, and easily confuse this feel-ing of well-being with a belief in the honesty, intelligence, capabilities, and political philosophy of the members of this group. On more than one occasion I have been told by Dominicans of this class, even of this group, that they never had difficulty "pulling the wool over the eyes" of American officials. Furthermore, and most important, their positions are enhanced and reinforced in each sphere of operation as a *result* of the status and prestige they are perceived to hold in the other.

Who, then, are the patrons, and who are the clients? Both parties have much to gain from each other, and each has a kind of power over the other. Dominicans of this class often feel that the relationship at the national level is one-sided, and they tend to resent the United States at the same time that they cultivate some Americans for their own purposes. Many of the Dominican leaders, while cursing U.S. imperial-ism in public, have at the same time sought loans from that country,

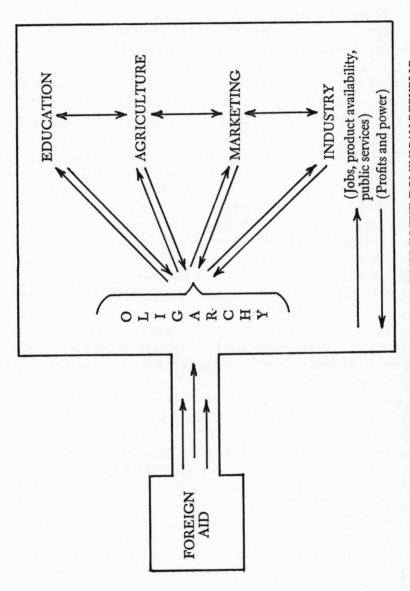

FIGURE 10: FLOW OF RESOURCES AND POWER IN THE DOMINICAN REPUBLIC

political intervention, and even outright annexation. There is also frequently a kind of ambivalence in the attitudes of individual Dominicans toward Americans. That is, they may stereotype Americans as being uncultured, avaricious, and stupid, but be personally friendly to individuals and fond of traveling and vacationing in the States.

This ambivalence is reciprocated. That is, resident and visiting Americans are frequently critical of what they believe to be character faults in Dominicans. They accuse them of dishonesty, graft, selfishness, lack of "culture," and conceit, among other things; yet they may relate perfectly well on an individual level. Indeed, some Americans believe that the members of the Dominican upper classes should be excluded from these criticisms. One young American woman told me that a certain Dominican gentleman was incapable of becoming inebriated because he was a member of the aristocracy! On the other hand, ironically enough, a relative of this man told me that the local aristocracy was generally disgusted with Americans who expect to be received among them on an equal social footing. As he put it, "No sabemos cuál pata puso ese huevo" (We don't know what duck laid this egg). (Although this is clearly a reference to the importance of family ties in determining social standing, it should be noted as an aside that the family trees of few of the so-called oligarchy can stand intensive perusal.) There is evidence from documents in the U.S. National Archives that official diplomatic Dominican-American affairs have been characterized by this ambivalence for some time.

Thus, in spite of the imponderable but clearly evident effects of one hundred years of American influence, cultural differences do remain. Ethnocentrism cannot be discounted in either of the two "parties" under consideration here. But it seemed to me in my observations that the Dominicans are more aware of the true nature of the system, and thus can better manipulate it to their advantage. For example, members of the Asociación, recognizing that Americans object to the principle of nepotism, purposely hide family connections when dealing with AID and State Department officials, yet consciously manipulate these same personal ties when operating within their own system.

Similarly, Dominicans have ways of avoiding the *appearance* of receiving graft while at the same time continuing to operate in terms of it. They have even turned this into a manipulatory device. AID has made large sums available for development projects that for some reason have remained idle. One informant, familiar with "palace" politics, said that the explanation for this was that for such projects the government would be required to put up matching funds and proposals would have to be sent for approval to AID. Since graft is virtually impossible under such conditions, the government prefers to use its own funds on purely Dominican projects over which AID has no control. The government officials and the businessmen providing the raw or building materials and services thus can get their customary and traditional cuts. I asked a high-ranking AID official whether this might be true. He replied that he himself had recently begun to wonder whether such an explanation might not account for the unused credits, which he assured me did exist.

ANALYSIS

In the preceding section I have tried to show how patron-client relationships between *representatives* of two national units nevertheless operate in terms of the standard idiom at the *interpersonal* level. So long as the local representatives of nations have any authority to grant or receive favors vis-à-vis the other party, the prevailing idiom will be important insofar as it determines their behavior. At another level, however, major policy orientations are completely out of the hands of individuals on either side, and can be best understood without recourse to the actions of individuals. In other words, an analysis of a system based only upon the use of case histories describing interpersonal relationships is likely to suffer from a confusion between psychology and sociology. Other social scientists, concentrating upon specific events or the behavior of specific people, have noted the apparent chaos obtaining in the Dominican Republic. There is, furthermore, a distinct tendency to view the United States and the Dominican Republic as independent volitional actors, a perspective that also leads to the "chaos" conclusion. For example, quoting Wiarda again, (1967:18):

. . . . the influence of the U.S. in Dominican affairs . . . has been enormous . . . but this influence has at times seemed inconsistent and uncoordinated. For a long time the U.S. bolstered the Trujillo dictatorship but later helped destroy it; afterwards the

U.S. worked for the establishment of a development-oriented constitutional democracy, such as that of Bosch; but some influential elements within the Embassy and in the United States favored an alternative government. At the time the revolution broke out, the United States was extremely close to the unpopular government of Reid Cabral and had maintained few ties with the dominant political party in the country.

So long as we continue to look at the United States and the Dominican Republic as mutually closed political systems, we will never find a way through this apparent maze of inconsistency and contradiction. Furthermore, this type of material alone will never give us a thorough understanding of the processes now operating in the Dominican Republic.

I suggest the following complementary analysis. We are dealing with the processes of development, among other things. From an evolutionary point of view, those structures or mechanisms that increase the adaptation of the whole system to its environment have positive survival value. And of course, for any given underdeveloped country, there are many development program possibilities, depending upon the values given to diverse objectives and to various policy instruments. It is a mistake, however, to assume that the United States has a wide range of choice as to which types of development programs may be selected for support. I suggest that the United States has very little choice owing to the fact that it is itself a part of a larger system embracing elements of both nations. Therefore—regardless of what individual well-meaning officials of AID, basing their conclusions upon nonpolitical factors such as social scientific surveys, rational thought, and good will, may suggest—ultimately the United States in this, as in other countries where the same relationships exist, will continue to support the programs and general policy backed by the oligarchical and establishment groups that have long been in power. Such programs are of a sort that has in the past served to improve and increase the adjustment of the Dominican Republic as a nation to the world industrial system, or at least to that system as it is represented in this hemisphere.

The history of the country during this century is one of continual development up to 1961. Under early U.S. influence it increased its average per capita income and improved or built public roads and highways, schools, markets, hospitals, and other such facilities. Literacy and general health rose in response to these measures. The Trujillo regime continued to promote development. Of course, population expansion occurred also, and here, as in many other areas of the world, the resultant increase has partially eclipsed the effects of economic development. Most observers agree that the lot of the Dominican masses is today not good, and there is little to suggest that it will soon improve. Indeed, the GNP increased only 3 percent between 1966 and 1967 and the per capita income actually decreased during the same period.

Yet between June 30, 1966, and November 30, 1967, a total of $79.9 million was made available through AID alone for development in the Dominican Republic (figures published in the *Listin Diario*, November 23, 1967, quoting Ambassador John Crimmins in a public speech). Although the published budget expenditures were conveniently grouped into six large categories, the list of activities and institutions actually receiving some help from AID in the Dominican Republic during this period is unbelievably large. The Banco Agricola (Agricultural Bank), Desarrollo de la Comunidad (Community Development), Plan de Emergencia (Emergency Plan), Mejoramiento Urbano de Santo Domingo (Improvement of the City of Santo Domingo), Nutrition Programs, and Training and Personnel are the general topics or categories affected by the funding. However, my research revealed assistance rendered in such diverse areas as agrarian reform, school construction, public water faucets and sewers, financing of large and small businesses and industry, labor unions, producers' cooperatives, leadership training schools, community-based improvement associations, scholarships to study in the United States, teacher-improvement at all levels, including college teaching, governmental administration in offices of all types, research projects on various aspects of Dominican culture, radio stations, tourist facilities, and on and on. Indeed, I found it difficult to find any area of Dominican life that was not touched in some way by the presence of the United States and at least partially dependent upon U.S. dollars. Tables 3 and 4 give some idea of the importance of foreign money to the country as a whole. In addition to AID, the Peace Corps made a large contribution to these and other facets of the Dominican scene, including the Boy Scouts and Girl Scouts,[10] birth control clinics, reforestation projects, and many others. The police and military bodies were heavily subsidized through grants for equipment and training of personnel. Finally, private U.S. organizations—CARE, various churches, and the League of Women Voters, among others—were involved in the general development effort.

TABLE 3

SUGAR PRODUCTION IN THE DOMINICAN REPUBLIC

Year	Short Tons (thousands)	Ownership (percent)
1881	6.4	
1889	25.0	90 U.S. capital
1911	95.0	10 Dominican, Canadian, Italian
1926	400.0	
1935	500.0	
1956	750.0	55 Trujillo
1960	1100.0	20 La Romana (U.S.)
		5 Vicini (Dom.-Ital. family)
		20 Seven independent growers (Dominican)
1967	1000.0	Same as above except that Dominican State now owns Trujillo interests.

Sugar investments over the years have increased, but note change in ownership during Trujillo regime. From: Bureau of American Republics, 1892; Coverdale and Colpitts, 1958; and U.S. State Department Records in National Archives, Washington, D.C., RG 38, 839.61351/67.

Certainly, at first blush, all of this sounds as though things should be going well for the country and for the United States' interests there. But there are some indications that problems may lie ahead. In one unpublished study done by an American scientist on the possibility of stimulating a cattle industry, the author says the following:

A developing country with serious immediate economic problems may have to concentrate much of its development assistance on the most progressive producers, even though it might not otherwise prefer to do so. Programs for assisting a country's most backward producers probably are more nearly a welfare expenditure than a development investment, and hardly can be made self-financing under existing cost-price conditions (Bilkey 1965:7).

The same writer, however, concludes his analysis by pointing out that any program aimed at helping only the most advanced producers would be undesirable in the long run both socially and politically, and eventually economically should the advanced producers use their relatively improved position to restrain the progress of the country's most backward producers.

Another writer points out:

> But the less developed the country, the more does the efficacy of planning depend on non-economic factors. Before concentrating on the purely economic factors, attention should be given to those social and organizational characteristics of the economy which have been critically important in impeding growth (Meier 1966:293).

Meier goes on to point out that frequently political interests in the developing countries themselves have run counter to the economic rationale of a particular development plan. Thus, some political parties have been too concerned with preventing a loss in social status or political power for certain groups in the society at the expense of effective implementation of a development plan.

TABLE 4

U.S. AID TO THE DOMINICAN REPUBLIC

Year	Amount of Aid ($ million)
Up to 1962	2.1
1962	26.0
1963	29.6
1964	0
1965	52.9
1966	93.9 [a]

[a] Total foreign aid for 1966 (*all* sources) $134.5 million.

Wiarda (1967:4), referring specifically to the Dominican Republic, backs up this point:

> When the Bosch government attempted to govern for the benefit of the poor, forgotten, or ignored sectors and to integrate these

groups into the national life while ignoring or curtailing the values or authority of vested interests, it met with the concerted opposition of the more traditional elements.

In conclusion, I would like to suggest that the type of patron-client relationship that has been a successful agent of development in the past no longer has adaptive value in the modern world. The system, highly specialized and highly adapted to the expanding industrial complex of the nineteenth and early twentieth centuries, may prove to retard future development in countries such as the Dominican Republic. Figures available on gross national product, per capita income, value of exports, etc., for the years since Trujillo's death (1961) do not indicate an increasing rate of growth (figure 11). On the contrary, there have been regressions in some years, and the overall picture is one of stagnation.

It serves nothing to blame these regressions upon revolutionary activity, riots, deficiencies of the Dominican character, and so on, as has so often been done in the popular press and even sometimes in more scholarly publications. On the other hand, the more scientific perspective would be to question why these activities now take place so frequently and with such regularity. The fact that alternative economic and political systems exist in the world, and the fact that they can make their impact felt, is certainly something we cannot ignore, and the fact that, in spite of massive amounts of U.S. aid money, discontent continues to grow also indicates disturbance in the system. Ideological pressures do not exist in a vacuum. They form an integral, but rarely determining, element in the sociocultural system itself. As with the "revolutionary" activity in the Dominican Republic during the nineteenth century, ideology is only the most visible superstructure, the economic and political bases often going unnoticed. Although the time period is still too short to be certain, it may be that the Dominican Republic is currently undergoing a struggle that will present the seesaw effect apparent in the nineteenth century history of that country. "Progression" and "regression" may alternate with each other for a time, thus precluding any real advance until new structural arrangements allow a way out of the impasse.

I would like to close by presenting the idea that the patron-client relationship as it has existed in the recent past between larger and

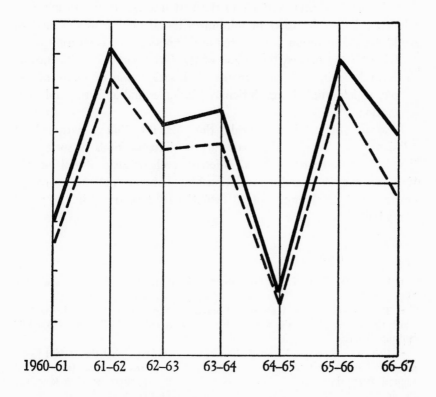

| 1960–61 | 61–62 | 62–63 | 63–64 | 64–65 | 65–66 | 66–67 |

Total product ━━━━━━━

Per capita product ━ ━ ━ ━ ━ ━

FIGURE 11. RATE OF GROWTH OF GROSS DOMESTIC PRODUCT, DOMINICAN REPUBLIC, 1960–67 (*Annual growth rates—natural scale*). *Source: Economic Survey of Latin America, 1967,* Part 2:11-187 (1968).

smaller nations no longer has evolutionary potential. By this I mean that the system works *contrary* to the best interests of the society as a whole, and thus decreases or minimizes its adaptation to the modern world. This conclusion is suggested and supported by decreasing levels of living for the masses, the failure of the GNP and per capita income to expand significantly, and increased dissatisfaction of many of the people, which erupts in revolutionary ideologies and activities and mass emigration.

It seems worthwhile to consider the possibility that as patron-client relationships between individuals vary in different kinds of societies—that is, in societies operating at different levels of sociocultural integration—so may patron-client relationships between nations evolve as changes and development of an evolutionary type occur in the world as a whole.

NOTES

1. For a discussion of the early sugar industry in Santo Domingo see Ortiz 1947:254ff.

2. This appears to be a Hispanicized version of the English "Saint Thomas," in which the accent falls on the first syllable of the second word. True Spanish would be Santo Tomás.

3. It is clear from speeches made by senators at the time that the United States recognized the benefit of having a "home" source of sugar, coffee, tobacco, and tropical fruits, but that the development of these resources *at that time* was simply not worth it. See *Congressional Globe*, 42d Congress, 1st session, 1871.

4. One famous caudillo, Desiderio Arias, is even today eulogized as having been anti-American to his bitter end—assassination by Trujillo men in the early days of the dictatorship.

5. Note that the interests of *individual* Americans or U.S. corporations were not always protected, just as not all segments of Dominican society benefited by the arrangement.

6. ADELA (Association for Development in Latin America, Asociación para el Desarrollo de Latino-América) is a private multinational organization of 154 banks, industrial companies, and financial institutions in the United States, Europe, and Japan interested in promoting development in Latin America. It is also commonly known as the Adela Investment Co.

7. At the turn of the century the dispatches of the U.S. consular service in the D.R. repeatedly refer to the presence of U.S. war vessels in Dominican harbors as "moral support" for whatever government we were helping at the moment.

8. One veteran farmer, a prominent liberal who had a totally different point of view on development, pointed out to me that tomatoes can be planted as early as August, although the tomato plant directors specified they must be planted starting

about the first of October and running through March. My informant speculated that the reason for this restriction was that the company wished to control production, concentrating the crop at one time to assure an oversupply and thus forcing prices down. He suggested collusion between the agricultural school's research lab and the tomato plant owners because the studies made by the former also indicated that October was the optimal planting time. Because the plant contracted for tomatoes at a set price per hundred pounds, an oversupply would not be likely to force the price down in any given season. Presumably it might do so in a succeeding year, however, by increasing the competition among growers for the contracts that assured them a market. Depending upon one's particular viewpoint, this could be argued either way.

9. Dominican investors dislike putting their money into any enterprise which does not secure them dividends of at least 10 percent. This fact was noted to me over and over again by various investors. The risk element in the country is considered to be so high that any lesser rate is poor business, they feel.

10. I cannot help noting that the Ford Foundation rents a house, for use by their officials and guests, on the corner of two streets named "Boy Scouts" and "Cub Scouts," respectively!

9

On the Nonoccurrence
of Patronage in
San Miguel de Sema

WILLIAM T. STUART

Department of Anthropology
Lawrence University

INTRODUCTION

In contrast with most of the other case materials in this volume, my data, collected in the Colombian *municipio* of San Miguel de Sema,[1] suggest a relative unimportance of the institution of patronage-clientage —in both the immediate instrumental and the eleborated "affect" senses in which we use the terms. I shall argue that relatively few activities and their integration are in fact best understood by employing these terms. I maintain that several factors in the sociocultural field of San Miguel de Sema militate against a significant set of patron-client relations.

First, in the case of San Miguel there are few advantages either to potential patrons or to clients for becoming involved in such precarious matters as those implied by patronage relationships. Second, even if a patron-client system of relationships were to appear useful from someone's perspective, the logistic base for it is absent. Third, the necessary sources of flexibility in the local peasant adaptation are largely kinship ties and generalized reciprocities. One may thus appreciate the relative unimportance, unnecessity, and in any event, impotence of would-be patrons in the sociocultural domains within which the residents of San Miguel interact.

A brief review of the social history of the *municipio* of San Miguel, in addition to some important considerations of the scale and distribution of sociocultural variables, suggests that the people of San Miguel have worked out an effective adaptation gambit of a peculiar sort. I call this gambit "retreatist" peasantry because it obviates the need for and possibility of establishing a system of pervasive patron-client-broker relationships whether internal to San Miguel or between it and the outside world.[2]

SOCIAL HISTORY

The municipality of San Miguel de Sema lies in the western panhandle of the department of Boyacá, some one hundred air miles (more by road) north of Bogotá. It lies essentially at the northern end of the Sabana de Bogotá, in the eastern Andean cordillera of Colombia. The municipality has been a separate polity only since 1960.

For several centuries after the conquest, the locale today called San Miguel de Sema was part of the larger region called Sema, a word apparently indigenous to the area and of uncertain meaning. Sema lay along the north edge of the Laguna de Fúquene. In 1909, the village (*centro*) of San Miguel was founded and put under the jurisdiction of the municipality of Tinjacá.[3] Then in 1924, owing to the efforts of some wealthy hacendados in the area and that of the adjoining *municipio*, Chiquinquirá, San Miguel became incorporated as a part of Chiquinquirá. This arrangement lasted for thirty-six years, until 1960. The years under Chiquinquirá's aegis were apparently highlighted by the growing resentment of the San Miguel people toward their political overlords. Particular resentments were focused on the issue of taxation for which there seemed to be little visible return. This was a result of the Chiquinquirá government's lack of concern for San Miguel problems, especially those having to do with roads and schools.[4]

With the decline of the influence of locally resident and influential parties tied to the larger city, a sense of identity grew apace among the peasants who lived in the minifundia surrounding the *aldea* of San Miguel. Rather important, most of these persons were members of the same ecclesiastical parish, also called San Miguel. Thus the role of the local priest and the agency of the church figured prominently in this earlier social process of independence, and they continue to loom large in local politics and entrepreneurship in San Miguel de Sema.

By the time of municipal independence in 1960, the trend toward the breakup and sale of some of the once-grand fincas in the rich bottomland of San Miguel had accelerated. In the early days, most of the bottomland, which lay proximate to the Laguna de Fúquene, was called Sema. It appears initially to have been joined in a single large hacienda. More recently, the grandest finca appears to have been Cascadas, owned by the family of one of the governors of the department of Boyacá in the 1930s. Later Cascadas, once over 1,000 hectares in size and comprising virtually all of what is now Sirigay[5] *vereda*, has been subdivided into the three fincas of Colonia, Puerto Rico, and Chivava. In addition, other Cascadas land has been sold and in other manners transferred to minifundia and intermedia lands of Sirigay *vereda*. In the Hato Viejo *vereda*, which now adjoins that of Sirigay, the once-impressive La Compañía hacienda has also been parceled. Some of the highlands have become smaller peasant landholdings and intermedia. The bottomlands have been subdivided into the commercial, mechanized haciendas of Paicaquita and El Rocodo. The latter, for instance, is but one of some forty-five fincas throughout Colombia owned by one man, an absentee owner and outsider to the San Miguel area.

Such has been the pattern of land fragmentation in San Miguel. Its importance for us here is that the recent owners of the fincas are relatively unimportant in the social life of the *municipio*.

A number of factors, undoubtedly, affected this breakup of the once-grand haciendas. One factor frequently mentioned in the literature for Colombia in general, and Boyacá Department in particular, is "La Violencia," the fratricidal warring that took some 150,000 lives (by conservative estimate) between 1948 and 1962. For instance, Fals-Borda (1957:33) argues that the insecurity that was the result of La Violencia may have induced depopulation in the peasant areas of Boyacá. It does, indeed, seem at least possible that such a factor may have been associated with demographic alteration in one of two ways.

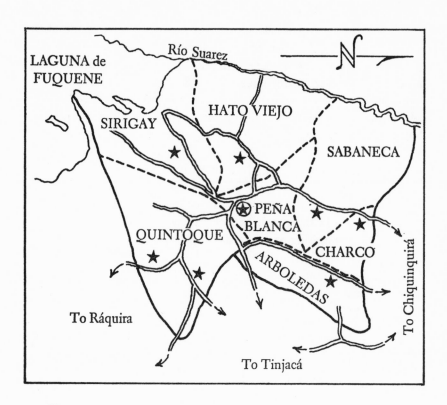

Key:

━━━━━ = unpaved roads of *municipio*

‑ ‑ ‑ ‑ ‑ = *vereda* boundaries

★ = *vereda* school

✪ = El Centro school

FIGURE 12. *MUNICIPIO* OF SAN MIGUEL (SCHOOLS AND ROADS)

First, La Violencia may have accelerated the breakup of "marginally productive and indefensible" fincas. Second, there may have been a flight from minifundia lands as well, as peasant refugees sought more secure places to live. The effects of such violence-induced emigration would probably have been to reduce land pressures. As plausible as such suggestions may be for other areas, they are not, I think, particularly germane for San Miguel de Sema, which was relatively well isolated, for very good reasons, from the violence.

Nonetheless, it must be admitted that low pressure on the land is characteristic of San Miguel; this is, I feel, the result of the operation of factors other than La Violencia. I shall consider some of them shortly.

By Colombian standards the *municipio* of San Miguel is a rather small polity. Its 1962 population was about 3,500. "El Centro," the central village, is laid out in the usual plaza form, and the surrounding countryside is divided into seven *veredas*. *Veredas* figure as important subdivisions of most Colombian municipalities. There are, however, some striking differences between the several *veredas* of San Miguel in terms of land tenure and size of holdings.

For convenience I shall discuss three general sorts of land parcel, the minifundia (five hectares or less in size), the intermedia (six to forty-nine hectares), and the latifundia (fifty or more hectares). The minifundia of San Miguel de Sema are typically located in the higher regions of uneven topography and poor fertility. They are relatively intensely exploited, especially for maize, potatoes, and to some degree wheat. Few cattle are found on holdings of this size; sheep are frequent. Those cattle that are on such holdings are important for the production of milk and cheese (both significant sources of cash, especially in years like 1962 when market conditions are bad for potatoes and wheat). Sheep are especially important sources of raw materials for home craft industries associated with the production of salable wool and *ruanas* (wool ponchos). Pigs and chickens are also kept in fair numbers. It is important to realize that even as these minifundia homesteads are widely scattered (we shall later consider the significance of this *granjas dispersas* pattern), the several tiny fields controlled by any single household may be rather widely scattered also, although they are seldom outside of the confines of a single *vereda*.

For the *municipio* as a whole, more than 95 percent of the popula-

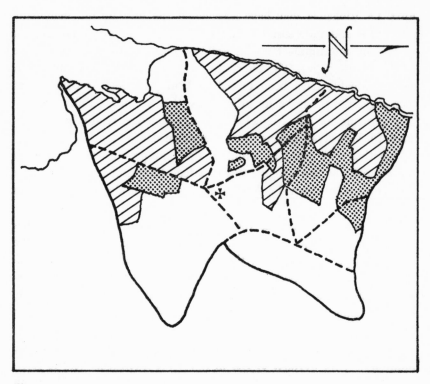

Key:

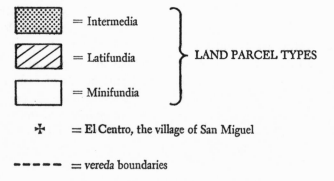

= Intermedia

= Latifundia

= Minifundia

} LAND PARCEL TYPES

✠ = El Centro, the village of San Miguel

- - - - - = vereda boundaries

FIGURE 13. DISTRIBUTION OF LAND PARCELS IN SAN MIGUEL DE SEMA. Many of the lands of San Miguel shown here as minifundia are in fact of little use either for agriculture or pasture. Source: Martin and Hanneson 1962.

tion lives on minifundia lands, occupying only about 47 percent of the total area of the polity (even if we extend the definition of minifundia to include holdings of up to ten hectares). If we limit our concern to those holdings five hectares or less in size, only 34 percent of the land area, and the poorest land at that, is accounted for by minifundia. Still the fragmentation picture is not as severe as it might seem to be and elsewhere in Colombia is. For, while it is generally true that those *veredas* that have been occupied longest (probably as a result of early proximity to ancient haciendas) are among the most densely populated and suffer most from soil erosion, most households exploit more than one land parcel. The distribution of minifundia lands by *vereda* and size of parcel is described in table 5.

TABLE 5
MINIFUNDIA OF SAN MIGUEL DE SEMA

| Vereda | Number of Minifundia | | |
	0–1 *Hectares*	1–3 *Hectares*	3–5 *Hectares*
Sabaneca	197(5) [a]	204(14)	51 (8) 27 [b]
Peña Blanca	58(2)	95(10)	46(10) 22
Hato Viejo	187(5)	224(25)	57(14) 44
Quintoque	97(3)	241(27)	76(17) 47
Sirigay	24(1)	70(16)	36(18) 35
El Charco	26(1)	69(26)	32(26) 53
Arboledas	12(4)	37(43)	15(35) 82

[a] Figures in parentheses show the percentage of total *vereda* land represented by parcels of that size.

[b] Figures in this column show the percentage of total *vereda* land classified as minifundia.

The most impressive aspect of the foregoing figures is the indication that, despite the fact that *veredas* vary considerably as to the percentage of land held in minifundia parcels, in most cases the profiles of minifundia for *veredas* are fairly comparable and indicate an intensity of occupation and exploitation somewhat more favorable than the extremes reported for other Colombian peasant areas. In addition to the shared characteristics of poor quality and often severe erosion, however, most minifundia lands are poorly supplied with reliable potable water sources.

Land holdings of the intermedia category are, in virtually all cases, the result not of entrepreneurial activity leading to the consolidation of minifundia but rather of the breakdown of finca lands according to the pattern mentioned earlier. Most of the intermedia are of post–World War II origin. There are several concentrations of intermediate-size lands. I have already mentioned one, that in Sirigay *vereda*, which exists as a result of the demise of Cascadas hacienda. At least a dozen parcels of intermediate size, from five to sixteen hectares, resulted from that fragmentation. In the adjoining *veredas* of Hato Viejo and Peña Blanca a similar process has occurred. In El Charco, and to some degree in all *veredas* that lie along or astride the recently constructed main road to Chiquinquirá, some new intermedia are common. In Sabaneca, which abuts the eastern border of the *municipio* of Chiquinquirá, one of the old fincas, La Granja, has been split up under the aegis of the Caja Agraria (a government-associated bureau) into a number of intermedia. Almost all of these, however, have been sold to absentee landholders living in Chiquinquirá; their owners are thus involved in few ways, except through taxation, in the life of San Miguel de Sema. As a general rule, however, all of the intermedia are worked, if not always owned, by families who live in somewhat grander houses (adobe brick with tile roofs, rather than wattle and daub with thatch) than those characteristic of minifundia. Some 250 parcels are classified as intermedia, and they constitute about 31 percent of the total *municipio* land. In those cases where they are worked by resident families, intermedia combine semimechanized cultivation with significantly more cattle grazing and dairying than is true for residents of minifundia. By contrast with the hacienda owners to whom we shall turn next, intermedia families, except for absentee owners in the former La Granja hacienda subdivisions, are usually tied through kinship and compadrazgo into one or more of the minifundia areas of San Miguel de Sema. Some of what would seem to be the best candidates for *patrones* are household heads associated with intermedia.

When we turn to latifundia lands we are dealing with the best lands, in terms of both fertility and commercially feasible size. Drainage remains something of a problem, but a few of the richer owners have joined to pump and drain swamp waters from their bottomlands into the Laguna de Fúquene. A mere sixteen latifundia parcels now make up about 35 percent of the *municipio* land. All lie in bottomlands except where, in several cases, the house sites themselves are located in the adjacent rolling foothills. In most cases, and the exceptions involve only the smallest haciendas (Puerto Rico and Colonia), the owners are not residents of San Miguel. Many of the latifundia hacienda owners are alien to the area, having bought up the best and largest portions of the earlier haciendas. It is not unimportant that the major haciendas that are commercially successful today are usually operated by strong mayordomos. Many owners inspect their lands only rarely. In the case of the very successful Paicaquita hacienda, the mayordomo travels each weekend to see the owner in the city of Ubaté, in Cundinamarca Department. The owners of Paicaquita (1,153 hectares) and El Rocodo (629 hectares) visit their holdings only twice a year. In fact, the hacendado of Chivava (431 hectares) is the only owner of a large finca who visits his holding every weekend. The only resident owners, of Puerto Rico (51 hectares) and Colonia (64 hectares), are now elderly and are selling their patrimony bit by bit merely to maintain their last days on these remnants of ancient holdings. Several products are commercially marketed by the larger fincas; these include large amounts of milk and, in better market years, wheat and potatoes.

TABLE 6

INTERMEDIA AND LATIFUNDIA IN SAN MIGUEL
DE SEMA

Vereda	Number of Holdings		
	5–10 Hectares	*Over 10 Hectares*	*Over 50 Hectares*
Sabaneca	30 (8) *	27(65)	8
Peña Blanca	29(11)	11(67)	2
Hato Viejo	26(10)	12(46)	1
Quintoque	56(22)	17(31)	2
Sirigay	13 (8)	4(57)	3
El Charco	20(28)	6(17)	0
Arboledas	3(10)	1 (8)	0

* Figures in parentheses show the percentage of total *vereda* lands represented by parcels of a given size.

With respect to the distribution of intermedia and latifundia lands by *vereda*, table 6 shows that the larger lands are clustered in certain *veredas* only.

In anticipation of some later considerations, it can be remarked now that, because of the social insularity of *veredas*, the political picture, especially as it pertains to social stratification and the potential for patronage, will vary widely from one *vereda* to another as we examine San Miguel de Sema.

In summary, the recent social, demographic, and land tenure history of San Miguel de Sema indicates that a diasproportionate amount of land is controlled by hacendados, who are, as a rule, not closely involved with the campesinos of San Miguel either commercially or civilly. The peasants, on their part, are characterized by significant but not particularly acute demographic pressures and shared poverty.

SOCIAL INTERACTION SPHERES

In order to appreciate the formal structuring of social interaction in San Miguel it is useful first to distinguish between several overlapping spheres of peasant interaction, and second to specify the "decomposable" units of small-scale groups and networks that may cross-cut, if not short-circuit altogether, the larger scale social and political entities. At the largest scale we are dealing with San Miguel both as a political entity and as a parish of the Roman Catholic Church. San Miguel as a kind of marketing "central place" represents still another *municipio*-wide domain. At lower levels of scale, we shall need to identify the *vereda* and the *granja dispersa* settlement patterns as well as to designate the socially instrumental networks that are described as kinship extensions and compadrazgo and imply friendship, mutual aid, and possibly patronage.

The political unit presently designated as El Municipio de San Miguel de Sema is relatively new. Nonetheless, it does possess some fiscal resources of its own, and some degree of political leverage derived essentially from the departmental and national levels. The political *municipio* does not, however, represent much of a basis for corporate identity. To some extent the struggle for municipal independence from Chiquinquirá control did encourage an enduring solidarity of affect; but few instrumental ties of the campesinos, other than those explicitly jural-political in nature, are integrated at the level of the municipal polity. Residing in the small administrative and service center housed in El Centro are some persons alien to the area. Some of them, the incipient *urbanos,* including civil servants of the town of San Miguel, have been able to divert some municipal funds from the *veredas* to building the comforts of city life. Nonetheless, I think the best way to appreciate the *municipio* of San Miguel as a social unit is to reiterate that it would probably never have attained political status except for its parochial and economic underpinnings.

The parish (*parroquia*) of San Miguel is thus more significant than the political domain for an understanding of how and why interpersonal ties operate as they do in San Miguel de Sema. For some time prior to independence, as well as since that time, several of the *veredas* of that area had been included in the parish of San Miguel. This parish is hierarchically subordinate to an office housed not in Chiquinquirá, which lies to the west of San Miguel, but in Tunja to the east. The local priest, who also came from the east (Tinjacá), led the pull away from Chiquinquirá hegemony. It may also have been critical that in the late 1950s, when the priest and others were working for independence, much of the population of what was to become San Miguel resided in Quintoque, eastern Sirigay, and Peña Blanca. In the absence of roads to Chiquinquirá, residents of these *veredas* were used to trading in the closer markets to the east of San Miguel, especially those in Tinjacá and Ráquira. At least two of the *veredas* of Ráquira belong to the parish of San Miguel. All of this means that the parish was the focus of much of the solidarity evidenced by residents of San Miguel in premunicipality days. The concrete symbol of this identity is the out-sized *templo* that was being constructed in the early 1960s. Attendance at mass in San Miguel is fairly regular for all the peasants of the *municipio,* with the important exception of the few residents of El Charco *vereda,* which remains in a parish under the direction of ecclesiastical superiors in Chiquinquirá.[6]

Economic factors are other essential underpinnings of the new political boundaries of San Miguel. An economic geographer, Hanneson (1969:73), describes San Miguel as a "social market" corresponding to the "minor markets" of traditional China, the "important Minor Markets" of Teotitlan and Huixtepac, and the "Minor Markets" of Oaxaca, Mexico, during the 1940s. This social market of San Miguel operates on Sundays and thus is aided by the simultaneous influx of churchgoers (and vice versa). Hanneson describes the market in these terms.

The most characteristic element of the San Miguel market is that it is a market oriented toward the purchase, in small lots, of exotic fruits of the *tierra caliente* and *tierra templada*. These include oranges, mandarins, mangos, tomatoes, bananas, and pineapples. Most often the fruit purchase is eaten in the plaza by the purchaser and his family. Prices do not vary greatly from the prices in larger markets even though quality, in terms of size and flavor, is inferior. . . .

The Social Markets are small, both in terms of numbers of people attending and the variety of goods for sale. They are held on Sundays and the rural movement to town represents a multi-purpose trip primarily for religious and social reasons. The economic activity is of secondary importance although the conviviality leads to the exchange of information on prices and crops (1969:51–52).

It should be added that some credit was available at the *tiendas* of the *municipio* in El Centro, much frequented during the market day. In addition, I think Hanneson may underestimate the significance of cross-cutting family and compadrazgo ties that are activated and validated by presence at and use of such local markets.

As we stress their economic, political, or religious systems, it is important to realize that each municipal domain is in some sense decomposable into lower order entities, usually *veredas*. This feature is most strongly pronounced in the political and economic domains, and least of all in religion.

STRUCTURAL POSES AND ADAPTATION GAMBITS

We may initially envision at least three kinds of structured responses that regulate the "adaptation gambits" of essentially subsistence-level campesinos to the outside world of state and regional politics. At one extreme is the well-documented form called "closed-corporate" peasant community, usually characterized by elaborated forms of leveling mechanisms. These constraints may be seen as instruments in the control of the parochial behavior of cohorts in the face of environments of the zero-sum sort, the idiomatic expression for which is often some kind of "image of limited good" (Foster 1961:177).

A second structural pose (Gearing 1957) involves the rather dramatic "open" peasantry where there are both the promises of and possibilities for individual exploitation of non-zero-sum environments.[7] The peasants can attempt to maximize their entrepreneurial options, which can entail wide-ranging ties of the patron-client sort, often at the expense of family solidarity. The associated ethic may be seen as a kind of "image of unlimited good."

Neither of these two forms, however, is adequately characteristic of the formal constraints of social systems in the *municipio* of San Miguel. I propose that San Miguel represents a third structural pose, what I earlier called "retreatist." In some respects this response lies between the two others already mentioned. Although the community as represented by the municipio, as a whole, can hardly be said to possess the extreme solidarity of a "closed corporate" sort, still many of the centrifugal tendencies apparent in the classic "open" case are likewise absent. Where the "closed" instance represents an increase in solidarity and integration and the "open" is assimilationist, our third type represents adaptive retreat.[8]

The immediate relevance of such defensive, retreatist strategies by the people of San Miguel is that they have circumvented the need to rely on widespread patron-client ties, which can be typical of either of the other two adaptation gambits. Such peasant behavior, which continues to be adaptive in contemporary circumstances, seems to have worked well in the San Miguel area for a very long time, well over a hundred years, in fact.

The Peasant Sector

From an economic perspective, the "peasant" sector of the economy of San Miguel is and has been rather restricted. Certain circumstances may force and others attract people into peasant pursuits, culminating in their increased vulnerability to market conditions. At least four sorts of pressures are reported for other parts of the world, including nearby areas of Colombia, that force subsistence-level farmers into a peasant existence: (1) high incidence of rented lands; (2) high reliance on neotechnic methods for agriculture; (3) extreme market vulnerability of the peasant crops marketed; and (4) government taxation and the like.

Only the fourth of these appears to have been significant in recent times in producing peasant adaptations in San Miguel; even here, however, the government policy of taxation, although demanding payment in money, is a progressive land tax instead of a regressive head tax. The quality of land is a prime determinant in tax rates, with the important result that peasant lands, generally inferior, are taxed much less heavily than those of the haciendas in the bottomlands. Regarding the other possible pressures:

(1) Most lands are held in freehold or worked in anticipation of imminent freehold inheritance; essentially all of the produce of the lands is available to the campesinos who work them, without exploitation by absentee owners.

(2) The reliance of campesinos on essentially paleotechnic agricultural methods represents a blessing in disguise. Although the use of fertilizers and pesticides and new hybrid varieties of crops might dramatically raise the carrying capacity of the land, the peasants then would be more tightly tied to the externally regulated market in order to obtain cash for the capital inputs needed for neotechnic farming. The minifundia of the campesinos of San Miguel are of low productivity, but the paleotechnic methods of the peasants leave them beholden to no one, even during market collapses (such as that of 1962, in which prices for potatoes and wheat fell to small fractions of their levels of the previous year).

(3) For the most part, the campesinos of San Miguel market food crops that are also subsistence crops. If market prices fall, they can at least eat the food—unlike peasants who grow specialized crops such as coffee or tobacco. Thus the campesino of San Miguel enjoys relative autonomy despite generally low levels of productivity.

The emigration of substantial numbers of people from the municipality may imply a homeostatically regulated population, with its demographic carrying capacity maintained at the expense of unregulated growth in urban areas and commercial plantation and other "rural proletariat" areas. The importance for San Miguel is that the relatively stable population there makes increased peasant activity and vulnerability unnecessary.

Thus the campesinos of San Miguel are not peasants in any extreme sense of market vulnerability. As for elements that might attract them into market activity, the unreliability of the market combines with the internal leveling and other features of social organization in paleotechnic subsistence agriculture at the *vereda* level to persuade the campesino not to become an entrepreneur at the risk of losing family support, so necessary in bad times. Extensive peasant participation would probably entail that sacrifice.

I have suggested that the people of San Miguel adopt a retreatist posture, which involves having as little to do with outsiders and their machinations as possible.[9] The limited extent of their peasant sector allows them to maintain such a stance.

Social Organization

The critical organizational units of San Miguel social life often have their loci elsewhere than on the level or scale of the *municipio,* often at the *vereda* level.

The settlement pattern typical of many Colombian Andean communities, including San Miguel and Boyacá as a whole, is that called by Fals-Borda the *Granjas Dispersas* pattern (1957:44, 47–48). This pattern of scattered homesteads seems to have its origin in pre-Columbian time. According to Fals-Borda, who is probably the best source on such matters of Colombian social history, the pattern was well established in the nineteenth century when, as a result of civil wars and general insecurity in the hinterlands, a depopulating of municipal central places was very common. It also seems likely that in the presence of the threat of widespread banditry and often quasi-governmental plundering of the villages as well, even the wealthier peasants responded by escaping to the hills and residing on their own lands. Although still vulnerable to attack, they then would have been unimportant targets for bandits and a negligible threat to government forces. In modern times, especially during La Violencia, the pattern has survived.[10]

The fact that scattered homesteads today constitute the basic units for San Miguel social life might be expected to incline the campesinos toward a kind of "amoral familism." Certainly, minimally extended families represent for many purposes the largest order action groups in San Miguel. Still, such corporate units remain tied to other such units through cross-cutting ties, often reciprocal labor exchanges. Generally these exchanges are based on extended kinship and the recognition of wide horizontal compadrazgo ties. Such ties do not usually extend far beyond the *vereda* boundaries (except along the boundaries of some of

them and with the important exception of the kinship ties of compesi-
nos to their somewhat more affluent relatives and compadres in the
Centro of the *municipio*).

Thus the *veredas* represent the maximal social universes in which
campesinos invest much affect. If the peasants keep open a variety of
options in affective and potentially instrumental ties, they do so within
fairly restricted interaction ranges—those of the *veredas*. Political affilia-
tions are also generally *vereda*-specific.[11]

Tiendas (small shops in which beer, *chicha*, some foodstuffs, and
other small goods are the main articles for trade) are important foci for
the actualization, and more importantly the validation, of the basic
premise upon which the *vereda* solidarities are based and maintained. In
much of the campo of San Miguel this fundamental similarity is that of
"shared poverty." For San Miguel, at least, a great deal of the customary behavior associated with the *tiendas*, especially that of excessive
drinking and the attendant excitability, belligerence, and often violence,
is best comprehended as informal leveling mechanisms by which peasants demonstrate and enforce their equality with their fellows through
a conspicuous sharing and buying of drinks. This may seem insipid in
comparison with elaborate, institutionalized conspicuous giving in closed
corporate circumstances (such as the "cargo" system Cancian reports
among the Zinacantecans). Still, the effects are, in some important
respects, largely the same. This pattern of often competitive and essentially reciprocal drinking is an important and necessary part of social
life in the campo. Few peasants who might later call upon the help
of others would dare to neglect the interaction of the *tienda* for the
self-fulfilling prophecy of shared poverty that such mutual carousing
represents.[12]

The *veredas* of San Miguel are not identical in peasant status differen-
tials. From appearances, the most flatly differentiated *vereda* is Arboledas. Its campesinos are uniformly described by residents of the *vereda*,
as well as by persons from other *veredas*, as "poor but equal." The
interesting point here is that I could not demonstrate any exceptional
degree of poverty as especially characteristic of Arboledas; the poorest
family there compared favorably with the poorest families elsewhere in
San Miguel. It appears that the *veredas* of, say, Sirigay or Hato Viejo,
by contrast with Arboledas, possess rather more dramatically skewed
status profiles. Nonetheless, even in those cases where some clear status

and prestige differences exist, they are not tied into a patronage system, except possibly in the most general and least significant sense.

Instead of providing a basis for pervasive patron-client relations, the status and wealth differences in San Miguel are effectively neutralized by a set of widespread validations and extended kin ties that preclude what otherwise might become balanced or negative reciprocities between patron and client. Kinship extensions and fictive kin ties of the compadrazgo sort in San Miguel involve "generalized" reciprocities.[13]

When we consider those *veredas* characterized by extensive hacienda land holdings, where the mayordomos might seem to be prime candidates for patrons, patron-client relations do not seem to have developed. Since the hacienda jobs are few, they go to the kinsmen of the mayordomo. Along with the rest of his fellows in San Miguel, he can hardly afford to give up the supportive ties of kinsmen, an almost certain result if he acted as a classical entrepreneurial patron (or client) and set up such contractual ties with nonkinsmen.

While they remain within San Miguel, the campesinos hesitate to set up ties with patrons, especially those who are alien to the *vereda*, since such relationships would imply "a set of countering liens" on local familial and possibly *vereda*-wide resources by the patron. The peasant typically perceives that he would stand only to lose, with the result of his and his family's further impoverishment.

It seems to me that the patterns of compadrazgo I witnessed in San Miguel are best identified with generalized or at most minimally balanced reciprocities. These can be correlated with the typical horizontal relationships between San Miguel compadres. The campesinos of San Miguel are also extremely reluctant to establish any balanced relationships, even those of vertical compadrazgo.[14] Until the repayment or payoff can be assured to his satisfaction, the campesino remains unwilling to run the risk, despite any potential advantages proffered by the patron. Quite simply, with respect to being able to collect, the campesino has no guarantor of his claims except himself; and since he possesses little resource clout he remains relatively impotent. To protect himself, he avoids entanglements; his recourse is withdrawal.

The absence in San Miguel of any clear-cut elite status categories helps to prevent the growth of ramifying patron-client ties. In any competition between the claims of kin and nonkin on the resources of people who might have opportunities to rise above their fellows, the claims of kinsmen prevail. The relative unimportance of status differences on the one hand, and the small municipal and *vereda* size on the other, consistently frustrate the development of a pervasive patronage system.

In summary, it seems to me that in San Miguel we have evidence of a defensive adaptation, a withdrawing on the part of the campesinos from the interaction spheres where they perceive (on balance, it seems, quite accurately) that they would stand to lose a great deal. Most internal relations, especially those between kin and fictive kin, are consistently characterized by generalized obligations. In those few cases of balanced reciprocities, the campesinos seem to seek an early liquidation of obligations. Aside from kinship and compadrazgo sodalities, the peasants seldom enter into entangling, long-term, balanced obligations of the patronage sort. They appear almost to prefer immediate money exchanges (in what Sahlins calls the sector of "negative" reciprocities), such as in the marketplace. Here, although afraid of and almost resigned to being exploited, the peasants conduct their business, take their expected but relative losses, and then retreat uncompromised to the campo, to the sanctity of their families and the security of familial resources.

CANDIDATES FOR PATRONS

An appraisal of the potential candidates for patron status will illustrate why it is that those people whom one might expect to become patrons cannot do so. In San Miguel the relevant categories are (1) bandit, (2) appointed government functionary, (3) hacendado and mayordomo, (4) petty entrepreneur and intermediate landowner, (5) elected local government officer and "elected" association leader, and (6) priest.

I can find no indication that regional leaders of the powerful kind suggested by Fals-Borda (1957:207), who were once common in other parts of Boyacá, have ever exercised much power in the vicinity of San Miguel. This is as true for *gamonales* and *caudillos* as for *patrones* of important blocs. During La Violencia, the only bandit in the area of San Miguel did not in fact operate from the sanctuary of this *municipio*. During my stay I could not see that he affected the body politic of San Miguel in any significant manner. At most, he and his small band of about six may have represented a vague collective force for his fellow Conservadores because his continued harassment of the peasant countryside was chiefly confined to action against Liberales or government troops.[15] Bandits are unimportant in San Miguel because the peasants represent small pickings, and this small-time leader was impotent in providing cohesion, defense, or any other valued service for potential clients.

Municipal and department employees, rather than being good candidates for patrons, are nobodies, party-appointed but in themselves unimportant people. Those from other parts of Colombia—schoolteachers and minor functionaries like the mayor and treasurer—have to expend some time and money (especially in *tienda* drinking bouts) [16] if they want to be accepted at all in San Miguel. They possess a few derived sanctions, but have few resources to exploit in bridging transactions of the patron-client sort. Small-scale government resources and activity are partly to blame, and the small size of the village and pervasive mutual familiarity regarding how the government is handling monies combine to prevent misappropriation and wheeling and dealing.

Although hacendados own a disproportionately large amount of the good land in the *municipio*, they are not important patrons. They find little in the rest of San Miguel to make such ties attractive to them. Commercial, mechanized agriculture on the haciendas means hacendados do not need peasant laborers, except for the few kin and compadres of the mayordomo. Even a mayordomo who is alien to the municipio and thus has no kin cannot develop his position into an entrepreneurial one, because he has too few jobs to distribute. Thus the mayordomo of San Miguel differs from his counterpart, the capataz, described by Strickon (chapter 3). The hacendados, for their part, are not involved in politics, and need no patron-client relationships for the purpose of securing votes. The campesinos of San Miguel have little to offer the hacendados, and are also reluctant to enter into any relationships with them.[17]

The petty entrepreneurs of San Miguel, to be successful, must be deeply involved with the campesinos of the *municipio*. But they are so well circumscribed by kin ties that it impedes them in any opportunistic recruitment of client followers. They cannot get far enough ahead in any entrepreneurial way to justify cutting their kin ties. The degree of success they do achieve (as owners of buses, *tiendas,* or other small stores in El Centro) suggests they must rely primarily on extended families in the *veredas* to turn a profit from their capital investment. The petty entrepreneurs can neither cut themselves off from kin ties nor achieve enough material success to elevate their kinsmen and themselves to a superior status. Any patronage that does exist is little different from pan-tribunal sodalities between kinsmen.[18]

Owners of intermedia in San Miguel, not hacendados but still relatively well-to-do, are not intimately involved in the economy of central-place *tienda* or other businesses. Many of them are absentee owners, of San Miguel. Others appeared time and again on my informants' lists of *principales*—important men—of the *municipio* and *veredas*, but most of these *principales* turn out in fact to be immediate kinsmen of campesinos in the district. They are important for their own kin and compadres, but not for extended patron-client relationships with others. They seem to be willing to exchange part of their superior wealth for the prestige of involvement and leadership in elective offices in sacred associations such as the *cofradías*, but not to take part in other matters of general San Miguel importance.

The *principales* and other "good thinking" men [19] of the *municipio* represent a kind of "firsts among equals." Whether intermedia property owners or petty entrepreneurs, however, they exercise little political power that is not severely constrained by pervasive kinship obligations. However desirable in the abstract, the rewards of independent action are insufficient motivation. The combination of *tienda*-associated drinking and *cofradía* membership seems to sap their extra capital, and such community-related activities may reduce the likelihood that any other than their kin and compadres will appeal to them for help as clients.[20]

Elected officials for municipal and *vereda* councils in San Miguel are poor candidates for the status and associated roles of patron. They remain so close to the controlling and ever-vigilant sectors of the body politic that any malfeasance in order to distribute patronage would be quickly discovered.

Still it should be noted that persons who occupy elective offices on municipal and *vereda* councils and responsible positions in quasi-governmental associations are in important respects unlike those who hold appointive positions. The former are, again, "good thinking" men.[21] Typically they are the center figures of particular kinship networks, deeply concerned with familiar matters, and they act as representatives of their respective constituents. Perhaps not surprisingly, I found no manipulations whereby one of them had tried to recruit extensive non-kin-based clientage obligated to him alone.[22]

I come now to San Miguel's only bona fide candidate for patron status, the priest of the *parroquia* of San Miguel. He exercises many kinds of power that, if coupled with his interest in doing so, might seem to imply a patron-client bloc of substantial proportions. He does not so much refuse to play the patronage game as find it unnecessary to do so. He is the beneficiary of a derived power far more ordered and reliable than the conditional sort that he could develop in personal patron-client ties. His position corresponds not so much to that of Melanesian "big man" as to that of redistributive "chief." He is also an effective connection with the outside world. Although he shows a certain degree of favoritism to those of his own Conservador party, he can keep in close contact with virtually all of the adult males in the *municipio*, except perhaps those who live in El Charco, which lies outside his parish. The relatively small population and area of San Miguel enable this priest to exercise more immediate, effective, and I think limiting influence on the campesinos during such disturbances as La Violencia than may have been true elsewhere in Colombia for the same time.

This particular man possesses a certain charisma generated by his youth, vigor, and especially his oratorical and organizational skills. The impressive new *templo* was his idea as the nearest thing to a collective representation for the *municipio*. The priest operates mainly through church-related groups, such as the *cofradías* (at both the *vereda* and the parish-wide level). Membership in the *cofradías*, especially the leadership in church-related fiestas, overlaps with membership in secular elective offices.

Through his several styles—oratory, visiting, ecclesiastical direction—the priest can affect significantly the secular policies of the *municipio*. Much of what becomes municipal policy first is hashed out in the informal pastoral visits and church association meetings. In a very important sense the church and its priest provide the ritual cement for what municipal solidarity exists, and the only successful cooperative effort in San Miguel operates under church aegis.

Thus this brief review of likely candidates for patrons in San Miguel reveals that none of them actually has become a patron. Only the priest

231

exercises strong integrative power in the municipality as a whole, and this he does more as chief than as patron.

SUMMARY

Eric Wolf (1965:16–18) has argued that for patronage systems to be sustained they must involve instrumental and/or affective ties which are of sufficient mutual advantage for *both* client and patron so that they will enter into this rather uncertain set of obligations. In the case of San Miguel, we may conclude that little is to be gained by either potential party in such arrangements (indeed, both peasant and potential patron may stand to lose a good deal). I have suggested that the strategic stance or gambit peculiar to what I call "retreatest peasantry" provides the necessary context for the explanation of this absence of patronage.

Specifically, the subsistence patterns among the peasants supply a major clue. Although not a "closed corporate" peasant community, San Miguel nonetheless is relatively self-sufficient, though poor. Disregarding the latifundia owners, there is little wealth differentiation in the area or dramatic status differences that would result from it. Farm work is successfully undertaken on an individual basis or in small reciprocal labor exchange terms. The economy is weakly monetized and the "peasant" marketing sector is often peripheral to the San Miguel subsistence activities, which emphasize kin ties and frustrate the establishment of patronage ties.

The basic social units of San Miguel are the *granjas dispersas* at the lowest level and the *veredas* a bit higher. The latter usually involve explicit national party identification as either Conservador or Liberal; and such political alignments are generally rooted in kinship and family tradition.

The peasants have few instrumental ties beyond the *municipio*. Where such ties do exist, their mode of articulation remains predominantly that of kinship ties. Even emigrants to other areas in Colombia, such as Bogotá, utilize this method of sponsorship rather than that of patronage. My impression is that few compadrazgo ties of the vertical sort exist between local persons and patrons. Certainly no patron blocs exist on the local level, nor does it appear that any individuals in San Miguel are important members of those elsewhere.

The Nonoccurrence of Patronage

The general picture we have of San Miguel suggests little need for, as well as lack of availability of, patrons. The local forms of sociocultural organization are kin-based, somewhat atomistic, and relatively egalitarian. There are accordingly few chances for big entrepreneurial gains of the patron-client sort.

Strickon has correctly assessed the problem of San Miguel when, in an interpretive statement prepared for symposium meetings, he noted:

> In essence the community, in terms of its resources, and in terms of it as a resource for outsiders, represented a kind of state of social, economic, and cultural entropy, with most of its resources and positions distributed evenly over the landscape. This provided little reason for the wheeling and dealing to gain access to different kinds of resources which is the hallmark of the patron-client relationship (Strickon 1969:8).

Some may object that I have argued an unnecessarily extreme case for the relative unimportance of patronage systems in San Miguel de Sema. Undoubtedly, my case is somewhat stronger or exaggerated than the same material might seem for others to merit. Nonetheless I hope that this paper may have the salutory effect of cautioning against using such a definition of patronage so weak or broad that we find it ubiquitous but of help in the explanation of very little. I am suggesting that we may not need to employ the concept of patronage as descriptive of behavior in many contexts and that, instead, we ought to reserve it for the special instances where it has greater explanatory relevance.

NOTES

1. I was able to conduct the fieldwork upon which this analysis is based as a result of the support given me, as a Summer Overseas Fellow, by the Carnegie Foundation. My fellowship was administered through the Department of Geography at the University of Oregon. The project in which I was involved was directed by Dr. Gene Martin of the Department of Geography, University of Oregon.

2. Many of the notions employed in this analysis of the San Miguel case are discussed in more detail and in broader reference in chapter 2 of this volume.

3. Tinjacá was then a *municipio* of somewhat different boundaries than in 1962. It lies to the north and east of San Miguel.

4. During my short stay in 1962, and according to the few documents I was able to examine, I was unable to determine the importance, if any, of the 1958 overthrow of the dictator Rojas Pinilla in the timing and ease with which San Miguel attained its independence.

5. Reference to the map of San Miguel de Sema will be of help to the reader in the following discussions and descriptions.

6. El Charco nonetheless remains included in the present-day polity of San Miguel despite its status as a kind of Chiquinquirá-oriented enclave. This was done, I think, to avoid excessive zigzagging of municipal boundaries. Such a geometric consideration seems to obtain elsewhere in the Colombian Andes. In addition, it is not unimportant that some peasant residents as well as petty entrepreneurs of that *vereda* appear to be tied by some kinship and economic interests to other areas in San Miguel, especially to El Centro.

7. Actually, the use of "zero-sum" and "non-zero-sum" is perhaps more crudely metaphorical than some readers would wish it. More accurately, I should note that it is not the environment, per se, which is itself one or the other sort of game; rather a particular set of environmental parameters may be said to condition a game of either zero-sum or non-zero-sum character.

8. Elman Service (1968:162–63) seems to me to be using a set of distinctions similar to mine when he suggests that some Indian groups of western North America can be seen in some instances to have attempted to directly assimilate to white culture, in other cases to have attempted to respond through tightening up their group identities (e.g., the Plains chiefdoms and corporate Pueblo communities), and in still other cases to have attempted a tactical retreat (e.g., the Diggers). I suggest that whichever response or adaptation gambit is selected is mainly a function of the peculiarities of the environment as well as the organizational and energetics capacities of the sociocultural systems themselves.

9. The defensiveness and suspicion implied in such an ordering of external relations is illustrated in the attitudes of San Miguel campesinos toward the education of their young. They appear very enthusiastic about such schooling and, unlike campesinos reported elsewhere, do not encourage truancy. They remarked, however, that to them the major attraction of formal education was that their children would, as a result, be less vulnerable than they to the trickery of the traders and merchants in larger marketplaces.

10. It is also plausible to suggest that terror tactics, such as those practiced or threatened during La Violencia, may have additionally served to caution the campesinos from investing their faith, and even more important, their time and capital, in government ventures where the capital and its products would be especially visible and large enough to be attacked, with profit, by bandits.

11. It appears that political affiliation with either of the two parties in Colombia, the Conservador and the Liberal, does not represent in San Miguel the volatile issue that it is elsewhere in Colombia. Nevertheless, it is not uncommon to find a sign in a *tienda* which admonishes against political discussions. Especially this is the case in *tiendas* along the boundaries of politically dissimilar *veredas*. In some respects, indeed, the *veredas* may be said to represent the essential loci of municipal factions. I have chosen, however, not to emphasize this aspect of *veredas*. For several reasons I feel that the *veredas* do not represent, in themselves, true factions but rather collectivities from which various kinds of action sets, including factions, may develop. In point of fact, factions, in the strict sense of the term, were absent in San Miguel; this was a result, I think, of the "retreatiest" adaptation so characteristic of the campo of San Miguel.

12. With respect to another set of cases of "Individualistic Culture," P. M. Gardner (1966) has demonstrated the effectiveness of a certain kind of retreatest response in the context of ever-present and ever-hostile environments faced by "refuge" populations. It would be intriguing to go with Gardner one step further and to speculate that campesino violence and brutality which is so common to Colombian peasantry makes sense, in part at least, as tension release in contexts of severe constraints on emotion and economic success in a Manichaean universe.

13. I am following Sahlins's (1965) formulations on reciprocities. While I am not using them in rigorous quantitative fashion here, I do feel they remain very useful for my argument.

14. It is true that in cases where the relationships between the parties of a dyad are asymmetrical, in terms of status, these are quite typically associated with "balanced" or even "negative" reciprocities. I am maintaining, however, that even such extensive balanced exchanges are not common in San Miguel; where they are found they are of short duration and quickly liquidated.

15. When it was ascertained, during the summer of 1962, that this particular bandit had by some error stopped the "wrong" bus (i.e., one carrying Conservadores) and killed some twenty or so of the passengers in the most brutal of manners, my San Miguel informants, at least the Conservadores among them, denied that this possibly could be the case. They maintained that this bandit "only shoots Liberales" and thus dismissed the issue. One of the vicitms, by the way, was the brother of a San Miguel schoolteacher, a Liberal and an alien to San Miguel.

16. For instance, the departmentally appointed treasurer was an outsider to San Miguel. Far from being able to use his position to any great personal advantage, he found it necessary to establish his harmlessness through his *tienda* behavior and associated public demeanor. In addition he found it necessary to set up a horizontal compadrazgo tie with a fellow Liberal party member who resided in one of the *veredas* of the campo.

17. In one case I was able to document the fact that an hacendado and his mayordomo had, some years before my arrival, acted in concert to try to establish a "cooperative" for their *vereda* in a fashion that would have involved the establishment of a true "patron bloc." They failed clearly and quickly. This may have been due to some *desconfianza* on the part of the campesinos of Sirigay *vereda* for this particular patron and his cohorts. However, I think it is more likely that simply none of the supposed advantages argued for the project seemed worth the obligations and vulnerability the project would have implied for the campesinos.

18. As I shall elaborate in the concluding section of this paper, I maintain that despite some similarities between the Melanesian Big Man and the patron, the two are significantly different when analyzed from a structural point of view. Specifically the critical difference revolves around the presence and relative importance of power derived from superordinate bodies or systems.

19. I am borrowing the term "good thinking" from Harry Basehart (1970:99) who has recently used the concept most effectively to describe the limited influence exercised by leaders of Mescalero Apache bands in New Mexico Territory during the nineteenth century.

20. It is worth recording at least one case of the ambiguous position of a petty entrepreneur intermedia landholder. In this instance, a milk cooperative was proposed, with the sponsorship of the local priest. Despite the latter's support and the explicit communal intent of the effort, at least two things intruded to insure the coop's defeat. First was the campesinos' suspicion of any endeavor that would demand their support, time, and resources but which would provide no clear-cut assurance that "lazy" peasants would not be able to get an undeserved slice of the profits, if any. Second, and more important, the campesinos refused to jeopardize their long-established relationships with traditional milk-transporters. Once again, the resulting failure of the coop represented a kind of self-fulfilling prophecy. The peasants continued to receive too little for their milk; but they lost little if anything else.

21. The fact that elected officials especially represent kinds of "good thinking" men indicates that wealth alone is insufficient to account for their esteemed positions. Once more, this may contrast with the Melanesian big man in some salient respects.

22. Rather than political entrepreneurs of a tribal sort, these council members are more similar to the lineage heads who are more constrained by kinship obligations and corporate restrictions than big men. Thus while the government of San Miguel may be well characterized as inefficient, it is also uncorrupted and accountable.

References

ADAMS, RICHARD N.
1960   "An Inquiry into the Nature of the Family," in *Essays in the Science of Culture in Honor of Leslie A. White* (New York: Thomas Y. Crowell).
1967   *The Second Sowing: Power and Secondary Development in Latin America* (San Francisco: Chandler Publishing Company).

ALBA, VICTOR
1968   *Politics and the Labor Movement in Latin America* (Stanford, Calif.: Stanford University Press).

ANDERSON, CHARLES W.
1964   "Toward a Theory of Latin American Politics," Occasional Paper no. 2, Graduate Center for Latin American Studies (Nashville, Tenn.: Vanderbilt University).

ANDO, ZEMPATI
1961   *Pioneirismo e Cooperativismo: Historia da Cooperativa Agricola de Cotia* (São Paulo, Brazil: Editora Sociologia e Politica).

ANDREWARTHA, HERBERT GEORGE
1961   *Introduction to the Study of Animal Populations* (Chicago: University of Chicago Press).

APARICIO, FRANCISCO DE AND HORACIO DIFRIERI (EDS.)
1959   *La Argentina, Suma de Geografia*, vol. 1 (Buenos Aires: Peuser).

BAILEY, F. G.
1965   "Decisions by Consensus in Councils and Committees: With Special Reference to Village and Local Government in India," in *Political Systems and the Distribution of Power*, ed. M. Banton (New York: Frederick A. Praeger), pp. 1–21.
1969   *Stratagems and Spoils* (Oxford: Basil Blackwell).

BALDE, BRANCO
n.d.   *Journal of the Cooperativa Central de Laticinios de São Paulo* (São Paulo, Brazil).

BANDELIER, ADOLPH
1910   *The Islands of Titicaca and Coati* (New York: American Geographical Society).

BANTON, MICHAEL (ED.)

1965a *The Relevance of Models for Social Anthropology* (London: Tavistock).

1965b *Political Systems and the Distribution of Power* (New York: Frederick A. Praeger).

1966 *The Social Anthropology of Complex Societies* (London: Tavistock).

BARNES, J. A.

1954 "Class and Committees in a Norwegian Island Parish," *Human Relations* 7:39–58.

1969 "Networks and Political Processes," in *Social Networks in Urban Situations*, ed. J. C. Mitchell (Manchester: Manchester University Press), pp. 51–76.

BARTH, FREDRIK

1966 "Models of Social Organization," Occasional Paper no. 23, Royal Anthropological Institute.

1967a "Economic Spheres in Darfur," in *Themes in Economic Anthropology*, ed. R. Firth (London: Tavistock), pp. 149–74.

1967b "On the Study of Social Change," *American Anthropologist* 69:661–69.

1969 *Ethnic Groups and Boundaries* (Boston: Little, Brown, & Co.).

BASEHART, HARRY

1970 "Mescalero Apache Band Organization and Leadership," *Southwestern Journal of Anthropology* 26:87–106.

BENEDICT, BURTON

1968 "Family Firms and Economic Development," *Southwstern Journal of Anthropology* 24:1–18.

BARTALANFFY, LUDWIG VON

1968 *General System Theory* (New York: George Braziller).

BILKEY, WARREN J.

1965 "Two Approaches to Stimulating an Industry in a Developing Country: The Dominican Beef Case," MS.

BOISSEVAIN, JEREMY

1965 *Saints and Firworks* (London: Athalone Press).

1966 "Patronage in Sicily," *Man* N.S. 1:18–33.

1968 "Networks, Brokers, and Quasi-Groups," MS.

BOLIVIA, REPUBLIC OF

1953 *Decreto Ley 03464, Reforma Agraria en Bolivia* (La Paz, Bolivia).

BOSERUP, E.

1965 *The Conditions of Agricultural Growth* (Chicago: Aldine Publishing Co.).

BOTT, ELIZABETH

1957 *Family and Social Network in East London* (London: Tavistock).

BUCKLEY, WALTER

1968 *Modern Systems Research for the Behavioral Scientist* (Chicago: Aldine Publishing Co.).

BUECHLER, HANS C.

1966 "Agrarian Reform and Migration on the Bolivian Altipalno" (Ph.D. diss., Columbia University).

1969 "Land Reform and Social Revolution in the Northern Altiplano and Valleys," in *Land Reform and Social Revolution in Bolivia*, ed. D. B. Heath et al. (New York: Frederick A. Praeger).

238

References

CALDERIA, CLOVIS
1956 *Mutirao: Formas de Ajuda Mutua no Meio Rural* (São Paulo, Brazil: Brasilians), vol. 189.

CAMPBELL, J.
1964 *Honour, Family, and Patronage* (Oxford: Clarendon).

CARTER, WILLIAM E.
1963 "The Ambiguity of Reform: Highland Bolivian Peasants and Their Land" (Ph.D. diss., Columbia University).
1964 "Aymara Communities and the Bolivian Agrarian Reform," University of Florida Monographs, Social Sciences no. 24 (Gainesville, Fla.).

CATTON, WILLIAM ROBERT
1966 *From Humanistic to Naturalistic Sociology* (New York: McGraw-Hill Book Company).

CAWS, PETER
1968 "Science and System: On the Unity and Diversity of Scientific Theory," *General Systems* 13:3–12.

COTIA, COOPERATICA AGRICOLA DE
1967 "Suplemento Estadístico: Ano de 1967," mimeographed.

COVERDALE AND COLPITTS
1958 "Report on Proposed Dominican Sugar Corporation," Cloverdale and Colpitts, Consulting Engineers, Study made at request of J. M. Troncosco, president, Corporación Dominicana de Centrales Azucareros, mimeographed (New York).

CTN
1970 *Codigo Tributario Nacional* (São Paulo, Brazil: Manuais "Utilitas").

DANDLER H., JORGE
1969 "El Sindicalismo Campesino en Bolivia," Instituto Indigenista Interamericano, Serie Antropologia Social, no. 11 (Mexico).

DIEZ DE MEDINA, FERNANDO
1956 *Thunupa* (La Paz, Bolivia: Gisbert).

ECONOMIC SURVEY OF LATIN AMERICA
1968 *Year 1967*, part 2, pp. 11–187.

EPSTEIN, A. L.
1961 "The Network and Urban Social Organization," *Rhodes-Livingstone Institute Journal* 29:29–62.

FALS-BORDA, ORLANDO
1957 *El Hombre y la Tierra en Boyacá* (Bogotá, Colombia: Ediciones Documentos Colombianos).

FIRTH, RAYMOND
1951 *Elements of Social Organization* (London: Watts and Co.).
1967 Ed., *Themes in Economic Anthropology* (London: Tavistock).

FORBES, DAVID
1870 "On the Aymara Indians of Bolivia and Peru," *Journal of the Ethnological Society of London* 2:193–305.

FORTES, MEYER
1970 *Kinship and the Social Order* (Chicago: Aldine Publishing Co.).

239

FOSTER, GEORGE M.
1953 " 'Cofradía' and 'Compadrazgo' in Spain and Spanish America," *Southwestern Journal of Anthropology* 9:1–28.
1960–61 "Interpersonal Relations in Peasant Society," *Human Organization* 19:174–78.
1961 "The Dyadic Contract: A Model for the Social Structure of a Mexican Peasant Village," *American Anthropologist* 63:1173–92.
1963 "The Dydadic Contract in Tzintzuntzan II: Patron-Client Relationships," *American Anthropologist* 65:1280–94.
1965 "Peasant Society and the Image of the Limited Good," *American Anthropologist* 67:293–315.
1967 *Tzintzuntzan, Mexican Peasants in a Changing World* (Boston: Little, Brown & Co.).
1971 "A Second Look at Limited Good," MS.

FREYRE, GILBERTO
1946 *The Masters and the Slaves*, trans. Samuel Putnam (New York: Alfred A. Knopf).
1963a *The Mansions and the Shanties: The Making of Modern Brazil*, trans. Samuel Putnam (New York: Alfred A. Knopf).
1963b *New World in the Tropics* (New York: Vintage Books).
1970 *Order and Progress: Brazil from Monarchy to Republic*, trans. Rod W. Horton (New York: Alfred A. Knopf).

FRIED, MORTON H.
1967 *The Evolution of Political Society* (New York: Random House).

FRIED, MORTON H., ET AL. (EDS.)
1968 *War: The Anthropology of Armed Conflict and Aggression* (New York: Natural History Press).

GALJART, BENNO
1964 "Class and Following in Rural Brazil," *America Latina* 7:3–24.
1967 "Old Patrons and New," *Sociologia Ruralis* 7, no. 4.

GARDNER, PETER M.
1966 "Symmetric Respect and Memorial Knowledge: The Structure and Ecology of Individualistic Culture," *Southwestern Journal of Anthropology* 22:389–415.

GEARING, FRED
1957 "The Structural Poses of 18th Century Cherokee Villages," *American Anthropologist* 60:1148–57.

GEERTZ, CLIFFORD
1965 "The Impact of the Concept of Culture on the Concept of Man," in *New Views of Man*, ed. John R. Platt (Chicago: University of Chicago Press).

GONZALEZ, NANCIE L.
1969 "The Problems of Relevance or: The Frustration of Seeing Many Sides" (Paper read before the meetings of the Society for Applied Anthropology, Mexico City, April).
1972 "The Sociology of a Dam," *Human Organization* (in press).

References

GRAHAM, LAWRENCE S.
1968 *Civil Service Reform in Brazil: Principles versus Practice* (Austin and London: University of Texas Press).

GREENFIELD, SIDNEY
1966 "Patronage Networks, Factions, Political Parties, and National Integration in Contemporary Brazilian Society," MS.
1969 "Patron-Client Relationships: The Significance of the Formal Structure," MS.

GREGORY, C. V.
1937 *The Distinction between Producer and Consumer Cooperatives* (Washington, D.C.: American Institution of Cooperation).

GUERREIRO RAMOS, ALBERTO
1961 *A Crise do Poder no Brasil: Problemas da Revolucao Nacional Brasileira* (Rio de Janeiro: Zahar Editores).

HAGEN, EVERETT E.
1962 *On the Theory of Social Change: How Economic Growth Begins* (Homewood, Ill.: Dorsey Press).

HALL, A. D. AND R. E. FAGAN
1968 "Definition of System," in *Modern Systems Research for the Behavioral Scientist*, ed. W. Buckley (Chicago: Aldine Publishing Co.).

HANNESON, BILL
1969 "Periodic Markets and Central Places in the Chiquinquirá-Ubaté Area of the Eastern Cordillera of the Colombian Andes" (Ph.D. diss., University of Oregon).

HEATH, DWIGHT B.
1966 "The Aymara Indians and Bolivia's Revolutions," *Inter-American Economic Affairs* 19:31–40.
1967 "Caste, Class, and Alcohol: Revolutionary Changes in Two Bolivian Communities," MS.
1969a "Two Routes to Justice: The Dual Legal System in Revolutionary Bolivia," MS.
1969b "Bolivia: Peasant Syndicates among the Aymara of the Yungas: A View from the Grass Roots," in *Latin American Peasant Movements*, ed. H. Landsberger (Ithaca, N.Y.: Cornell University Press), pp. 170–209.
1971 "Peasants, Revolution, and Drinking: Interethnic Drinking Patterns in Two Bolivian Communities," *Human Organization* 30:179–86.

HEMPLE, CARL G.
1965 *Aspects of Scientific Explanation* (New York: Free Press of Glencoe).

HICKMAN, JOHN M.
1963 "The Aymara of Chinchera, Perú: Persistence and Change in a Bicultural Context" (Ph.D. diss., Cornell University).

HUIZER, GERRIT
1965 "Some Notes on Community Development and Rural Social Research," *America Latina* 3:128–44.

HUTCHINSON, BERTRAM
1966 "The Patron-Dependent Relationship in Brazil: A Preliminary Examination," *Sociologia Ruralis* 6, no. 1.

241

JAGUARIBE, HELIO
1968 *Economic and Political Development: A Theoretical Approach and a Brazilian Case Study* (Cambridge, Mass.: Harvard University Press).

KAPLAN, DAVID, AND BENSON SALER
1966 "Foster's Image of Limited Good: An Example of Anthropological Explanation," *American Anthropologist* 68:202–6.

KENNY, MICHAEL
1960 "Patterns of Patronage in Spain," *Anthropological Quarterly* 33:14–23.

KLEIN, H. S.
1968 "The Crisis of Legitimacy and the Origins of Social Revolution: The Bolivian Experience," *Journal of Interamerican Studies* 10:102–16.

LA BARRE, WESTON
1948 "The Aymara Indians of the Lake Titicaca Plateau, Bolivia," American Anthropological Association Memoir no. 68 (Menasha, Wis.).
1950 "Aymara Folktales," *International Journal of American Linguistics* 16:40–45.

LA UNION
1969 Newspaper editorial, Catamarca, Argentina, July 5, 1969.

LANDE, CARL
1964 "Leaders, Factions, and Parties: The Structure of Philippine Politics," Yale University Southeast Asia Studies Monograph no. 6 (New Haven, Conn.).

LEEDS, ANTHONY
1964 "Brazilian Careers and Social Structure: An Evolutionary Model and Case History," *American Anthropologist* 66:1321–47.

LEFF, NATHANIEL H.
1968 *Economic Policy-Making in Brazil, 1947–1964* (New York: John Wiley & Sons).

LENSKI, GERHARD E.
1966 *Power and Privilege* (New York: McGraw-Hill Book Company).

LEONS, M. BARBARA
1966 "Changing Patterns of Stratification in an Emergent Bolivian Community" (Ph.D. diss., University of California, Los Angeles).
1967 "Land Reform in the Bolivian Yungas," *América Indígena* 27:689–713.
1970 "Stratification and Pluralism in the Bolivian Yungas," in *The Social Anthropology of Latin America*, ed. W. Goldschmidt (Los Angeles: University of California, Latin American Center), pp. 256–82.

——— AND WILLIAM LEONS
1969 "Peasant Economics in North Yungas," MS.
1971 "Land Reform and Economic Change in the Yungas," in *Beyond the Revolution*, ed. J. M. Malloy (Pittsburgh), pp. 269–99.

LEONS, WILLIAM
1970 "Modelos Cambiantes de Organización Laboral en una Comunidad Boliviana, *Estudios Andinos* 1, 2:49–60.

LITJANS, JOAO
1964 "Núcleos de Colonização Holandeza nos Estados de São Paulo e Paraná— Holambra," in *Organização e Desenvolimento de Emprêsas e Núcleos Agro-*

industrials: *IV Congresso Brasileiro de Organização Científica* (São Paulo, Brazil: Instituto de Organização Racional do Trabalho [IDORT]), pp. 39–63.

LOGAN, RAYFORD W.
1968   *Haiti and the Dominican Republic* (London: Oxford University Press).

MANGIN, WILLIAM
1967   "Las Comunidades Alteñas en América Latina," Instituto Indigenista Interamericano, Serie Antropología Social, no. 5 (Mexico).

MARSCHALL, K. B.
1970   "Cabildos, Corregimientos y Sindicatos en Bolivia despues de 1952," *Estudios Andinos* 1, 2:61–78.

MARTIN, GENE AND BILL HANNESON
1962   *Un Analisis Regional Preliminar de San Miguel de Sema, "Boyacá"* (Bogotá, Colombia: C.A.R.).

MARTIN, JOHN BARTLOW
1966   *Overtaken by Events: The Dominican Crisis from the Fall of Trujillo to the Civil War* (New York: Doubleday & Company).

MARTINS, ARAGUAIA FEITUSA
1962   *Mutirão Cafeeiro*, 3d ed. (São Paulo, Brazil: Editora Brasiliense).

MAURER, THEODORO HENRIQUE, JR.
1966   *O Cooperativismo. Uma Economia Humana* (São Paulo, Brazil).

MAYER, ADRIAN
1966   "The Significance of Quasi-Groups in the Study of Complex Societies," in *The Social Anthropology of Complex Societies*, ed. M. Banton (London: Tavistock), pp. 97–122.

McCLELLAND, DAVID CLARENCE
1961   *The Achieving Society* (Princeton, N.J.: D. Van Norstrand Company).

McEWEN, WILLIAM J.
1969   *Changing Rural Bolivia* (New York: Research Institute for the Study of Man).

MEAD, MARGARET
1953   "National Character," in *Anthropology Today*, ed. A. Kroeber (Chicago: University of Chicago Press), pp. 642–67.

MEGGITT, M. J.
1965   *The Lineage System of the Mae-Enga of New Guinea* (New York: Barnes and Noble).

MEIER, GERALD M.
1966   "Progress and Problems of the Development Decade," *Social and Economic Studies* 15:285–304.

MINTZ, SIDNEY W. AND ERIC R. WOLF
1950   "An Analysis of Ritual Co-Parenthood (Compadrazgo)," *Southwestern Journal of Anthropology* 6:341–68.

MITCHELL, J. C.
1966   "Theoretical Orientations in African Urban Studies," in *The Social Anthropology of Complex Societies*, ed. M. Banton (London: Tavistock), pp. 37–68.

1969 *Social Networks in Urban Situations* (Manchester: Manchester University Press).

MORALES, JOSE AGUSTIN

1929 "Monografía de las Provincias Nor y Sud Yungas," MS (La Paz, Bolivia).

MOURA, VALDIKI

1965 "Legislação Federal sobre Cooperativismo: Específica e Aplicada," Ministério da Agricultura, Servico de Informação Agricola (Rio de Janeiro).
Colombia: C.A.R.).

MURATORIA, B.

1969 "Participación Social y política de los Campesinos de Nor Yungas, Bolivia," *Revista Mexicana de Sociología* 31:909–45.

NADEL, S. F.

1954 *Nupe Religion* (Glencoe, Ill.: Free Press).

NAGEL, ERNEST

1961 *The Structure of Science* (New York: Harcourt, Brace & World).

NEWMAN, ROGER

1966 "Land Reform in Bolivia's Yungas" (Master's thesis, Columbia University).

NUNES LEAL, VICTOR

1948 *Coronelismo, Enxada e Voto: O Município e o Regime Representativo no Brasil* (Rio de Janeiro).

ODUM, EUGENE P.

1959 *Fundamentals of Ecology*, 2d ed. (Philadelphia: Sanders).

ORTIZ, FERNANDO

1947 *Cuban Counterpoint: Tobacco and Sugar* (New York: Alfred A. Knopf).

PADILHA, DRAZIO LEME

1966 *Sociedades Cooperativas: Organização, Contabilidade e Legislação* (São Paulo, Brazil: Editora Atlas).

PAINE, ROBERT

1969 "In Search of Friendship: An Exploratory Analysis in 'Middle-Class' Culture," *Man* 4: 505–24.

1971 Ed., "Patrons and Brokers in the East Arctic," Newfoundland Social and Economic Papers no. 2 (Memorial University of Newfoundland).

PARSONS, TALCOTT

1947 "Introduction" in *The Theory of Social and Economic Organization*, by Max Weber (New York: Free Press of Glencoe).

PATCH, RICHARD W.

1960 "Bolivia: U.S. Assistance in a Revolutionary Setting," in *Social Change in Latin America*, ed. R. N. Adams (New York: Council on Foreign Relations).

PETTERSON, PHYLLIS

1964 "Institutionalized Confusion," in *Political Systems of Latin America*, ed. M. C. Needler (New York: Harcourt, Brace & World).

PINHO, DIVA BENEVIDES

1962 *Dictionario de Cooperativismo*, 2d. ed. (São Paulo, Brazil).

1963 *Cooperativismo: Seleccão Bibliografica* (São Paulo, Brazil).

References

PITT-RIVERS, JULIAN
1961 *The People of the Sierra* (New York: Phoenix Books).
POWELL, JOHN D.
1970 "Peasant Society and Clientalist Politics," *American Political Science Review* 64, no. 2.
PLUMMER, JOHN F.
1966 "Another Look at Aymara Personality," *Behavior Science Notes* 1:55–78.
PRESTON, DAVID A.
1969 "The Revolutionary Landscape of Highland Bolivia," *The Geographical Journal* 135:1–16.
1970a "New Towns: A Major Change in the Rural Settlement Pattern of Highland Bolivia," *Journal of Latin American Studies* 2:1–27.
1970b "Negro Enclaves in the Andes," MS.
RIGGS, FRED W.
1964 *Administration in Developing Countries: The Theory of Prismatic Society* (Boston: Houghton-Mifflin Co.).
ROMERO, EMILIO
1928 *Monografía del Departamento de Puno* (Lima: Imprenta Torres Aguirre).
ROOSEVELT, THEODORE
1910 *Presidential Addresses and State Papers*, vol. 3 (New York: P. F. Collier and Son).
SAHLINS, MARSHALL DAVID
1962 *Moala: Culture and Nature on a Fijian Island* (Ann Arbor, Mich.: University of Michigan Press).
1965 "On the Sociology of Primitive Exchange," in M. Banton, ed., *The Relevance of Models for Social Anthropology* (London: Tavistock).
1968 *Tribesmen* (Englewood Cliffs, N.J.: Prentice-Hall).
SAITO, HIROSHI
1964 *O Cooperativismo e a Comunidade: Caso de Cooperativa Agricola de Cotia* (São Paulo, Brazil: Editora Sociologia e Politica).
SCHNEIDER, JANE
1969 "Family Patrimonies and Economic Behavior in Western Sicily," *Anthropological Quarterly* 42:109–29.
SCHNEIDER, PETER
1969 "Honor and Conflict in a Sicilian Town," *Anthropological Quarterly* 42:130–54.
SCOTT, JAMES C.
1970 "Patron-Client Politics and Political Change," MS.
SERVICE, ELMAN
1968 "War and Our Contemporary Ancestors," in *War: The Anthropology of Armed Conflict and Aggression*, ed. M. H. Fried et al. (New York: Natural History Press).
SHEPHERD, GEOFFREY S.
1955 *Marketing Farm Products—Economic Analysis* (Ames, Iowa: Iowa State College Press).

SHIRLEY, ROBERT W.
1970 *The End of a Tradition: Culture Change and Development in the Município de Cunha, São Paulo, Brazil* (New York: Columbia University Press).

SIMON, H. A.
1965 "The Architecture of Complexity," *General Systems* 10:63–76.

SOARES, GLAUCIO ARY DILLON
1966 "Classes Sociais Rurais e Cooperativismo Agricola: Nota de Pesquisa," *Revista de Direito Público e Ciência Politica* 9:68–77 (Rio de Janeiro: Fundação Getulio Vargas).

SQUIER, E. GEORGE
1877 *Peru: Incidents of Travel and Exploration in the Land of the Incas* (New York: Harper & Brothers).

STAVENHAGEN, RODOLFO
1965 "La Comunidad Rural en los Países Subdesarrollados," *Ciencias Politicas y Sociales* 11:57–71.

STRICKON, ARNOLD
1962 "Class and Kinship in Argentina," *Ethnology* 1:500–515.

1965 "The Euro-American Ranching Complex," in *Man, Culture, and Animals: The Role of Animals in Human Ecological Adjustments,* ed. A. Leeds and A. Vayda, publication no. 78 (Washington, D.C.: The American Association for the Advancement of Science), pp. 229–58.

1969 "Patron-Client Relationships: The Analysis of Situations," MS.

STUART, W. T.
1962 "Algunas Instituciones Sociales Variables en San Miguel de Sema," in Martin and Hanneson.

TSCHOPIK, HARRY S.
1951 *The Aymara of Chucuito, Peru: I, Magic,* Anthropological Papers of the American Museum of Natural History, vol. 44 (New York).

U.S., DEPARTMENT OF AGRICULTURE
1958 *Three Principles of Agricultural Cooperation,* Farmer Cooperative Service, Educational Circular no. 13 (Washington,, D.C.).

U.S., DEPARTMENT OF STATE
1967 National Archives, Record Group 38; 839.61351/67.

VASQUEZ, MARIO C.
1952 "La Antropologia Cultural y Nuestro Problema del Indio," *Peru Indigena* 2, nos. 5–6:7–158 (Lima: Instituto Indigenista Peruano).

VAYDA, ANDREW AND R. A. RAPPAPORT
1967 "Ecology: Cultural and Non-Cultural," in *Introduction to Cultural Anthropology,* ed. J. A. Clifon (Boston: Houghton-Mifflin Co.), pp. 476–97.

WARD, BARBARA
1960 "Cash or Credit Crops? An Examination of Some Implications of Peasant Commercial Production with Special Reference to the Multiplicity of Traders and Middlemen," *Economic Development and Cultural Change* 8:148–63.

WATSON, JAMES
1963 "Caste as a Form of Acculturation," *Southwestern Journal of Anthropology* 19:356–79.

References

WEBB, MALCOLM C.
1965 "The Abolition of the Taboo System in Hawaii," *Journal of the Polynesian Society* 74:21–39.

WEBB, SIDNEY AND BEATRICE WEBB
1921 *The Consumer's Cooperative Movement* (London: Longmans, Green, and Co.)

WEBER, MAX
1947 *The Theory of Social and Economic Organization* (New York: Free Press of Glencoe).

WEINGROD, ALEX
1968 "Patrons, Patronage, and Political Parties," *Comparative Studies in Society and History* 10:1142–58.

WHITE, LESLIE A.
1949 *The Science of Culture* (New York: Grove Press, Inc.).

WIARDA, HOWARD J.
1967 "From Fragmentation to Disintegration: The Social and Political Aspects of the Dominion Revolution, *America Latina* 10:55–72.

WINCH, PETER
1958 *The Idea of a Social Science* (New York: Humanities Press, Inc.).

WOLF, ERIC R.
1956 "Aspects of Group Relations in Complex Societies," *American Anthropologist* 58:1065–76.
1966a "Kinship, Friendship, and Patron-Client Relations in Complex Societies," in *The Social Anthropology of Complex Societies*, ed. M. Banton (London: Tavistock), pp. 1–22.
1966b *Peasants* (Englewood Cliffs, N.J.: Prentice-Hall).

WOLFE, ALVIN W.
1970 "On Structural Comparisons of Networks," *Canadian Review of Sociology and Anthropology* 7:266–44.

Index

ABCOOP (Aliança Brasiliera de Cooperativas), 154
ACAPESP (Aliança das Cooperativas Agropecuarias do Estado de São Paulo), 154
Actor-oriented analysis, 4, 10, 11, 12, 13, 14, 15
Adaptation gambits, 31, 212, 222; "retreatist" system, 223, 225, 227, 228, 232
ADELA, 192
African societies, studies of, 5, 38
Agency for International Development, 130. See also AID; USAID
Agrarian reform, Bolivia, 101, 110, 112, 124, 126, 130, 132
Agrarian reform act of 1953, 112, 124
Agricultural school, Dominican Republic, 194–97
Agriculture, Argentina, 48, 52, 59–63, 64, 65, 159, 164, 168; irrigation, 162, 163; role of contractors, 60–63; and Sociedad Rural, 58. See also Subsistence farmers
Agriculture, Bolivia, 102, 103, 104, 107, 118–19, 224; marketing procedures, 111, 118, 119, 130, 132. See also Aymara campesinos
Agriculture, Brazil, 149, 150; cooperatives and, 141–56 passim; laws governing, 144, 146, 151, 155, 156; marketing and, 139, 146, 147, 151; modernization of, 144, 149, 150, 151, 156. See also Coffee production, Brazil
Agriculture, Colombia: commercial farming, 213, 219, 229; crops, 215, 219, 224; dairies, 215, 218, 219; livestock, 215, 218

Agriculture, Dominican Republic, 184, 185, 186, 190, 192, 198, 224. See also Sugar industry; Tomato-paste industry
AID, and assistance to Dominican Republic, 192, 194, 195, 196, 197, 200, 203. See also Agency for International Development; USAID
Alcoa Company, 190
Alliance for Progress, 79, 80
Altiplano region, Bolivia, 103, 104, 107
American Can Company, 197
Andes Mountains, 102, 104, 212
Arboledas vereda, 226
Argentina, governmental channels, 63–65; history, 159; military junta of 1966, 66. See also Perón administration
Arrenderos, 109, 116, 124
Asociación para el Descarrollo (Development Association), 191–98 passim; enterprises, 192, 194, 195, 196, 197; manipulations of, 192, 194, 196, 197, 198
Athos, 77, 78
Aymara campesinos, 15, 101–34 passim

Bacharéis, and consumer cooperatives, 143
Banana plantations, 186, 190
Banco Agrícola (Agricultural Bank), 203
Banco de Catamara, 162, 172
Bandits, 225, 228
Bank of Nova Scotia, 190
Basic Law of Cooperation, 144
Bela Horizonte, Brazil, 151
Beni province, Bolivia, 103
"Big Man," Melanesian, 19, 35, 36, 231

Index